Advance Praise for *MAKE ME A STAR*

"They say a smart man learns from his mistakes but a wise man learns from another's mistakes. Some pitfalls are necessary for an artist's development, but not all. The stories and advice within these pages are not merely rhetoric or theory—they are hard-fought and hard-won experiences from those who've been in the trenches."

—**Keith Urban**

"I find the book to be wonderfully straightforward, savvy, and easy to digest. I believe aspiring artists and those of us in the biz would benefit from reading it. I've not read anything as practical or reliable about this indescribable business and its process.

—**Gary Borman** (manager of Faith Hill,
James Taylor, and Keith Urban)

"I'm always impressed but never surprised with Anastasia's level of success in the entertainment industry. Her years with our company in the 1990s gave her the expertise to be able to offer great advice on making it in the music industry on the national stage. Her management experience, coupled with her more recent endeavors as a celebrity talent judge, owner of an entertainment technology company, and role as a music supervisor for film and television, will give the reader many rare and insightful tips for making it in the music business."

—**Miles Copeland**

"This book is SO GREAT! All of the interviews added a lot of great insight, and the information included was really useful and enjoyable to read. This book is cutting edge—not the old-school 'how to get a record deal' approach—it reveals realistic but brilliant ideas about how to get your music heard and how to launch a career."

—**[illegible]g** (aspiring singer,
songwriter, actor)

MAKE ME A STAR

Industry Insiders Reveal How to Make It in Music

MAKE ME A STAR

Industry Insiders Reveal How to Make It in Music

ANASTASIA BROWN

WITH BRIAN MANSFIELD

THOMAS NELSON
Since 1798

NASHVILLE DALLAS MEXICO CITY RIO DE JANEIRO BEIJING

Published in Nashville, Tennessee, by Thomas Nelson. Thomas Nelson is a registered trademark of Thomas Nelson, Inc.

Thomas Nelson, Inc. titles may be purchased in bulk for educational, business, fund-raising, or sales promotional use. For information, please e-mail SpecialMarkets@ThomasNelson.com.

Page design by Kay Meadows

Library of Congress Cataloging-in-Publication Data

Brown, Anastasia.
Make me a star : industry insiders reveal how to make it in music/
Anastasia Brown with Brian Mansfield.
p. cm.
Includes bibliographical references.
ISBN 978-1-4016-0404-2
1. Singers—Vocational guidance. I. Mansfield, Brian, 1963- II.
Title.
ML3795.B827 2008
781.64023—dc22

2008005353

Printed in the United States of America

08 09 10 11 12 13 RRD 9 8 7 6 5 4 3 2 1

CONTENTS

SOURCES
267

Credit: Trey Fanjoy

Dedicated to Tony and Wilson.
My safe harbor and source of true happiness.
I love you unconditionally.

INTRODUCTION

Anastasia Brown and Waylon Jennings

I am a fan of artists and the music they create, so much so that in 1998 when a tornado caused destruction throughout downtown Nashville and Music Row, I almost got sucked out of the music industry and into the storm. I didn't listen to the radio too much in the 1990s—I listened to demos, rough mixes, and CDs in my car. I soaked up the music of the artists with whom I worked 24/7. On April 16, 1998, as I listened to the roughs of Waylon Jennings's (God rest his soul) last studio record, *Closing in on the Fire*, I didn't notice the menacing skies and hadn't heard the tornado alerts on the radio. As I parked, I finally saw that the sky had turned a dark, pea green, but I didn't give it another thought as I walked into my 17th Avenue office—which was empty. I called out for Roger Osborne, and he screamed, "Get downstairs now!" That's when I heard the rumbling wind pass us by and felt a chill run down my spine. Music certainly can take us to an elevated place where we escape reality!

To me, music is so powerful that I went straight to it after my husband, Tony Brown, suffered a traumatic brain injury and almost died. All I knew to do was pray and play music to him while he was in a coma for weeks. He's a miracle, 100 percent recovered, and I believe music played a hand in it.

As a music supervisor for film and television and a judge on *Nashville Star*, I not only get inspired by music, I pay my bills with it. So I take it seriously and respect the truly gifted artists who create it. Yet having worked with aspiring artists and legends during the last sixteen or so years, I've noticed that there isn't a "school" or a how-to book available for artists with nothing but a dream. It's pretty much just the school of hard knocks, trial and error, and/or music contests for 99 percent of these people. So I decided to reach out to my friends who have knowledge to share, collect their pearls of wisdom, and offer this wisdom to the world.

As first a fan of *Nashville Star* and, later, one of the show's judges, I've watched firsthand as singers like Buddy Jewell, Miranda Lambert, and Chris Young have gone from aspiring entertainers to full-fledged artists. As a manager, a record-company executive, and a person who's worked in the music industry for almost twenty years, I've seen friends and clients succeed, and I've seen others struggle. I've had artists ask for advice, and I've seen others regret not having asked for help.

Since shows like *American Idol* and *Nashville Star* began, thousands—maybe even hundreds of thousands—of aspiring stars have auditioned, each one hoping to become Kelly Clarkson, Clay Aiken, Carrie Underwood, or Jordin Sparks. Each year, as I watch the audition rounds of the show, I see all these young, innocent, vulnerable kids. Some of them don't have talent, and some of them just haven't had it nurtured enough that it can withstand the heat of the television lights. I see pain and misery in their faces when the judges pass on them.

I remember thinking, "I wish there were a book to help these young women and men know what they should expect from these auditions and how to deal with them." There ought to be a book with simple lessons from respectable people in the music business. Opinions are a dime a dozen, but opinions from safe, reputable people are much harder to come by.

Artists often don't have business degrees, but they do need good, honest guidance. Though several universities offer excellent music-business programs, there is no school for most aspiring artists. But as in any business, the music industry has plenty of pitfalls; if you are an artist, having the right people help you avoid those traps can be invaluable.

So this book is for anyone—singer, songwriter, or musician—who wants to pursue an artistic dream. "Where do I start? Do I go this direction or that? How will I ever get any traction?" If you are asking these questions, this book is for you.

Because I live in Nashville and most of my best friends live here too, the examples in this book often come from that world. While some of the particulars may change depending on where you live and the style of music you sing—you won't play a lot of songwriter nights if you're an R&B singer in Atlanta or fronting a rock band in Boston—the general principles almost always still apply.

INTRODUCTION

There are two things this book is not—a textbook or a checklist. I don't go into great detail about controlled compositions and cross-collateralization (though, eventually, both those concepts become important). At the back of this book, you'll find a sample recording contract, but I'm not going to take you through it step by step. No matter how much I tell you about those contracts, you will still need professional help when it comes to negotiating the deal. Get a good lawyer—a music-industry lawyer. Negotiating contracts is part of the lawyer's job.

And please don't go through this book checking off things as you accomplish them. If you gauge your progress simply by when you hire a manager, when you sign a publishing contract, when you get a record deal, you'll have missed the whole point of the book and set yourself up for disappointment, too.

This book should inspire you, frighten you, and entertain you. It should open your eyes. Every person in the music industry has stories that can make you laugh or cry or cringe—or pat yourself on the back. It amazes me how some people come from nothing and overcome tragedies and heartache and still come out on top. Others make disastrous decisions and have to live with them for decades, never able to recover fully from them.

In a desperation to succeed, young artists can make terrible decisions—taking the money of a backer with no real ties to the industry, giving away the publishing rights to a song or songs, signing a production deal with someone who claims influence he or she doesn't actually have. One bad contract can haunt a singer for years.

Remember: It can take five *years* to build a reputation, but five *minutes* to lose it. We've all heard stories about artists who have made mistakes on the road, said or done the wrong thing in an interview, or behaved badly at a public event, and it took them years to recover. One mistake can really set back a career, and some mistakes are too big to ever completely overcome.

But everyone in this business has made mistakes—and everyone has made some great decisions. This book is for people who have a dream and want to pursue it, who are willing to learn from the experiences of others who've pursued the same dreams—some who've reached their dreams and some who have not.

My grandmother used to say, "Anastasia, you have two ears and one mouth." She wanted me to listen more than I talked. I learned her lesson well. When I'm around people who have more experience than I do, I'm all ears. One of those people is Miles Copeland—the well-known entertainment executive who founded I.R.S. Records (R.E.M., Black Sabbath, Fine

Young Cannibals) and managed the Police, the Go Go's, and others. Because I listened to Miles, I learned to follow my gut, to let artists and their music guide my decisions, and to think long term.

After working with Miles in the 1990s, I decided I wanted to work as a music supervisor, the person who picks and licenses music for films and TV shows. Most music supervisors live in Los Angeles or New York, but I wanted to stay in Nashville. Everyone but my family told me it couldn't be done out of Nashville, but Miles always told me, "The risk-takers are the ones who score and succeed big." Those words echoed in my mind every time I flew to Los Angeles trying to get movie work. That one sentence—and he's proof that it's true—kept me going. Now it's a reality—my reality. It's not a dream any more; it's my life, and I love every minute of it.

I also love every minute of *Nashville Star*, especially when I see a true artist on stage—even if he's scared out of his mind and his voice is wavering. If I see a little spark in him, even one obscured by imperfections, I know that he just needs to be nurtured and developed. It may be just one artist a year, but I love to see that one special artist who's a diamond in the rough. It's inspiring. It's exciting. Those artists don't know it, but I read every article about them during the season and after it ends. I track their careers—and it's fun. It's more enjoyable for me than watching most TV shows. And when I see someone's career actually work—when that special artist makes it—it's amazing. Those moments plant a big old smile on my face that stays there all day long.

On *Nashville Star*, I see many people I want to learn more about. I want to see whether they've got that "it" factor. But a minute and a half often isn't enough time to do that. And half the time, the most talented people might not represent themselves well in that environment. If there's one thing you have to do on these talent shows, it's make a great first impression. That's what I want this book to do for you—help you make a better first impression—not just in your auditions but in every phase of your performing life.

A Tim McGraw song asks, "How Bad Do You Want It?" As an aspiring entertainer, you need to ask yourself that question every single day. Becoming a star requires much more work than you can possibly imagine. Your desire and your work ethic will do as much or more to increase—or decrease—your chances for success than any talent, natural ability, or bankroll you might have.

When I was working as an artist manager, I loved to ask potential clients, "What's your

Plan B?" If they had one, I knew they weren't for me because music would always be more of a hobby for them. Maybe they had talent and maybe they wanted to be famous, but they probably didn't have the necessary drive inside themselves to overcome obstacles, to endure pain and suffering on the way to success, or to have the confidence to survive. There are people singing on stage today who aren't artists, but they're famous. That's certainly a route to take, especially these days. But that dream doesn't interest me. If artists have a Plan B, I'll never really believe in them because they don't really believe in their art. Key tip: *If you have a Plan B, it most likely will become your Plan A!*

Parents hate to hear me say that because they usually know better than their children just how long the odds are for anyone wanting to make it in the entertainment business. They're also afraid they'll wind up with an unemployed thirty-year-old living in their house. But this business is for people who cannot or will not do anything else—and nearly every artist we interviewed for this book told us exactly that in some form or another.

When I was young, I never dreamed about being a star. I sang in bands, and I loved it. But I knew singing was not the dream that would make me give up everything else. I knew all the sacrifices I would have to make, all the blood, sweat, and tears. I was never able to write a song, and while performing didn't motivate me, music did. I was already thinking Plan B before I ever seriously pursued singing. I did dream about impacting people, but I didn't know how I would do it. Not until I started developing artists and helping them get their music out did I realize, "I'm impacting people behind the scenes—and they don't even know it." That's when I knew I'd found what I was supposed to be doing, what I had always *really* wanted to do.

This past year on *Nashville Star*, one of my early favorites, David St. Romaine, had a nice voice, but he played guitar like an amateur. Once you're on television, whatever talent you choose to tap into, it's got to be great. Don't reveal any talent on camera until it's polished. David didn't play guitar well enough, and I told him on the air. He came up to me afterwards and said that his gut had told him not to play guitar, but he thought that, in Nashville, it would hurt him not to have a guitar in his hands. I told him, "It only hurts you if you're not good at it." It's better to play to your strengths, especially at the beginning, rather than trying to fit in.

At times like that, when contestants come up to me and say, "You have really made a difference for me, and, thank you, I'm going to take your advice," it hits me that I'm actually doing what I was dreaming about doing when I was a kid. I'm making an impact on people. That's when I know I'm in the right place.

Are you in the right place? You know that feeling you have when you're at home and you're comfortable in your own skin—as opposed to those moments where you're jumping out of your skin because you're so uncomfortable? Listen carefully to your body, pay attention to those telltale signs, and you might avoid years of heartache. Too many times, we don't listen to our gut—to our own subconscious. Then we have to endure a lot of setbacks. If you're not listening to your gut, you're not pursuing what you need to pursue. The gut has a good way—I believe it's God's way—of saying, "No, go *this* way."

It's like when you have your dog on a leash and you're pulling him to the right but he insists on going to the left and then gets choked. The older and more experienced you become, the more you'll learn to trust your gut. The less confusing it becomes, the fewer times God will have to tug on your slip collar.

I hope this book helps you start doing what you're supposed to do sooner rather than later. I hope it gets you to dig deep and find answers to your questions: "What is my path? Am I trying to chase someone else's dream and not my own? What is *my* dream?" When I was managing and working with Miles Copeland, I wasn't miserable and I wasn't wasting time. I enjoyed it, I was making an impact, and it was great. But it didn't make me feel the way that what I'm doing now makes me feel. I'm a round peg in a round hole, and it feels really comfortable.

The majority of people who read this book dream of being a rich and famous singer—but many will eventually be weeded out of the star system. Some of you will make that decision on your own. Others will have the decision made for you. I hope this book helps you go further and make better decisions every step of the way. As you learn how to go through this crazy business in a less-crazy manner, I hope you'll be convinced to pursue your dream even harder—even if it means changing your dream altogether.

CHAPTER 1

THE GOLDEN AGE OF TALENT CONTESTS

A QUICK OVERVIEW OF TV TALENT SHOWS

American Idol wasn't the first talent show on television, though it has turned out to be the biggest. Competitions like *Idol* have been around as long as television. Some actually predate it. And credible artists have come out of these contests for decades.

Tony Bennett, Connie Francis, Patsy Cline, Roy Clark, and Don Knotts were just a few stars-to-be who got a boost from appearing on *Arthur Godfrey's Talent Scouts.* Godfrey, a media personality who brought his show from radio to TV in 1948, made *Talent Scouts* one of the most popular programs during television's first decade. The show brought rising entertainers from across the country to New York to perform for a national audience, with winners being chosen by an "applause meter."

Ted Mack's Original Amateur Hour made its television debut the same year as *Arthur Godfrey's Talent Scouts* and lasted even longer. Like *Talent Scouts, Amateur Hour* began as a radio show. Instead of professionals, though, Ted Mack's show featured amateurs, and viewers voted for their favorite acts by mailing postcards. Gladys Knight, Ann-Margret, Teresa Brewer, and Pat Boone all got breaks on *Ted Mack's Original Amateur Hour* before the show went off the air in 1970. Frank Sinatra performed as part of a quartet on the radio version of the show, emceed by Major Edward Bowes, in 1935.

Chuck Barris, the game-show producer who created *The Dating Game* and *The Newlywed Game*, came up with *The Gong Show* in the 1970s. *The Gong Show* combined the talent competition with laughs, much the way the audition rounds of *American Idol* do. Celebrity judges drowned out the worst performers by striking a large gong—just as *Amateur Hour*'s original radio emcee Major Bowes had. Singer Cheryl Lynn, who had a disco hit in 1978 with "Got to Be Real," appeared on *The Gong Show*, as did an early version of the new-wave band Oingo Boingo, whose members included future film composer Danny Elfman.

Star Search, the immediate predecessor to *Idol*, was initially hosted by *Tonight Show* sidekick Ed McMahon and ran on syndicated television from 1983 to 1995. It was revived briefly after *Idol* took off. Though only a handful of *Star Search* winners, including country group Sawyer Brown, received recording contracts as a direct result of the show, the impressive list of future stars on the show included Alanis Morissette, Aaliyah, Christina Aguilera, Beyoncé Knowles, LeAnn Rimes, Jessica Simpson, Britney Spears, and Justin Timberlake, as well as Diana DeGarmo, Nadia Turner, and Jessica Sierra, who all went on to become *Idol* finalists.

Idol combined key elements from many of its predecessors and then raised the stakes. Like *Amateur Hour*, it put unknown stars in front of viewers from across the country and then let the audience pick the winners. It used comedic relief like *The Gong Show*, essentially giving *Idol* two shows: the auditions, where the odd and merely deluded parade before the cameras between the emotion-packed back stories of the potential finalists; and the finals, where the real competition begins. As on *Star Search*, the best performers return from week to week, though *Idol*, in a flash of brilliant inspiration, formatted the contest more like an athletic season and less like a game show where a challenger could always send a popular champion home. With *Idol*, audiences have more time to identify with their favorite singers. The contestants who best cultivate those relationships and give the strongest performances continue to compete from week to week. Only the weakest performers disappear.

THE TRUTH ABOUT (NOT SO) CONSTRUCTIVE CRITICISM

If the 1950s were the golden age of televised talent shows, we're now living in the golden age of talent-show judges. *American Idol* took judging to a whole new level with Simon Cowell. Judging became brutal, almost painful for some people. Before Simon, we had *The Gong Show*, where the worst humiliation came in the form of a few slapstick jokes and a swipe at a gong—almost a badge of honor.

But Simon has taken rejection to a whole new level. I praise Simon for being honest, and a lot of the time, I agree with him. Occasionally, he'll miss something good—he's sometimes reluctant to embrace country music, for instance, but he generally knows what he's talking about. He's got great taste in music, obviously—his track record says it all. As a mother, though, I look at some of those children on the receiving end of his verbal jabs, and I feel for them. I worry about their spirits recovering.

I've been called the Simon Cowell of *Nashville Star*—which I find a little odd since I don't insult contestants or crush dreams every few minutes. I guess it's because I'm always honest, so I naturally evolved into that role. I've tried to be really honest with all my artists over the years. I've had to present information that isn't positive news. Rather than sugarcoat it, I have tried to give my artists all the information.

Now on *Nashville Star*, when I have to say something in sixty seconds, sometimes I can't put it gingerly. But I've never told someone he or she looked like "one of those creatures that live in the jungle with those massive eyes." I've never told anyone they were ugly or fat. I might criticize his or her wardrobe, I might question his or her song choices, but I won't go after the person. I've never done that, and I never will do that.

I'm not busting Simon—as he likes to say, "I'm not being rude"—I'm just pointing out differences in philosophies. *American Idol* has the ratings it does in large part because of Simon and his insults, so more power to him. And he'd be the first to tell you that his comments serve a purpose—and he's right. In the music business, you'll be judged every day, and judged every bit as harshly as you would be by Simon Cowell. Minus the insults, you will encounter people as blunt as Simon in every facet of the music industry, every single day of the week. The higher up the ladder you go, the blunter it gets. There's too much at stake and the executive's time is too valuable to be wasted dancing around people's feelings. No matter how nicely you try to phrase it, rejection—and there's way more rejection in this industry than there is acceptance—is a brutal business, and you have to learn to accept it. It's better just to pull the bandage off quickly.

When I went to negotiate a new record deal for John Berry after he had his chart-topping country hit with "Your Love Amazes Me," I took a couple of his new songs to Tony Brown. (This was before he and I ever started dating.) Tony was an executive at MCA and one of the biggest producers in town, and he had a simple answer for me—no. He didn't add flowery words to lessen the sting. Fortunately, we secured a deal with Lyric Street Records, and John got multiple endorsements, a few more singles on the charts, and a few more years of recording for a major label.

REJECTION IS A BRUTAL BUSINESS, AND YOU HAVE TO LEARN TO ACCEPT IT.

No one beats around the bush. No one sugarcoats a "no" because they don't have time for that. It's just "No, and this is why"—and the explanation might not be something you want to hear. Or it might be "no" with no explanation at all.

Like the old saying goes, "It ain't show friends; it's show business." Very rarely will you get someone to say, "Well, do this and do that, and if you work a little harder here—" They're just going to give you a *yes* or a *no.*

This is a big, expensive, high-stakes industry, and you've got to expect a business interaction about your art. It's not about emotions and feelings—when you create the music, that's your job. But you have to put yourself in the executives' shoes and understand what they're looking for. They're looking for a natural. They're looking for someone who is seasoned and has been slugging it out in bars, honky-tonks, or recording studios since they were in high school. They're looking for someone who is gifted at songwriting, like Taylor Swift. They're looking for someone who can wow an audience just by walking into a room, like Garth Brooks or Bruce Springsteen. That's the kind of people who make them want to invest millions of dollars. It's a business, so expect nothing less.

THE BENEFITS OF TALENT SHOWS

Talent contests can be great places to develop your talent. Not only can contests help an artist gain exposure, but the auditioning process can help a fledgling performer gain experience. Entering as many competitions as possible will not hurt you if you have talent. It will hurt you if you don't.

Some people—usually jealous ones—call shows like *Nashville Star* and *American Idol* "shortcuts" to stardom. People behind the scenes are more likely to call them "boot camp." If you're lucky enough—scratch that, if you're *good* enough—to make the final round on one of these shows, you'll likely be paired with vocal coaches, choreographers, performance coaches, stylists, and music directors. They'll work with you to teach you how to maintain your voice, how to pick songs, how to present yourself on stage, and how to conduct yourself in an interview. All the lessons that most artists have to learn by trial and error over the course of several years, talent-show contestants—at least the ones that are going to last—have to learn in a matter of weeks.

"IT AIN'T SHOW FRIENDS, IT'S SHOW BUSINESS."

There's a story in Nashville about Carrie Underwood and another artist doing a day of media and radio interviews in Nashville's RCA offices at the same time, shortly after Carrie had won *American Idol*. The other artist—one of country music's biggest stars—wanted to make the new singer in town feel welcome and made a small-talk comment about how hard these types of days were. Carrie, who'd already been through the grinder of *Idol* press, basically replied that this was nothing compared to what she did for *Idol*.

Shows like *American Idol* and *Nashville Star* are ideal for people in small towns. Few storylines are more deeply ingrained in America's collective consciousness than that of the small-town boy or girl who suddenly rises to fame and fortune. Just ask Carrie Underwood, a native of Checotah, Oklahoma, which has a population of about 3,500.

The contests are also great vehicles for singers who have absolutely no connections within the industry. They may have the dream, they may have the talent, but they have zero relationships. Developing those relationships can be one of the hardest parts of starting a singing career. You'd be amazed how much easier it gets after a few weeks on national TV.

While the contests might seem to favor small-town singers who might not otherwise be "discovered," people in big cities can make use of them, too. Competition for exposure and record deals is really stiff right now, and any performer who isn't exploring every possible avenue isn't doing his or her job. So don't write off the talent shows just because you live in New York, Los Angeles, or Nashville.

It's true that television shows and big record companies alike favor a certain type of look—a gorgeous size two or four in a woman, a V-shaped man with six-pack abs. And that's understandable, to a degree: after all, if you're about to sink a few million dollars into a product, you want every advantage you can possibly have. So if you're not relatively young—in your mid-twenties or younger—and you don't have a classically good-looking appearance, it's hard to go the record-company route. You're just not going to get much attention. Television's a little different, though. While TV certainly favors people who are easy on the eye, it also likes the occasional exception, like Taylor Hicks and *Nashville Star*'s first-season winner, Buddy Jewell.

Hicks turned twenty-eight during *American Idol*'s fifth season, making him the show's oldest winner at the time, and he wasn't a good-looking guy in the classic sense. He didn't have a traditional way of dancing. His music didn't fit the current trends. All in all, he's a pretty odd entertainer. But middle America liked him. They identify with the underdog. They want to root for someone with soul who is not a typical all-American hottie. When I was an A&R executive with Ark 21 Records, I would never have invested a million dollars in Taylor Hicks. And I still wouldn't. But by the time he'd made it through *Idol*, he'd had millions of dollars' worth of marketing and promotion and had created a ready-made fan base.

Jewell was forty-one when he won *Nashville Star* in 2003, and he'd been kicking around Nashville for a decade. His vocals were spot-on and his confidence was there because he'd been singing jingles or demos every day. By traditional Nashville standards, though, he was already old when he got to town. By the time he auditioned for *Nashville Star*, Jewell's shot at getting a hit record through the traditional methods was long past. But all the showcases he had played where record labels had passed on him time and again gave him the experience and the confidence to shine on *Nashville Star*. That was really his only option to grab a bigger audience. Had *Nashville Star* not come his way, he would've continued recording demos and singing nights in little honky-tonks.

By comparison, Chris Young—the show's fourth-season winner, in 2006—could have gone either the record-company or the talent-show route. He was young, he had strong vocals, and he showed promise at writing songs, so he had the option of taking the traditional path, which would have been a little slower, or trying *Nashville Star*.

People like Young have a hard time deciding whether to go the contest route. They wonder if it will help them or hurt them. I think talent shows can only *help* you—if you have talent. Even if you don't make it on television, auditioning for these shows can give you invaluable experience. If you simply haven't had the experience of getting in front of people other than your friends and family and singing, auditioning can give you that chance. If you're not in a situation where you can get a lot of honest, reliable responses to your performances, you'll get them—and *fast*—in the early audition rounds. They're a great place to try out songs, to try out looks, and to find out what works for you and what doesn't.

TALENT SHOWS CAN ONLY HELP YOU— IF YOU HAVE TALENT.

Also, you never know who's in the audience. If one of the judges thinks you have potential, even if it needs development, they may remember your name and keep an eye on you. I've certainly done that.

Even if you're already playing around the region where you live and beginning to develop a fan base, trying out for these shows can be good for you. If you ever audition for the head of a record company, there's a good chance you'll be asked to play for him or her—just you and maybe a guitar or piano. Even if you're used to playing for hundreds or thousands of people every night, singing in front of one or two people in an office is an *entirely* different dynamic. Aside from having a potential record deal on the line, it's not as nerve-wracking as standing in front of a panel of judges singing *a cappella*—the musical equivalent of naked. If you've mastered that, you'll be in good shape when you're faced with the other auditions.

Time and again I've seen artists overanalyze what they do and talk themselves out of perfectly good opportunities. If you are a singer, then the contest route can be a really great route—as long as you're singing jingles and performing live and doing everything else you can think of to make progress in your career and to make a living.

The contest route can also help you learn to handle stress. Auditions are unknown, uncomfortable situations. The more you place yourself in those kinds of situations, the more comfortable they'll become to you. The more you have to sing off the cuff in a pressure-cooker environment, the better you'll be. The first ten times you do it, you're not going to be your best. Eventually, though, you'll be able to rise to that occasion when necessary. It's a great dry run for the real world.

You've got to be able to handle stress because if the contest route doesn't work for you, your next path probably will be doing showcases for labels. Do you think there's no pressure to that? There's *a lot* of pressure with showcases because label executives are even more jaded than TV producers.

WHEN A TV TALENT SHOW *ISN'T* RIGHT FOR YOU

Judges see people at every stage of the game, and we see every personality under the sun. The painfully shy ones break my heart. If you're afraid of heights, why make yourself climb Mount Everest? They're often on the verge of tears. It makes me wonder why they put themselves through the pain.

I also see the overly confident. I see people who are just star seekers who want to be on TV. These people probably auditioned for *The Bachelor*, for *Big Brother*, for *The Apprentice*, for every single contest. With as many reality shows as television offers these days, that's a big trend—people who just want to be on TV, all personality with no talent to back it up. If you don't have the goods and you're just using TV to get ahead, you can really wind up making a fool of yourself. Of course, some people don't seem to mind that.

If you're cocky or if you're a diva, you won't come across well on TV. You've heard people say the camera adds ten pounds to your weight? It does the same thing to your personality. Your personality traits expand on television. Look at *American Idol*, *America's Got Talent*, any audience-voted TV show: those who are cocky and "too" gorgeous—boom, they're gone. They may last a few weeks while the audience waits to see the train wreck they know is coming, but they never get far. Kelly Clarkson isn't cocky. Carrie Underwood doesn't come off like a diva. Clay Aiken isn't rude. Chris Young doesn't act like a jerk. Do you really want to be Omarosa?

SONGWRITERS AND SINGING CONTESTS

Most music-based talent shows favor singers. Entertainers who write their own songs clearly have a disadvantage. The contest route can be a good option if you're a singer/songwriter, but it might not be your number-one option. You need to work with other songwriters, to play songwriter nights, to really develop that craft. That's what's going to get you ahead. You can, however, still use the auditions to hone your performance skills, and a more diverse talent pool of contestants can only help the shows.

There are a few types of artists that these contests wouldn't help and might even hurt. A complicated and volatile personality like Ryan Adams, introverted poets like Bob Dylan and Lucinda Williams—for those kinds of artists, contests are not the right route to take. They're troubadours, poets and philosophers, and their art just wouldn't fit easily into the limits of a televised competition. They're not like Garth Brooks or Beyoncé, where it's all about entertainment. Not that Garth and Beyoncé are one-trick ponies—they're two of my favorite artists. Not everyone is a Bob Dylan or a Ryan Adams—and it wouldn't be good for the music business to have everyone that way. But rather than pursue the talent contests, they just need to slug it out like so many of the artists who have come before them.

Occasionally, I'll see songwriters who focus too much on contests and performing, even though I know that writing is their strength, that their voice is not their "ace in the hole." The only time I see them light up on stage is when they're singing their own songs. Those people really need to diversify their approach, either finding contests that allow them to perform original songs or, perhaps, writing for TV and film to get noticed.

The more talented the artists who audition for these shows, the better the shows will be. These days, you have to be a triple threat—whether it's acting, dancing, and singing or singing, writing, and playing the guitar. You're at a much greater advantage if you've got more than one talent—even if a given outlet doesn't showcase every one of them.

KNOW YOUR PASSION

Many people don't know their true strengths and don't want to admit their weaknesses. It's harder to know what our strengths and weaknesses are when we're young because we haven't made as many mistakes as those who've been around the block a few times. As we gain experience, we realize that the areas of our lives where we make the fewest mistakes are probably the areas where we're gifted. We've got to work harder, highlighting our strengths while minimizing our limitations and hiding our Achilles' heels, to become successful. But when we're young and full of enthusiasm and passion, it's hard to figure out that one thing we're best at. This is one of the most challenging aspects of finding your way to success—and you are not alone!

Ask yourself: "What is the single thing I am most excited about, most passionate about? What is my first thought in the morning? Is it writing a song? Is it grabbing my guitar? Is it singing to someone?" Whatever your answer is, that's probably where you need to focus your energy. If you want to be a singer, sing more. If you want to be a songwriter, write more songs.

Television producers keep saying they need someone who "pops" on TV, but I'm screaming that we need great artists. Sure, on these shows, you need to get yourself noticed. But if you're a great artist *and* you're able to get yourself noticed, all the better. Just ask Tony Bennett.

Credit: Juan Pont Lezica

JENNIFER HANSON:
HOW COMPETITIONS HELPED MY CAREER

Country singer and songwriter Jennifer Hanson used pageants as the launching pad for her career. Named Miss California in 1994, Hanson competed in the Miss America pageant. She had a Top 20 country single in 2002 with "Beautiful Goodbye." Later, she wrote Bucky Covington's debut single "A Different World" and the Wreckers' number one country hit, "Leave the Pieces." She currently records for Nashville-based Universal South Records.

I was fifteen when I competed in my first beauty pageant, and the only reason I even considered it was because there was a talent contest associated with it. I ended up getting second place in the pageant, but I won first place in the talent portion. And that's what started me on the pageant journey.

When I graduated from high school, I became aware that the Miss America pageant had a scholarship program. My incentive for entering the pageant was to earn scholarship money so I could afford to go to college. The Miss America program also had a talent competition, which counted for 40 percent of a contestant's score, so that motivated me as well. I thought the talent event could be a stepping stone for me if I ever got to the state level.

I was eighteen when I entered the Miss Orange County pageant, and I won. I went on to the Miss California pageant, and I won the talent award, but I didn't place in the top ten. I took the scholarship dollars I earned and attended college for the next year or so, and when I ran out of money, I thought I'd try again. In 1994, when I was twenty, I won Miss Garden Grove, went on to Miss California and won that, and then competed in the Miss America pageant.

I learned a lot during that time about how to carry myself as a person. Competing in a pageant is a great way to discipline yourself, and I gained a lot of different skills.

(cont.)

From a music perspective, the thing I gained most was performance experience, as well as finding my voice and the songs that suited my voice.

Music was a passion for me—I started performing in clubs when I was about fourteen years old. I majored in music in college, and I took as many music courses as I possibly could. I also sang in a vocal group. I was constantly honing my craft. Every time I stepped on the pageant stage, I gained more experience performing, as well as connecting and communicating with an audience. Having an outlet in which to perform was huge—to be able to get up in front of people and sing and to be critiqued like that was a growing experience for me.

Judges consider all aspects of your performance—how great your pitch is, how moving your performance is, your song selection, how you're dressed, what you look like on stage, all of it. For a contest, you have to master a two- or three-minute performance—you get that short amount of time to win over the judges and the audience. So you try to make the most of your two-and-a-half minutes on stage. Any time you're in a competitive scenario like that, you just try to put your best foot forward. It's similar to *Idol*—every single time those contestants get on stage, they've got to pick a song that will showcase their voice.

When you're competing, I think the most important thing you can do is be true to yourself. So many times, girls would go into the pageant and try to dress a certain way and be what they thought everyone was looking for. I found that I did best when I stayed true to myself, not only musically but in the clothes I selected, the way I did my hair, all those things. I think anytime you let yourself shine through and come across as genuine, you're going to be more successful. But you've got to work hard and be committed to it.

ARTISTS WHO HAVE APPEARED ON TV TALENT CONTESTS

ARTIST	SHOW
AALIYAH	STAR SEARCH
CHRISTINA AGUILERA	STAR SEARCH
CLAY AIKEN	AMERICAN IDOL
ANN-MARGRET	TED MACK'S ORIGINAL AMATEUR HOUR
TONY BENNETT	ARTHUR GODFREY'S TALENT SCOUTS
BO BICE	AMERICAN IDOL
PAT BOONE	ARTHUR GODFREY'S TALENT SCOUTS, TED MACK'S ORIGINAL AMATEUR HOUR
TERESA BREWER	TED MACK'S ORIGINAL AMATEUR HOUR
IRENE CARA	TED MACK'S ORIGINAL AMATEUR HOUR
NICK CARTER (OF THE BACKSTREET BOYS)	THE ORIGINAL AMATEUR HOUR (1992 VERSION)
ROY CLARK	ARTHUR GODFREY'S TALENT SCOUTS
KELLY CLARKSON	AMERICAN IDOL
PATSY CLINE	ARTHUR GODFREY'S TALENT SCOUTS
ROSEMARY CLOONEY	ARTHUR GODFREY'S TALENT SCOUTS
BUCKY COVINGTON	AMERICAN IDOL
VIC DAMONE	ARTHUR GODFREY'S TALENT SCOUTS

ARTIST	SHOW
CHRIS DAUGHTRY	AMERICAN IDOL
BILLY DEAN	STAR SEARCH
FANTASIA	AMERICAN IDOL
LOUIS FARRAKHAN (AS VIOLINIST LOUIS WOLCOTT)	TED MACK'S ORIGINAL AMATEUR HOUR
JOSE FELICIANO	TED MACK'S ORIGINAL AMATEUR HOUR
CONNIE FRANCIS	TED MACK'S ORIGINAL AMATEUR HOUR
GEORGIA GIBBS	TED MACK'S ORIGINAL AMATEUR HOUR
JOSH GRACIN	AMERICAN IDOL
TAYLOR HICKS	AMERICAN IDOL
JENNIFER HUDSON	AMERICAN IDOL
BUDDY JEWELL	NASHVILLE STAR
GLADYS KNIGHT	TED MACK'S ORIGINAL AMATEUR HOUR
BEYONCÉ KNOWLES	STAR SEARCH
MIRANDA LAMBERT	NASHVILLE STAR
CHERYL LYNN	THE GONG SHOW
ALANIS MORISSETTE	STAR SEARCH
JOHNNY NASH	ARTHUR GODFREY'S TALENT SCOUTS
OINGO BOINGO (AS THE MYSTIC KNIGHTS OF THE OINGO BOINGO)	THE GONG SHOW
FREDA PAYNE	TED MACK'S ORIGINAL AMATEUR HOUR
KELLIE PICKLER	AMERICAN IDOL

ARTIST	SHOW
LEANN RIMES	STAR SEARCH
DIANA ROSS (AS A MEMBER OF THE PRIMETTES)	TED MACK'S ORIGINAL AMATEUR HOUR
SAWYER BROWN	STAR SEARCH
JESSICA SIMPSON	STAR SEARCH
JORDIN SPARKS	AMERICAN IDOL
BRITNEY SPEARS	STAR SEARCH
JIM STAFFORD	TED MACK'S ORIGINAL AMATEUR HOUR
RUBEN STUDDARD	AMERICAN IDOL
JUSTIN TIMBERLAKE	STAR SEARCH
CARRIE UNDERWOOD	AMERICAN IDOL
PHIL VASSAR	STAR SEARCH
ELLIOTT YAMIN	AMERICAN IDOL
CHRIS YOUNG	NASHVILLE STAR

CHAPTER 2

GET READY TO AUDITION

The process of preparing for an audition begins long before the actual audition day. Some people think, "I'm just going to go for it." That's fine, but go for it *after* you prepare. Going for it after you've prepared is just as exciting and exhilarating as winging it—more so, even, when you don't fall flat on your face.

FIRST THINGS FIRST: DISCOVER YOUR UNIQUE STRENGTHS

The first thing you want to do is figure out what your strengths are. That's the beautiful thing about this art—everyone has his or her different strengths. Just look at the different *American Idol* success stories: Jordin Sparks's fresh teen appeal was very different from Fantasia's commanding R&B diva presence, but both women made it to the winner's circle; likewise, Clay Aiken's emotional ballad style was very different from Taylor Hicks's throwback soul. Those singers played to their strengths—and in Taylor's case even played up a "weakness," his awkward, everyman dance moves. The better you understand what you do well, the better you'll do during your auditions and beyond.

I find that artists almost always know what's best for them—artistically, if not commercially or financially. Some artists start their careers with a clear idea of what their sound is. For that kind of artist, the early years are filled with a process of learning to create the sounds she hears in her head. It can take years for an artist to develop the talent, the tools, and the team to put together the style that expresses her true personality through music.

THE BETTER YOU UNDERSTAND WHAT YOU DO WELL, THE BETTER YOU'LL DO DURING YOUR AUDITIONS.

Having worked with Keith Urban during his experimental years, I saw firsthand how much time he took creating his demos. He played all the parts on most of them, and he could point to them as examples of the way he wanted his records to sound. He tried different amps and microphones and studios and producers for years until he finally hit on the best balance. If you listen to Keith's early albums, you can hear him developing the sound he has today, the one that he'd been looking for all his life. It took him years to break through on radio, but now other artists copy his "ganjo" licks and try to emulate his sound. I believe Keith will enjoy a longer career because he took the time to identify and to develop his vision.

At the very beginning of their careers, artists can be confused about what their art really is. Confusion is different from weakness. It's also different from desperation—"I'll do anything. I'll do whatever a label, or the people I'm working with, tell me to do." Other people can help you find your sound, but they can't tell you what it is. You've got to dig for it.

Creating your sound is creating who you are. The digging helps you solve the confusion and find clarity. If you're a singer, it's not as easy to dig deep and figure out what makes you different as an artist as it can be if you also play an instrument or write your own songs. You have to test your voice. You have to figure out if you're a pop singer, a jazz singer, or a bluegrass singer. Sing as much as you can, and sing as many different styles of music as you can, especially when you're by yourself or working with friends.

As you test your voice, look for music that feels natural when you sing it. When you find a song that feels natural, look for other songs with similar melodies or rhythmic patterns. When you've gathered a few of those songs, find an accompanist and sing the songs in several different keys. Avoid the keys that make you strain for high or low notes and that make your voice feel tired after you've sung the song. You'll notice that some keys sound better to you, while others sound worse. You may not sound best in the same key that the original artist recorded in.

After that, if you find a song with lyrics that seem perfectly suited to you, go back to that accompanist and rearrange the song so that you can sing it in the style of music that already feels comfortable to you.

The music you grew up loving might not always be your strength. Sometimes the music you love is not the music you sing well. Waylon Jennings used to say he couldn't go pop with a mouth full of firecrackers. All he had to do was listen to himself sing to know he should be singing country. Brooks & Dunn's Ronnie Dunn was the same way. He sang a lot of rock songs when he started out, but eventually he gravitated toward country. The melodies and the lyrics just suited his voice better.

Some people don't know what kind of music they sing best, and that's okay. That's why you want to surround yourself with people who question you—so you can learn to answer your own questions. Some people are kind, and they'll tell you you're good—parents, especially. But you can usually tell the difference between someone who's genuinely excited about something they've just heard and someone who's just being nice. People always want to hear that they've done well, so they'll often rationalize: "They must have really liked it. They said they did." You've got to get out of your own head. Learn to read body language and become perceptive about the world around you.

When you sing for people and have to push a high note or go *a cappella* (sing with no musical accompaniment) watch their body language. Look for their response. If your audience spontaneously claps in the middle of your song, what were you doing just at that moment? If people suddenly become still and quiet when you sing an emotional ballad, you've probably got them in the palm of your hand; if you hear a lot of chatter, though, you've got a problem. Do you notice people leaving the venue during a particular song each night? That song might need to exit your set list. If suddenly the crowd gets up to dance, maybe you should perform more songs like that. These audience cues will help you determine your strengths and weaknesses as a singer.

Nashville Star's fourth-season winner, Chris Young, had been singing a lot of songs with an "outlaw" edge to them, like Tim McGraw's "Real Good Man" and Charlie Daniels' "Drinkin' My Baby Goodbye." But the night he sang the song he wrote, "Drinkin' Me Lonely," it was just Chris and his guitar. All of a sudden, his voice was delicate rather than just deep, aloof, and strong—and that's when the whole audience exploded with applause. It was a magical moment and his defining performance on the show. You can't buy that. You can't force it. You just need to read moments like that and remember, "That's a strength."

AUDIENCE CUES WILL HELP YOU DETERMINE YOUR STRENGTHS AND WEAKNESSES AS A SINGER.

I've told many people, "I think you're pursuing this the wrong way." During the third season of *Nashville Star*, I told Jayron Weaver I believed he would make a better Christian artist than he would a country artist. I didn't say that as a derogatory statement. He had a voice like an angel—clear, gentle, and peaceful—and he didn't have any swagger or cockiness at all. He had an air about him that reminded me of Michael W. Smith and Steven Curtis Chapman. He made no secret about his faith, and I felt he wouldn't need to change much about himself for a Christian audience to find him authentic.

Unfortunately, he took my recommendation as an insult. He'd talked on the show about his Christian faith, and he and his family believed I said he should be a Christian artist because he'd talked about his faith. Then his mother said, "It's like you don't deserve to win just because you are a Christian. That's what it sounds like Anastasia's saying. People are really getting aggravated with her. We're ready to pull her hair out." They thought I was rude for saying what I did. But I didn't want him to pretend to swagger or wear a hat just to fit into the country genre. I wanted him to find a way to get his music and his personality across authentically. I wanted him to be true to himself, and I thought pursuing a Christian-music career would be the best way for him to do that.

Jayron tried for years to get a country deal. He is still looking for a deal. Watching his strengths, I knew he wouldn't succeed. He wasted good years pursuing the wrong path. If he was in a honky-tonk singing "She Thinks My Tractor's Sexy" and getting no applause—well, that's a sign he needed to listen to.

Maybe Jayron was looking at a particular artist as an example of the career he wanted. It's fine to let other artists inspire you, but you've got to create your own path. You've got to do what's best for your talent rather than trying to follow the herd or thinking, for example, that country music could be more lucrative than Christian music and therefore going for country even though that's not what you do best. Too many people think that way. They think, "I'm not going to pursue jazz because there's no money in jazz." Well, guess what? If you're not doing what you're meant to be doing, you're probably not going to make money anyway—and you're certainly not going to be happy doing it. Follow your heart more than your head, and the right success will follow.

IT'S FINE TO LET OTHER ARTISTS INSPIRE YOU, BUT YOU'VE GOT TO CREATE YOUR OWN PATH.

Emmylou Harris has one of the most beautiful, fulfilling careers of any artist in the history of our industry. She's had hit records, and she's won Grammys. She's not selling out arenas, and she's not selling 5 million records. But I'll bet that at the end of her day, she feels fulfilled. Had she said, "I really need to take this path to sell more records," then we would have lost one of our best artists. So you really have to get your head out of your heart!

FIND THE RIGHT SONG, PART I

As an auditioning artist, you need to think very carefully about what you sing. One of the most common mistakes throughout the contest route is song selection—a singer picking the wrong style of music for her voice, the wrong song for his persona. The right song can make you stand out from everyone around you. The wrong song can make you seem just like everybody else or can hurt your chances of getting to the next level.

Few young artists pick their material well, but that's hardly a recent problem. In a 1954 *Time* magazine article, the associate producer of *Ted Mack's Original Amateur Hour* complained about the lack of imagination contestants displayed in their choice of material. "For a while all amateurs were singing 'Believe,'" she said. "Then they were all singing 'Stranger in Paradise;' now it's either 'Answer Me,' 'My Love,' or 'Secret Love.' They always sing the top hit song."

The songs may have changed since the era of Doris Day and Nat "King" Cole, but the problem remains the same. Too many singers believe the quickest road to success is to sing a song somebody else has just made a hit. That thinking may work well at clubs and parties where people expect to hear the latest radio hits, but if you're trying out for *American Idol*, it's the quickest way to make sure you sound exactly like ten thousand other people who will wind up on the cutting-room floor.

The only way to make a Rihanna song work in an audition for a TV talent show is to be able to sing it better than Rihanna. If you're a better singer than Martina McBride—and, trust me, you're probably not—*then* you can try "Broken Wing." Otherwise, you're better off staying away from it. Opt for a song you can make your own.

SING A SONG THAT YOU LOVE, THE KIND OF THING YOU CATCH YOURSELF SINGING WHEN YOU DON'T REALLY REALIZE YOU'RE SINGING.

So what should you sing? Sing a song that you love, the kind of thing you catch yourself singing when you don't really realize you're singing. Pick something that shows off the best qualities of your voice, not something you think shows the judges what they want to hear. Most judges want to hear something they've never heard before. They've already heard Alicia Keys; they've already heard Chris Brown—if you're just mimicking them, we don't need you.

Consider looking for material a little off the beaten path. One of the most wonderful moments in any *American Idol* audition round came in 2006 when seventeen-year-old Paris Bennett tried out with the Dixie Chicks's "Cowboy Take Me Away." The judges knew to expect something good from the girl—after all, her grandmother was gospel singer Ann Nesby, who'd performed with the Sounds of Blackness—but none of them expected her to lead with a country song. She completely shattered any presuppositions they might have had about her. She did it again when they asked her to sing a second number and she countered with "Take Five," a jazz classic with an unusual time signature. Nobody imagined that a teen-aged black girl would choose either of those songs, much less have the confidence and the nerve to put them together. Picking those two songs sent a strong message—"This girl can sing anything"—and it was one of the best one-two punches in the show's history.

Another *Idol* contestant from that season said he had more trouble grasping the concept of song selection. "The whole time I was on the show, I was like, 'I just don't get it,'" says Bucky Covington. "Some songs suit your voice better than others. A lot of times, other people can tell you what the right song is better than you can. It's hard to say yourself."

Some people try to outthink a show's producers. They'll think, "They had a country winner last season, so they won't want one of those this year. I'll do pop." They try to predict what the judges want to hear. Instead of thinking outward like that, I recommend artists look inward and ask themselves different questions: "When have I felt most confident, and what was I doing then? Was I singing a ballad? Was I dancing and singing uptempo? Was I in an intimate environment singing a love song? Where was I the most confident, and what gave me the best reaction?" Those are the questions you should ask. Being the best self you can possibly be is the only way you'll move forward.

When I was working as a music supervisor, looking for music for movies, songwriters would ask me, "What kinds of songs are you looking for right now? What should I write? What topics are you looking for?" They would try to predict what I was looking for, and that's impossible. A moment will freeze for me when I hear something brilliant, and it won't matter if I'm looking for that or not—I'll save it till I need it. So looking inward rather than outward is an important exercise for an artist. Keep asking those questions: "What was I singing when I felt most confident? How was I performing when I got the best crowd reaction?" Analyze what's worked well for you. Whatever is best for you, do it, and don't waver. Commit to it.

A NOTE ON YOUR APPLICATION

The application is the way you introduce yourself, so make it count. The judges will see thousands of them. How will you stand out? Your audition begins with your application, so try to find somewhere on that application to help the judges remember who you are.

If there's a place for background information, write down something interesting and be sure to mention it during your audition. Even if there's not a blank, there's always room on the side, but keep it neat.

One of the most memorable *Nashville Star* auditions I've seen took place during the third season's regional round. A beautiful young lady wearing a knit hat performed "Ring of Fire" like I'd never heard it before. She turned the song into the sexiest waltz I'd ever heard. Later, when I tried to find her application, I couldn't figure out who she was—she hadn't worn the hat in the picture she submitted, and she hadn't listed the song she planned to perform. I always wished she had made it to the TV show, and to this day, I refer to her as The Ring of Fire Girl.

Whether it's a song you'll sing or something you know you're going to wear or say to the judges, put it on your application. Make sure your application connects you to your audition so the judges or the show's staff will be more likely to remember you just by looking at that sheet of paper.

CLOTHES CAN MAKE (OR UNMAKE) THE CONTESTANT

When picking out an audition ensemble, remember the words of author Fran Lebowitz: "If people don't want to listen to you, what makes you think they want to hear from your sweater?"

Don't let your outfit overwhelm your personality or, worse, your voice. Beware of the temptation to try to look so good that you get away from what works for you. Some women try to get noticed by going really sexy. Some men try to go too trendy and put on something they'd never wear otherwise. Women also tend to apply more makeup than they normally would because they're going to be on TV. But if you don't know how to do TV makeup right and you just put more on, you look worse. In general, there's too much makeup on at auditions, and the clothes often don't work. They give me the impression the singers just ran out and bought something they saw on *American Idol* last season.

THE MORE YOU ARE YOURSELF, THE BETTER.

If you get on the show, you'll work with professional stylists. Some singers are confident enough to use the stylists' expertise to complement what they already know. That's what I loved about Miranda Lambert. She was exactly who we see today, even back in 2003 on *Nashville Star*. But 2006 winner Angela Hacker let herself be put in some dresses that I'd bet a thousand dollars she'd never wear anywhere else. Those clothes took away what had made her stand out. Angela's a swampy, soulful redneck, and she shouldn't be singing in a fluffy, bright yellow dress.

If you're not comfortable, guess what? Your performance will be stiff. Take Gretchen Wilson—no one has convinced her to wear Prada dresses or Christian Louboutin pumps. She's known for jeans, tank tops, and boots. So you inform the stylist, "This is what I'm known for—can you find something like this rather than taking me in a whole different direction?"

Start from your personality. If you're a jock, say you're a jock. Josh Turner is not like John Rich, wearing rhinestones up the side, or like Kenny Chesney, wearing jeans and tight-fitting T-shirts. Josh keeps his image understated and classic, drawing attention to his voice.

You've got to listen to your gut. A lot of times, people don't trust themselves and they don't want people to see them as difficult, so they acquiesce. Be open to new ideas, sure, but you can also say, in a nice way, "I don't think I'm going to be comfortable singing on national TV in this outfit. Let's look for an alternative." Don't you regret every time you ignore your gut? I do. Trust your gut—trust yourself. The more you are yourself, the better. And the less you'll look like the singers auditioning before and after you.

GET SERIOUS ABOUT GETTING READY

Studies show that most people make remarkably accurate assessments of new people and situations within five to ten seconds. That's especially true of auditions, where judges train themselves to identify talent quickly and to make snap decisions. Contestants must make each second count, and the best ones eliminate as many potentially negative variables from the audition process as much as possible.

CONTESTANTS MUST MAKE EACH SECOND COUNT.

So spend a lot of time getting ready for those few seconds.

As a rule, "new is not best" when it comes to auditions. Experience is your best guide. People often try to do something new when they get to a critical juncture—a new hairdo, a new style, a new song—but when you're under pressure, you'll be better off going with what you know.

We've all made that mistake. I've tried something new because I was going to be appearing on a big TV show, doing a photo shoot for an important magazine, or meeting a new person. But I ended up awkward and uncomfortable that way, and who I am didn't come across. So use what's been successful for you in the past. That's your strength, and that's your first card to play because you've proven time and again that it works for you.

This holds true for music choices, as well as looks. If you have the option of choosing a song you've already performed, go with that. Double-check to make sure it's the best key for your voice. You might even alter the arrangement. If you don't have that option, go through the list of approved songs beforehand. Choose a song and change it—change the key, change the arrangement, turn it into a waltz, make it soft or angry. There are many ways you can interpret a song.

Then test some of those songs in public. Sing them at your church or a little club; sing them at your school talent show. Sing them to your music teacher. Sing them on videotape. See where you get the loudest clapping, where you get the most autograph requests, where you get the most girls' phone numbers. Perform them a few times before you sing them for Randy Jackson, for me, or for a TV audience. If you're getting a good reaction, maybe you're on to something.

When you're trying out material, don't ask your parents for their opinion. They love you. I love my son, and I'm going to do everything I can to keep his confidence at an all-time high at all times. I'll be honest with him, but he's still my son whom I will always love and protect. Here's the person whose opinion you want to ask: the person who'll tell you, "Yes, it makes your butt look big."

"Your parents always tell you you're good," says Dierks Bentley, who's had several number-one country hits with songs like "What Was I Thinkin'" and "Long Trip Alone." One of Dierks's first encounters with honest, helpful criticism came from songwriter Brett Jones, whose hits include Lee Ann Womack's "A Little Past Little Rock" and Tracy Lawrence's "Better Man Better Off." The two were at a Nashville song-publishing company with several songwriters who were more experienced than Dierks.

"They said come upstairs; we're passing some songs around," recalls Dierks, who was just starting out in Nashville at the time. "I go up there, and there are about five people in the room. Everyone's passing songs around. It comes to me, and I pull out my biggest song, which I thought was great. One woman said, 'I just didn't really get the hook.' Brett said, 'Yeah, and it took forever to get there. People would walk out if it took that long.'

"It was the first real criticism of any of my songs. Up until then, everyone had said, 'Oh my gosh, you're so great, blah blah.'

"Brett told me, 'Write about five hundred songs. Then put them in a drawer and forget about them. Once you do that, give me a call because I think you've got something and you probably just need to work on it.'

"I was thinking, *five hundred songs?* At that point, I'd probably written thirty songs, and they were all in a nice notebook. The idea of just writing songs and tossing them in a drawer then going on to the next one was really foreign to me. But it ended up being some of the best advice I got. At the time, I thought he was being a jerk. Later, I realized you need that hard criticism because you're not going to get that from anyone else."

Some people, especially hard workers, tend to be most critical of themselves. They can hear nine positive comments on work they've done, and the single negative comment is the only one that makes any impact. They're just obsessed with trying to do better.

FIGURE OUT HOW TO BRIDGE FROM A SURPRISE QUESTION TO THE MAIN POINT YOU WANT TO GET ACROSS.

Of course, you also have to be aware of jealousy and competition, so think about the person you can really trust—the one who let you know about the spinach stuck between your teeth or told you when you hurt her feelings. Then grab a video camera and record your run-through—even the part where you enter the room and walk up to the judges' table—and let your super-honest friend play the role of the judge. Have your friend videotape you in the outfit you plan to wear; hand her the application you're going to give the judges. Have her test how you're going to be remembered, whether you're saying, "Yes, I just got out of jail last weekend," or "I'm going to sing 'Ring of Fire' like you've never heard it before." Test yourself with your honest friend—all the way through the performance—then watch the tape to see what worked and what didn't. Then do it again and again until you're completely comfortable with what you see.

It's also a good idea to practice a little chit-chat for the judges. Even if you're used to playing music and talking with your friends and fans afterwards, you might be thrown by a few pointed questions. If you make it through the first audition rounds to meet with the show's judges, you know you're going to be asked, "Why do you think you're the next big star?" Have an answer ready that doesn't make you look arrogant or inarticulate.

When Senator Ted Kennedy was seeking the Democratic nomination for president in 1980, he sat for an interview with CBS newsman Roger Mudd. The interview was going along great until Mudd asked the simplest of questions: "Senator Kennedy, why do you want to be president?" Kennedy gave Mudd a deer-in-the-headlights look, then tried to stutter and stumble through an answer that ended up being completely incomprehensible. People watching the interview thought, "If he doesn't know why he wants to be President, why on earth should I vote for him?" If you want people to vote for you in a talent show, be ready to give them a reason they should.

Some of the most talented people in the world are introverts, and it's often hard for them to communicate when they're not singing. I'd bet that applies to more than half of the people who read this book. If you're an introvert, you need to sit down the same way you do when you write a song or decide how to sing it—and just map out a plan. Literally, think to yourself: "If I am asked this question, I'll say this." Write out the answer, practice it, and have it prepared. Figure out how to bridge from a surprise question to the main point you want to get across. The more introverted you are, the more difficult those types of questions will be. The more prepared you are, the more in control you'll feel.

WHEN YOU PRACTICE FOR YOUR AUDITION, FOLLOW THE RULES OF THE COMPETITION.

Carrie Underwood, for example, is extremely bashful, and her shyness was painfully obvious to many of the people who met her in the months after her *American Idol* win. She's not always comfortable when meeting strangers, particularly members of the press, and she's had to work hard to be able to give good interviews. She can be a wonderful interview now, but reporters who don't know her well occasionally perceive her as over-rehearsed. That's just a result of Carrie's compensating for her shyness.

I can't believe more people who audition don't record themselves beforehand. But most people don't. It's like trying to wing an exam where only the top grade passes or playing in the state football championship without practicing the week before.

When you practice for your audition, follow the rules of the competition. You can't practice with a guitar then think you're going to be fine without the guitar during the audition. It frustrates me to no end that contestants aren't allowed to use accompaniment for auditions. I understand why producers do it—they want singers who can carry a show (and a tune) without any help; they want performers who can turn their energy on as easily as they flip a light switch; and they want to put contestants in one of the toughest possible settings to help weed out people who might freeze on live television—but some people cannot sing without a guitar, so we're not allowing them to be themselves. But if your tools are being taken away from you because of the contest rules, try to bring the tools along just so they're near you. They'll help you feel safe and add to your comfort level. Bring your guitar, or have your harmonica in your pocket. And bring that honest friend with you.

A FINAL NOTE: CLEAN OUT YOUR INTERNET CLOSET

If you seriously plan to face the challenges of stardom, start maintaining your public image now as if you were already a public figure. Don't get drunk and clown around with a video camera. Don't let your girlfriends talk you into taking racy photos during a sleepover. Don't let a security camera catch you shoplifting from a mall. In the Internet age, there's no such thing as privacy, so if you don't want everybody in the world to see you doing it, don't do it in the first place. I don't want to sound preachy, but there are more important reasons to refrain from this type of behavior than a TV contest.

If you've got pictures on Facebook® you wouldn't want to see on *Entertainment Tonight* or if you've posted things on somebody's message board you wouldn't want to see reprinted in *USA Today*, find them and delete them before you make the show. If you wait until you've made it through a few rounds, somebody on the show's staff will have already found them and made copies. If you wait until you're on the show, they'll be part of your history forever.

If you don't think this sort of thing matters, go Google these words—"Antonella Barba photos." Now . . . do you remember what she sang?

Credit: Andrew Southman

COLBIE CAILLAT: LEARN TO PLAY AN INSTRUMENT

For years, my parents told me I should learn to play an instrument. They told me if I wanted to be a singer and have a career then I should learn to play an instrument and write my own songs. They gave me piano lessons, but I kept quitting. I could've started when I was fourteen or fifteen and been really good now, but I didn't. If I'd focused when I was young, then I would be better than I am now. At the beginning it's very tough—your fingers hurt when you play guitar, and you can't sing and play at the same time. But you get past that after, like, a month. So just push through it.

CHAPTER 3

THE AUDITION

So this is it—the big day. You've prepared for today's audition for weeks, maybe months—maybe, indirectly, for years. You know you're ready to sing, but you're still a bundle of nerves. That's good. If you can harness your nerves instead of letting them take control of you, that anxiety will heighten your awareness and help you do better. It's your body telling you it's ready to perform.

BEFORE YOU GO IN

Get the best night's sleep you can before your audition. That probably won't be easy, but at least save the parties for afterwards.

If this is your first major audition, consider it nothing more than a rehearsal. Don't approach the day as your big chance; approach it as your learning experience, especially if you haven't sung much in public. It's not the end of the world if the judges send you home after thirty seconds. This is not your only chance in the spotlight.

If the thought of singing in front of strangers sends your nerves into overdrive, pick a heartening person (or even a pet!) and think of that audience as you prepare to sing. That way, you're singing in front of a friend rather than an intimidating, unfamiliar person.

Treat your fellow contestants kindly, and try to make a positive impression on the show's producers and judges (without overdoing it, of course). The one person to whom you reveal your inner diva or your secret jerk will be the person you're most likely to encounter at some point in the future. Feel free to watch what everybody else is doing, but don't make any last-minute decisions or changes to your audition based on what everybody else does.

Credit: David McClister Photography

BO BICE ON HIS AUDITION

Bo Bice placed second behind Carrie Underwood on American Idol*'s 2005 season. He'd gotten his start in a school competition at age thirteen, and he had fifteen years of playing throughout the Southeast by the time he auditioned for* Idol.

By the time I got to Orlando, we were probably eight hundredth or nine hundredth in line. Some 21,000 people had shown up—17,000 got wristbands to audition. They had karaoke booths set up in two corners of the venue, so 17,000 people were trying to sleep on the floor with full-time karaoke going. I was just sitting there, thinking, "Oh, this is bad. I don't know why I am here. I don't know anything about this pop stuff. I don't even watch *American Idol.* My mom better see something that I don't." I never in a million years dreamed I was going to make it as far as I did. My true intention that day was just to get in front of whomever I needed to get in front of. They were going to tell me, "You're all wrong for this television show—it's a pop show. But call this guy and maybe he'll help you further your career." I was looking to do what I still think are two of the most important things in this business—networking and making contacts. I wasn't looking for the fast train I ended up getting through *Idol.*

GET OFF TO A GOOD START

"If you don't grab the attention of the producers in the first five seconds, you will not make it to the next round," says *Nashville Star* executive producer Jeff Boggs, who also has helped *American Idol*'s producers develop CMT's *Can You Duet.* "That goes from local auditions to home video tapes. There has to be something in the first five to ten seconds that makes the producers listen longer; otherwise, they just tune out.

"You can tell right away if that person is going to be a star. You can't pull it out of them; that person has to be a star from the first second that we see them."

With the stakes that high, how can you maximize that minimal amount of time?

When you go in for your audition, smile at the judges and make eye contact with them. Be friendly, but don't overdo it. Some guys think that flirting with a female judge will help them. It doesn't, and it's kind of creepy. Even if we're older than you, it doesn't help your cause. The same thing goes for women who undo an extra button on their blouses or wear their clothes a couple sizes too tight. You want the judges to remember your voice and your personality, not your breasts—you can buy those anywhere. Act like a professional, and get down to business. Don't suppress the excitable qualities of your personality, but keep them in check—as you might do if you were going on a job interview.

STICK WITH WHAT YOU'VE PRACTICED AND REHEARSED, AND COMMIT TO IT.

The first year of *Nashville Star*, I didn't judge on the show, but I helped with some early rounds that weren't on TV. During the third, fourth, and fifth seasons, I traveled to a couple of regional competitions. Afterwards, the judges and show's producers watched the final forty contestants on tape, and we made our decisions together. Then I saw who made the show when the rest of America did. So I've seen all the different stages of auditioning. It's a pressure cooker for all of us.

I've seen people cry. I've seen people unable to finish their songs. I've seen them start the song in the wrong key, so they'd have to stop when the melody got too high or too low for them. That's where practicing is important. That first note has to come naturally, but in order to make it look easy, you need to prepare, rehearse, and prepare some more.

I've seen people change their minds about their audition song at the last minute. That's just asking for problems. Stick with what you've practiced and rehearsed, and commit to it. Commitment in everything in life is important. Once you dig deep and know where your strong point is, commit to it. Wear blinders. Don't let other auditioners influence you. Just focus on yourself and your plan.

Keeping in mind Jeff's statement about how little time contestants have to impress audition judges, don't think you have to start your number at the beginning. You've picked your best song; now get to the best part quickly. If there's a spot in the chorus that shows the strengths in your voice—sometimes called the "money notes"—begin the song there.

"If you're singing a song like Martina McBride's 'Independence Day,' I probably would start with the big part instead of the verse," Jeff says. "Everyone can sing that part. When you have only a few seconds, start with the big 'let freedom ring' and blow the judges away."

LOOK FOR SUBTLE WAYS TO DISTINGUISH YOURSELF DURING YOUR AUDITION.

That small, single action sends multiple messages. Not only do you immediately show the judges your voice's best qualities, you also let them know you're not messing around. One minor adjustment will separate you from most other people the judges see that day.

"It sounds simple, but 90 percent of the people who sing that song start at the beginning and never get to the big part," Jeff says.

I've noticed that many contestants who get to the big part sing it too loudly. They think if they sing high and loud and go full-throttle for the entire song, they're going to get further ahead. That couldn't be further from the truth. Volume does not equal talent.

I'm not saying you have to whisper; I'm just saying that louder doesn't equal better. It's a rookie mistake. I've done the equivalent on the business side, where my passion was so huge

I was going to conquer the world and produce a big European tour, but it was too early for me to do something of that magnitude, and I announced it too soon and fell flat on my face.

When you're developing, realize that you're learning. Like my grandmother said, you have two ears and one mouth. Listen more than you talk. Be a sponge.

Whenever I'd sit in on the early audition rounds for *Nashville Star*, I'd try to give contestants a little feedback. If I didn't plan to move someone along, I'd try to tell him why not. That's not always an option, though. Especially in the pre-television audition rounds, judges need to move as many people through the queue as quickly as possible, and there's just not time to give each contestant even the tiniest bit of personal attention. Judges just have to trust their guts and make decisions.

Look for subtle ways to distinguish yourself during your audition. One male artist auditioning for *Nashville Star* talked about his time in jail. He'd included that innocent and hilarious story on his application. I was sitting there reading his application, watching him sing, and I totally remembered him during recap meetings. Even just a couple of sentences on your application can help people remember you.

Obviously, you want to follow the rules, but know when you can bend them. For example, the first round of *American Idol* auditions doesn't allow you to sing with a guitar. I had an intern who tried out for the show, and I suggested she take her guitar anyway to send the message that there was more to her than just her singing. She didn't get on the show, but she is performing live, writing songs, and using that experience to move forward. Pushing the boundaries is okay, like bringing that guitar to send the message that you're multitalented. Even if they don't let you use it, they notice it.

ANOTHER SONG IN YOUR BACK POCKET

In most TV contests, you have to choose your audition material from a preapproved list of songs. Perhaps none of those songs suits you perfectly. This is nonnegotiable, so deal with it or choose a different route to get your start. But as you move along in the audition process, there is a chance a judge will ask you to sing one of your favorites, so always have a backup song prepared that you can sing at the drop of a hat. It should be something that shows your versatility, too—something tried and true. Don't start with your backup; don't even volunteer. Just have it ready in case somebody asks you. It doesn't happen often, but judges do like to test somebody and see her come through.

In the first season of *Nashville Star*, one contestant in the early rounds of auditions had patterned his style after early honky-tonk singers like Hank Williams and Ernest Tubb. He clearly wasn't going to make it to the finals, but he was a good singer, if a bit nasal, and he was extremely personable. He did all right with his audition performance, but the song obviously didn't suit his voice. The judges noticed and asked him to sing another song—not necessarily something from the approved list, just whatever he'd have used to audition if he'd had his choice. He didn't miss a beat. I don't remember his audition piece, but I still remember the song he chose: Wynn Stewart's "It's Such a Pretty World Today," a big hit back in 1967. It's a great country song, but one obscure enough that most of today's stars would have trouble singing it at the drop of a hat. He didn't make the show, but he blew the judges away and they moved him on to the next round. One of them even approached him later to ask for a demo. He eventually went on to work in Loretta Lynn's road band.

HOW YOU HANDLE A MISTAKE WILL TELL THE JUDGES MORE ABOUT YOUR POISE AND CHARACTER THAN ANYTHING ELSE YOU DO.

At the other extreme sits 2006 *American Idol* auditioner Josh Flom. You may remember him as the hoarse-throated rock singer who professed his admiration for Chris Daughtry before shouting his way through a Fuel song. More amused than impressed, the judges asked him how he'd handle ABBA week, singing like he did. Josh, of course, didn't know any ABBA songs, so Simon challenged him to go learn one, then come back in fifteen minutes and audition again.

Josh had his golden opportunity, the second chance *Idol* contestants almost never get. Simon had given him enough rope to hang himself—or to swing into Hollywood. Josh raced out of the room, found someone who quickly taught him "Dancing Queen," then came back—and sang it just like he'd sung the Fuel song. He proved the judges' assertion that he wasn't versatile enough to be an *American Idol.* If he'd nailed "Dancing Queen," adapted his style to the song in a creative way that shone new light on him *and* the song, he'd immediately have become a favorite of fans and judges alike. He might even have had enough momentum to propel him into the finals. Instead, he showed his own limitations, and he went home.

By the way, if you want to hear an approach that might have proved successful, search for the cover version by the Yayhoos, which features former Georgia Satellites singer Dan Baird.

WHAT THESE SHOWS ARE REALLY ABOUT

Contrary to what Simon Cowell likes to say, these shows are *not* singing competitions. First and foremost, they're TV shows—they just happen to be TV shows about singing competitions.

So, sure, producers and judges want singers. They also want people with presence and identity. Know your personality—what makes you unique—and play to it in a way that would make the one person you most want to impress proud to see it on television. They want to create compelling television with a well-rounded cast. You wouldn't want an *American Idol* with Melinda Doolittle, Lakisha Jones, Mandisa Hundley, Jennifer Hudson, Kimberly Locke, and Fantasia Barrino at the same time, and you wouldn't want to put Carrie Underwood, Kellie Pickler, Bucky Covington, and Josh Gracin together in the same season. But a soft-spoken Indian-American teenager? A white guy with prematurely gray hair who sings old-school R&B but can't dance? A large guy with glasses who went to Bob Jones University

ALWAYS HAVE A BACKUP SONG PREPARED THAT YOU CAN SING AT THE DROP OF A HAT.

and shoots wisecracks back at Simon? You don't get too many of those, and they'll add a little spice to any season.

When judges listen to so many people sing for such a short time, only a very few will stand out for any reason, good or bad. Most contestants fall into the "Yeah, they're okay, but they don't do anything for me" category. That happens for a variety of reasons. Maybe they're too nervous. Maybe they didn't prepare enough. Maybe they didn't pick the right song. Maybe they're just not that talented. For whatever reasons, they wind up being part of the pack. When that happens—and, honestly, it happens most of the time—there's not much to say to a contestant.

If you get any constructive comment from a professional judge in an early audition round, consider yourself fortunate. You made an impression. Even if they're telling you something you did wrong, you need to listen rather than try to mount a defense. You can count on one hand—and you'd probably still have a couple fingers left over—the number of times a contestant has explained her choices or her actions to a judge on one of these TV shows and changed the judge's mind about her performance. By that point, the judge has made his mind up, and pleading will do a contestant as much good as a baseball player arguing with an umpire: all it'll do is get him tossed out of the game earlier. Keep this in mind: unless that judge is telling you to look for a new line of work, his criticism probably means he saw something promising in you that compelled him to comment.

WHEN YOU GET THE NEWS—PASS OR FAIL—REACT WITH POISE, THANK THE JUDGES, AND MOVE ON.

If the judges pass on you, don't ask for a second song. You'll look desperate and insecure when judges are looking for confidence. You won't leave a good impression, and the judges are likely to remember how badly you acted if you go in front of them again. When you get the news—pass or fail—react with poise, thank the judges, and move on. Less is more.

Sometimes you can do everything in the world right but your timing's off. On *Nashville*

Star, sometimes we have too many girls and too few guys. In that case, the bar gets set much higher for women, and some really good ones go right past us. Maybe it's just bad timing for you because the show needs another guy, or they need an R&B singer and you do country.

Some people will do extreme or extremely stupid things to get on one of these shows. If you're just trying to get your thirty seconds on national TV, that's fine, but if you really think you've got a shot at the finals, tone it down. And keep in mind: it's almost as hard to be memorably bad as it is to be memorably good. You think it's easy to be as bad as William Hung or Martik Manoukian (the crazy panther guy from *Idol*'s Season 6)? Those guys worked hard at what they did. Go back and watch Martik's audition video. He wasn't improvising—he'd been rehearsing that bit for *years*. If that's your thing, have fun with it.

RENEE LAYHER:
DRESS TO IMPRESS AT THE AUDITION

Wardrobe stylist Renee Layher worked at Ralph Lauren before moving to Nashville, where she has styled singers like Kellie Pickler, Alison Krauss, Wynonna Judd, and Gary Allan. "I don't think the wardrobe makes the deal for you when you walk into a meeting or audition," she says. "You do that, but you have to look put together to do it. Most of the time when a record label gives you a deal, they're going to change your look anyway to fit the marketing. I think you just have to be well put together and have a good fit." Here are Renee's recommendations for making that great first impression.

1. **KEEP IT SIMPLE.** People feel as if they need to invent themselves before they go in for these things, and they end up taking on trends and doing silly things that just don't look attractive. What you want to do is get your talent across. So keep it as simple as possible, and don't try to go after trendy stuff. It's all about simplicity and not overdoing it, especially at the beginning.

(cont.)

2. **WEAR SOMETHING THAT FITS.** If you don't know what fits your body well, talk to someone who does. Get an opinion from somebody who dresses well, or go to a personal shopper in a department store and ask what works for your body type. If you're a young woman, go into the juniors department to find that; don't go to the misses dresses.
3. **KEEP THE JEWELRY TO A MINIMUM.** Don't accessorize yourself to death because it takes away from what you're trying to do. Once again, think simplicity.
4. **AVOID PRINTS.** Don't do stripes or dots either because they're going to moray out on camera. That's the distracting, out-of-focus-looking video pattern you sometimes see in amateur videos. White isn't good either because sometimes it looks too stark on camera. You can wear a variation of white, like a cream, but it's got to be soft.
5. **COVER YOUR BELLY BUTTON.** The whole midriff thing is so 1990s—and it is not attractive; I don't care how great your body is. It's not about showing as much skin as possible. My mother always said you don't have to show skin to be a beautiful woman, and I've always followed that motto. If you have the right fit for your body, everyone is going to see how beautiful you are.
6. **WEAR UNIQUE PIECES.** Find things that are interesting and not just things you can buy off the rack. Think about your music, what you're trying to get across, what makes you stand out from everybody else. Wardrobe-wise, if you do have one thing you're in love with, like really interesting necklaces, then play on that vibe.

7. **TAKE A PHOTO OF YOURSELF.** See how your outfit, including the undergarments you plan to wear, translates on camera. Most people don't know about lighting, but it's so important when picking what you wear. Stand in direct sunlight—this will give you a good idea of how your outfit will look under TV lights.
8. **GET OPINIONS FROM PEOPLE YOU TRUST.** Remember, your parents are not always wrong. They are there to help and guide you. Now, if you look at your mother and think, "There's no way I'd wear that in my entire life," then don't get advice from mom. But there are peers in your life to whom you can turn for advice.

WHAT TO DO WHEN THINGS GO WRONG

If you go to enough auditions, you'll eventually have a bad one. Even the best singers in the world forget a lyric or miss a note. I'm always curious to see a contestant's reaction when he makes a mistake. It's a great gauge of how mature or immature the singer is.

So you go for a high note and go bust. Just keep on singing. Do not cry, do not laugh. How you handle a mistake will tell the judges more about your poise and character than anything else you can do. Sometimes, you can turn an accident into something beautiful, showing poise and grace along the way. Don't act embarrassed or silly; just keep on singing and try to make the last portion of your song even more beautiful than the first part. If you forget the words, don't blink. Keep in mind that the judges sometimes don't know the words to the song any better than you do, so they might not notice if you recover quickly enough. And if you make up something good on the spot, you just might impress them.

Some people start then want to stop and start again. Sometimes you can get away with doing that once. You could casually, without embarrassment, say, "Wrong key, could I try again? Do you have time?" or "Wrong words, may I start over?" Show your poise, though. Don't ask in an embarrassed or ditzy manner. And if you botch it the second time, don't ask for a third chance. Just chug right through. When they send you home, just say, "Thank you—I'll try a different city one day."

Judges probably won't remember your mistakes (we've seen plenty of successful artists have a bad day), but they will remember if you act rudely or improperly during your audition. The next time you show up in front of them, you won't even need to sing because you've burned that bridge. There's a good chance they'll also remember you if you handled a bad audition with professionalism. In that case, you'll either have someone rooting for you because they've seen you crash and burn and recover like a pro, or you'll have a blank slate. And if they don't remember you because you quietly eased out after making your mistake, then you'll still have a fresh start.

If you're auditioning for a show that holds casting calls in multiple locations, keep open the possibility of auditioning in more than one place, if the rules allow that. Miranda Lambert finished third on the first season of *Nashville Star*, but she didn't make it to even the final forty when she tried out in Dallas.

"She bombed," her mother, Bev Lambert, recalls. "She sang a Shania Twain song, and it wasn't the right song for her. She didn't have the song ready, and her heart wasn't in it—it was just not good at all. When we went home, she said, 'I am never doing another contest.' And I'm like, 'Let's try it in Houston, but go like you mean it. Walk in there to win.'

"That's what changed from the first time to the second time. When she walked into Houston, she walked in with such confidence people just moved out of her way. The producers saw it and told me later that they noticed it. And she went in with the right song—she sang Patsy Cline's 'Crazy,' and she ripped it."

Not every artist is cut out for auditions like this. Colbie Caillat eventually used MySpace® to build her audience and had a huge radio hit in the summer of 2007 with

"Bubbly." Colbie also suffers from stage fright, and she recalls her unsuccessful *American Idol* audition as being "a torturous experience."

"We had to audition twice," Colbie says, "and we had to sleep out on the street to wait in line two days before. So we brought our sleeping bags. It was me and my friends and my mom. Then, the day of the audition, we got ready and we waited in that huge line with thousands of people. They gave us ten seconds to audition, and we were just outside in all the loud noise.

"I sang my little part of my song, and they said, 'No, you don't have what it takes.' Which I totally understood, because I wasn't outgoing or anything. I just sang quietly and stood there."

Colbie didn't go home and sulk when she realized she'd never be the next *American Idol.* She started focusing on her MySpace© page. Last we checked, she had about 30 million plays there, her album *Coco* had gone gold, and more than a million people had downloaded "Bubbly." Not bad for a talent-show reject.

Credit: Emily Netterville

Anastasia Brown (L) and Debbie Dover (R)

DEBBIE DOVER:
STAND OUT AT THE AUDITION

Hair and makeup stylist Debbie Dover has created standout styles for artists like Trisha Yearwood, Dixie Chicks, James Taylor, Alison Kraus, Brooks and Dunn, Wynonna Judd, Sara Evans, Jo Dee Messina, and Kellie Pickler. Here are her tips for getting noticed—in a good way—on TV.

1. **DON'T OVERDO THE TAN.** Daily self-tanning and lying in a bed making yourself look like a different ethnicity is totally out. Plus, film can make self-tanners look orange. At the most, go for a little bit of a golden sun-kissed look, maybe one shade darker than your natural skin color, not super tan.

(cont.)

If you get a Mystic Tan™, ask for a one or two rather than a three. If you buy self-tanner, get light or medium, not dark. Exfoliate and use moisturizer before you put tanner on your face; otherwise, it makes the brow area bright orange.

2. **GO DEEP, BUT NOT TOO DEEP.** Even out your skin tone using foundation or tinted moisturizer a half-step deeper than your skin color, and use the same color powder over it. It looks better with those hot lights. If you go the same shade as your skin color or lighter, you'll look like a ghost.
3. **THINK BEYOND THE FACE.** Continue the foundation underneath your chin and blend. On camera people tend to get nervous and flush red in the chest and neck area, but if you're a deeper color in your face, viewers won't notice the flush as much.
4. **KEEP THE FACE POWDER LIGHT.** You want a little bit of dew—even on guys—not a cardboard matte look. A light dusting goes a long way. If your skin gets shiny, take a rice paper or tissue and blot off the excess oil instead of adding more powder on top. Just pat the paper on your forehead, chin, and nose—don't rub. You don't have to reapply a bunch of powder. If you do, you'll look dirty on camera—especially with high-definition television, which shows every particle of makeup.
5. **HIDE THAT PIMPLE.** If you have a pimple, it's actually better to use a deeper concealer beneath your foundation. The camera light reflects off the lightest thing on your face, so if you put on a very light concealer, the light will make it stand out. If the pimple is red, use concealer with a green base to take the redness away. Remember, you can change the color but you can't change the texture, so don't pick at it and make it worse.
6. **LADIES, ALWAYS WEAR MASCARA.** Always.

7. **KEEP THE EYE SHADOW VERY CLEAN.** If you worry about your eyes not showing up, eye shadow is not the answer. Curl your eyelashes—you too, guys! If they stick straight out, a little curl makes the eyes look more open, and that's more eye-catching. Ladies, add a good coat of black mascara.
8. **DON'T LET YOUR BROW BEAT YOU.** Make sure the brows are neatly arranged, but they don't have to be perfect. Over-groomed brows on men look a little too neat and tidy and sweet. I don't recommend waxing at all. It's too clean and too perfect. I always recommend tweezing for men. For women, my first recommendation would be to get your brows done by a professional, and then leave them alone. Tweeze rather than wax. You can be a little more artful with tweezing, and waxing is very irritating. If you have over-tweezed, definitely see someone who can show you how to fill in a little bit. I do that a lot for clients—show them how to fill in with pencil and not look like Groucho Marx.
9. **CONSIDER SAVING YOUR SHAMPOO.** It's best if your hair is not freshly washed because a little texturing on hair looks good on camera. Not three days dirty, but maybe one day dirty—it makes the hair nice and smooth. Maybe just a little dollop of Frizz-Ease or a light, light bit of hairspray just to calm flyaways. Nothing super-strong. Once again, less is more.
10. **AVOID THE TEMPTATION OF BIG HAIR.** We always think, "I want to stand out, so I'll make my hair giant." But big hair is really just distracting. You want people to listen to you and not be distracted by your hair. You should have a style in which you feel confident but totally undone, nothing overly dramatic.
11. **STAY OUT OF THE SALON ON AUDITION DAY.** Don't experiment on audition day. Don't go out and get a new haircut or spray tan or whatever right before your audition. Just stick with what you've got.

CHAPTER 4

MAKING THE SHOW

Let's say you've passed all your auditions and you've been picked for the show. Congratulations, and get ready, because you're about to be busier than you've ever been in your life. You might even feel like the dog that chased the bus and caught it.

LEARN TO LIVE UNDER A MICROSCOPE

Carrie Simons, who runs Triple 7 Public Relations in Los Angeles and in Nashville, has worked on both *American Idol* and *Nashville Star.* Soon after *Nashville Star* would name a new group of finalists, Carrie would sit them down for a talk about opportunities and responsibilities.

"Your life is now under a microscope," Carrie would tell them. "What you do, what you say, and how you act is up for public critique, public commentary, and press fodder. You need to be responsible—you need to be professional and 'on' at all times because anybody can get on their cell phones or computers and make or break your public persona very quickly.

"Think of every single thing you do going forward as something that's setting the path for your career," she'd continue, "Everything is important, whether it's an interview, a radio tour, or an on-camera appearance. Be on time, and be respectful of other people's time—they're using that time to promote you. In any interview you do, be sober, be on time, give answers of more than one word, and have your personality come through. That's especially important in a show where America is voting, so figure out what your personal character is and what you want everybody to know about you so that it shines through everywhere you go and in everything you do. Remember that anything you do can be known to the public and to the press, and it will have ramifications for the rest of your career."

The judges are expected to conduct radio interviews to promote the show—I did them early in the morning every week. One day, the DJ on the other end of the line was a complete jerk to me, and I had no choice but to ask him—on air—why he had woken up on the wrong side of the bed. He replied that one of our contestants blew off his interview, and he proceeded to throw that contestant under the bus the entire time we talked. Needless to say, I was happy when that call ended and not surprised when the singer got booted off the show the next week.

THINK OF YOURSELF AS YOUR OWN CHEERLEADER.

Check with the show's staff to make sure you're operating within the boundaries of the contract you signed with the show. That contract, for instance, may limit the show-related topics you're allowed to discuss publicly and when you're allowed to discuss them. You will likely also be prohibited from doing anything for a sponsor not affiliated with the show.

You do, however, want to use every resource placed at your disposal. *Nashville Star* gave contestants the opportunity to send text messages via a carrier that sponsored the show. Some people sent their text messages, and others didn't. The short-term thinker says, "I'm tired, and I don't want to bother." The big-picture thinker stays up a little longer and takes advantage of the opportunity.

Carrie recommends that you think of yourself as your own cheerleader. Call everybody in your extended family, all your friends, and any fans you've made along the way—and ask for their help. If you've made the acquaintance of people at your local radio station or done interviews with your hometown newspaper, it's time to place another call to them. Get your extended family to call the stations and newspapers in their towns. If you don't already have profiles on social-networking Web sites like Facebook, MySpace, or Friendster®, get them up and running. If you've got even a couple hundred friends, you're just one link away from several thousand people, and if you can recruit those several thousand people to your cause, you can connect, at least indirectly, with a few hundred thousand.

"Never forget a name, save every phone number, never forget to say 'thank you,' and always have a door to come back into the next time," Carrie advises. "That's really the priority because, as those of us who have done this a long time know, the press and your public image determine your future. Many radio stations have people come in every day, but the ones who are gracious and appreciative are the ones they want to help and support. You want to have everybody want to help you succeed."

IT'S NOT A PARTY, IT'S WORK—REALLY HARD WORK

Bev Lambert warns contestants against taking a lighthearted approach toward appearing on the show.

"It probably looks like a lot of fun, but you have to be ready to put in several weeks of some of the hardest work you'll ever do," she says. "It's not being on TV for a few minutes. The music business is a lot of work. Shy Blakeman [from *Nashville Star*'s fourth season] thought he'd go to Nashville and party for a few weeks. We're like, 'No, Shy, it's not like that.'

"Miranda [Lambert] got so little sleep we worried about her at the end. She was sleeping about four or five hours a night, and she was used to normal sleep patterns. They worked her really hard. So that's the first thing: get ready to work, and don't think you're going to go there and drink and party for nine weeks. It's not like that."

Carrie says that some contestants have a hard time understanding how much perseverance is required to succeed on a show. Some may have thought of getting on the show as the goal and never given much consideration to the demands of life on national television.

"You get on camera and you get that production going and you're rehearsing and you're tired and you're doing everything morning to night, and you forget how much more there is to do even beyond that," Carrie explains. "The ones that didn't get it, I don't think it's that they didn't get it; I just don't think they understood that they needed to take an extra five steps beyond the five steps they'd already taken.

"You have a limited window of opportunity here. If it means not going out or losing sleep in order to take advantage of that opportunity, then you need to be eating, breathing, and sleeping the show."

YOU NEED TO BE EATING, BREATHING, AND SLEEPING THE SHOW

Some of *Nashville Star*'s first-season contestants took the competition more seriously than others, according to eventual winner Buddy Jewell.

"We had a curfew and were supposed to be in the house by a certain time, and there were several nights some of them showed up way after the curfew," he says. "A lot of times, especially on a Monday following a Saturday show, we had to get up at six o'clock to do morning radio interviews, and there were people who had stayed out too late the night before and slept through their interviews.

"Even though we were on TV, it took radio to make that show work, and I don't think some of them quite understood the power and importance of getting radio behind them.

"Being in town for ten years and seeing what it took to get a foot in the door, I wasn't going to waste it. I took it very seriously. It's hard sometimes to maintain that level of professionalism because all that attention is focused on you and you're the darling of the day. You can forget that it's a business first and you're out there to make a living at it and get some longevity out of your career."

Carrie Simons points to Kacey Musgraves of *Nashville Star*'s fifth season as someone who understood how to take advantage of the opportunity. "Her grandmother called me before we had even announced the top ten and said, 'What can I do now, when can I start being proactive, when can I send an e-mail blast from the chamber of commerce to everyone in my small town in Texas?'" Carrie recalls. "Her mom called and said, 'Kacey is good friends with Miranda Lambert—when can Miranda put something on her Web site?' From day one, Kacey was very aggressive, as was her family, in a good way."

One of Kacey's fellow contestants, David St. Romaine, learned how to play the game, even using his two-year-old daughter to give him an edge. "He knew how to work the phones, he knew how to work his resources, he knew how to ingratiate himself, he knew how to make people fall in love with him," Carrie says. "He really understood capturing a persona for the audience. Having his little girl in a different T-shirt with a different saying every week really emphasized his love for his family. It also ingratiated him with the public, as did his graciousness and gratitude when doing interviews with the press.

"Those two contestants really stuck out for me. They were always on time. They were always professional. They knew how to work it in public no matter the hour of the night or the location of the bar. They set the standard that others tried to emulate.

"A few people along the way had had opportunities before the show started, and they had a team around them already. They didn't feel the need to do anything beyond the nationwide exposure that the show offered. That can be a good thing, but it can also be a bad thing because it means you're not working as hard you could have been. You could have had an even greater impact."

YOUR NEW BEST FRIENDS

No television show goes on the air without a huge staff. When you start production on the show, you'll meet a bunch of new people—from directors and producers to make-up artists, musical directors, cameramen, and production assistants. They all have the same goal—to put on the best show possible. They all have a different expertise, so they all have something to teach you. And they're professionals, so if you stay in this industry, you'll likely encounter them again and again throughout the course of your career.

(cont.)

"Two years after *Nashville Star*, I did something at the Academy of Country Music awards, and the guy filming me was one of the guys who filmed me for *Nashville Star*," says Chris Young. "You're around people who are going to work in the music industry for a long time."

Additionally, staff members talk—among themselves and with others. And you never know whom they're talking to or what they're saying about you.

Carrie Underwood told *USA Today* she made a point of being nice to everyone who worked on the show. "I wanted people to say, 'Carrie's easy to work with. She follows direction and she pays attention,'" she told the paper. "I want people to say that about me so that years down the line when somebody says, 'I grew up listening to Carrie Underwood,' somebody else can say, 'Oh, she's great.'"

DAYS ON AND OFF THE SET

For Buddy Jewell, days on *Nashville Star* typically began early with radio and press interviews. After that, contestants might work on picking their outfit for that week's show, doing photo shoots, and taping teasers for the show and commercials for sponsors. And, of course, there were always rehearsals.

"We'd go to the Acuff Theater a couple days before the show and do run-throughs," Buddy says. "We'd be over there all day long blocking—like, 'Here's where you stand when we're doing this segment, and this camera will be on you when you're doing your song.' We spent a lot of time in the theater running through the show, making sure we had the pacing and all that. We'd get over there at 7:30 or 8:00 in the morning, and we'd finish up at 6:00 in the evening."

Chris Young says that performing in front of a camera is completely different from playing a standard show. Learning the difference is a time-consuming process. "There are a million factors involved in what you're doing," Chris says. "Say you want to run out into the audience during a song: You don't want it to be contrived, but you have to tell the crew.

If you don't tell the guy who's filming you, you just run out of the frame. All of a sudden, you're not on TV and people are wondering what you're doing.

"There are so many things like that—trying to find the camera without looking like you're chasing it, because there are ten cameras in the room and at any given time one of them has the red light on and nine others don't. You have to find unique ways to find the red light and look at that camera. It's something you just have to learn, and that's a learning curve in and of itself."

The work week often wouldn't end after the show. "One night after a show, they took us out in some Chevy Silverados," Buddy says. "We had to keep driving those trucks through the drive-thru at a McDonald's. We probably spent two hours just circling—it's not easy to get a long pickup truck through a drive-thru. When everybody else had gone to bed, we were still up at one o'clock in the morning filming a commercial that I don't think they ever used."

By the time Carrie Simons joined the *Nashville Star* crew, the show aired on Tuesday nights, so Monday would be the day for final rehearsals, and they would last long into the evening. On Tuesdays, Carrie says, "Contestants limited using their voice as much as possible before the show, except for the run-through on the set earlier in the day.

"On Wednesday, you started figuring out what your next song would be and working with the team on how you're going to do your arrangement. Thursday, Friday, Saturday, and Sunday were spent practicing your song, figuring out how you were going to do it, and shooting the reality pieces—going to Sonic and having burgers, or shooting a print ad for Chevy, whatever.

"There are a lot of requirements, but it's just making the choices between whether you go outside and throw the football or go to the private room and start calling more people and taking the time to further your career."

Credit: David McClister Photography

BUDDY JEWELL: MAKING THE MOST OF YOUR TIME ON THE SHOW

Buddy Jewell won the first season of Nashville Star *in 2003. He followed that win with a Top Five country single, "Help Pour Out the Rain (Lacey's Song)," which he had performed on the show, and a gold album.*

1. **IF YOU DON'T HAVE A WEB SITE, GET ONE.** People will want to learn more about you and maybe buy some product, so make sure they can find you on the Web.
2. **IF YOU'VE GOT A SHOT AT GETTING ON ONE OF THOSE SHOWS, GET SOME ORIGINAL MUSIC ON YOUR SITE TO SELL BECAUSE IT WILL DEFINITELY ENHANCE YOUR INCOME.** The night I won, I made enough money in T-shirt and CD sales to pay off all my credit cards.
3. **CREATE A MAILING LIST.** Because of my guestbook, I had a huge database of fans after the show was over. These were people who came looking for me; I didn't go looking for them. Even if you don't win, you know who your fans are.
4. **MAKE A COPY OF YOUR MAILING LIST.** I turned my guestbook over to Sony to help them market my first album, and they lost it.
5. **IF YOU WRITE SONGS OR KNOW SOMEONE WHO'S WILLING TO WRITE WITH YOU, WRITE AS MUCH AS YOU CAN.** My first single was something I'd written myself, and there's a lot of money in that.
6. **BE COACHABLE.** People from record labels are watching, and it gets back to them if you're hard to work with, lazy, or a pain in the butt.
7. **BE NICE TO THE GUY WHO'S SETTING UP THE CATERING, THE CAMERAMAN, AND THE PRODUCTION ASSISTANT.** You never know where you'll see them again or who they'll tell about you. By the way, that's not just a good business thing; that's being a good human being.

FIND THE RIGHT SONG, PART II

If rehearsals take up the biggest chunk of time during the week, picking songs probably creates the most stress. We discussed the importance of song selection in an earlier chapter, but choosing material takes on new dimensions once you've made the show.

"The public never knows what goes into picking the song," Bev Lambert says. "They have no idea how many phone calls are made, how many parents are consulted. It's like live or die in a minute and a half. Probably the most common thread among all contestants is the amount of time that goes into choosing that song. No one is ever flippant about it. Ever. I probably talked to Kacey Musgrave ten times a day, with her playing songs over the phone and just stressing out.

"My stomach gets in a knot just remembering how I felt when Miranda called, saying, 'Mom, I'm not sure about "The Fightin' Side of Me;" I know I've been singing it my whole life, and I know Merle Haggard like the back of my hand, but is it the right song for me?' Saying, 'Yes, baby, it's the right song for you,' is tough because she's leaning on me and her dad to help her. We knew she could deliver it, but was it going to help her win the show?"

Buddy Jewell focused on finding ways to impress the audience in a short time. "I had to pick a song that was going to show any vocal prowess that I might have, and I had only a certain amount of time to do it," he says. "That was my main focus—was it something that fit me as an artist? I love Keith Urban, but there was no sense in me singing a Keith Urban song. That wasn't who I was or what I was about. So I tried to pick songs by artists that I identified with, like Alabama and Don Williams. Plus I'd try to pick something that would allow me to show a little bit of vocal gymnastics if I were given the opportunity."

Buddy says *Nashville Star* contestants received a list of approved songs a week before each show. "We seldom were allowed to go outside of that list," he says.

"The house band was a lot of help. We'd have thirty minutes to rehearse with them every day leading up to the show. I remember the show where we were doing Southern rock. I had chosen 'Gimme Three Steps' by Lynyrd Skynyrd. I knew I couldn't go out and do it exactly like Skynyrd or the judges would pooh-pooh me for not being original. Somehow, I dreamed up this version of the song where it had the Stevie Wonder 'Superstition' feel. I told the band, 'Let's pretend that ZZ Top and Stevie Wonder are trying to rip off Lynyrd Skynyrd.' Those guys took it, and we came up with an adaptation that people liked so much I still play it in my shows today."

To further complicate the matter of choosing material, contestants can't just sing any song they'd like to sing. In order for a television show to use a song, the show must receive permission, or a license, from the music publisher that holds the copyright to the song. To use a particular recording of a song, the show's producers must obtain *two* licenses—one from the song's publisher and one from the company that owns the recording.

When singers want to record a song, the publisher is required to grant them a license at a certain payment rate—it's called a *compulsory* license—but the producers of a television show or a movie must negotiate the rate they'll pay the publishers. Because no publisher wants to get paid less money to use its song than the other publishers get paid for theirs, each license includes what's called a "most favored nations" clause. That means that the publisher gets paid as much as the publisher receiving the most money—in essence, ensuring that all publishers are paid the same.

YOU CAN GIVE A SONG YOUR PERSONAL STAMP BY DRASTICALLY CHANGING ITS ARRANGEMENT.

If one publisher's rate goes up, so does every other publisher's—and that can break a show's budget very quickly. That's why a singer can't say, "It's just one song." If every publisher is getting, say, $10,000 per song and one singer really wants "My Heart Will Go On" but that costs $20,000, then every other publisher would get $20,000, too. So it's not just one song—it affects every other song performed.

If a publisher agrees to let its songs be used with a "most favored nations" clause, that publisher's songs have been *cleared* for use on the show. If a publisher doesn't agree to that rate, no material from that publisher can be used. A publisher can refuse to license a song for any number of reasons, ranging from the fee the show is willing to pay to the songwriter's opinion of contests.

Bucky Covington recalls talking to a woman who worked at *American Idol* and had met a top star who wouldn't allow Bucky to sing one of his songs on the show. "She asked, 'Why won't you clear any of your songs? I had a guy who wanted to sing one of your songs.' He said, 'I don't want to have somebody's dreams shattered over one of my songs.'

"You can't argue with that kind of logic."

Working within that list of cleared songs is the biggest challenge for some artists, especially singer/songwriters used to singing only their own material or fringe artists with unusual singing styles. If you're that kind of artist, you may have to work extra hard to find a song that you can give your personal stamp.

You can also give a song your personal stamp by drastically changing its arrangement. You could change a song as familiar as "Free Bird" to the point where it wouldn't even be recognizable. I've seen that sort of thing done for television, movies, and records. In fact, for one of my films, we were searching for a female singer/songwriter for one of the lead roles. At one point in this film, the actor sings "Free Bird," but not in a way you've ever heard. When we auditioned artists, we requested they change the song's arrangement and perform it for me, the director, and the studio. An artist named Joey Martin not only changed it, she changed us! Time froze for all of us when she softly and wistfully sang the Southern-rock anthem as a waltz. You've just got to use some imagination and be willing to take a song into a new place.

Some people have egos so big they say, "I don't sing any of these songs. You've got to clear this song—it's my song." They wait until the last minute, hoping their song will clear, without preparing a backup. Instead of waiting and not preparing, look through that list of approved songs and find one where you can change the arrangement so that it's close to one you *do* sing. Change the key, change the tempo, change the style—you can change all these things. You've just got to open your mind.

IT'S A GAME—LEARN TO PLAY

Some people have strategies they think will help them win. My suggestion is simply that you put your best foot forward every day. Don't hold anything back. Leave everything you've got out there on the stage. Find ways to distinguish yourself every time you perform, and keep in mind the words of British journalist Malcolm Muggeridge: "Never forget that only dead fish swim with the stream."

If you're an artist who's good enough to win, you'll come up with something even better for next time. If you think you're going to have to save something so that you can finish strong, maybe you don't belong at this level in the first place.

One season on *Nashville Star*, Justin Davis gave lackluster performances during the first few episodes, and I told him so. I told him he was barely showing up, he was phoning in his performances. I was pretty hard on him. The next week, he stepped up to my challenge, playing the mandolin and giving me the passion and the emotion I'd been craving. I told him just that. He replied that his strategy was to hold back until the middle of the season then start giving his all and pull ahead of the pack. I told him he had to give his all every time he showed up. Never pull back. Never perform halfway, I said. If people are buying $10 tickets to see you perform, don't give them a $5 performance. How are you going to get ahead, I asked, when you're only giving everything you've got some of the time?

THE PERFECT CONTESTANT STARTS WITH A GREAT LOOK AND A GREAT VOICE.

You've also got to know your audience. Buddy Jewell brought it every show, and he really analyzed his audience. That's really smart.

"We were on Saturday nights," Buddy says. "I knew that the people watching were a little bit older. On a Saturday night, the twenty-somethings are out in the clubs. They're not home watching television. That had a lot to do with my song choices.

"Had they had that show during the week when a younger audience was home, I don't know if I would've won. Miranda or Jamey Garner might have."

Think about the demographic of your show's viewers. Is it mostly male? Mostly female? Average age twenty-five? Thirty-five? All those things can make a difference in what people want to hear and see. If you're a beautiful, curvaceous girl who likes to show off your body, are you still going to want to do that if your show's viewers mostly consist of moms chasing young kids? By the same token, *American Idol* has a younger viewer, so you wouldn't want to show up singing Frank Sinatra every week.

So now that we've gone over many of the different facets of performing on the shows, what kind of person is the ideal contestant? Obviously, the perfect contestant starts with a great look and a great voice. According to Carrie Simons, the perfect contestant is also the person who knows who she is and knows the image she wants to portray to the public. It's the contestant who knows his story and what makes him different from the rest of the contestants. She's on time to every radio and every print interview and has thought in advance about what she's going to say. He's always awake, always professional, always respectful. She asks, "What suggestions do you have for how I can improve?" He has an extra level of conscientiousness that makes him want to do better the next time.

The perfect contestant is the one who always asks, "What else can I do?"

Photo courtesy of Anastasia Brown/Meg Davis

Reba, Ronnie Dunn, and Anastasia Brown at a late-night CMA party

REBA McENTIRE: TIPS FOR PERFORMING

Few singers approach performing with the professionalism of Reba McEntire, who has mastered the concert stage, Broadway, television, and film during a career that dates back to the 1970s. Here, Reba offers some very specific pointers for entertainers looking to make a better connection with their audience.

1. **WHEN YOU GET THROUGH SINGING A SONG, STAY FOCUSED ON THE CROWD.** Stay in the moment until the audience completely stops clapping,

then say, "Thank you very much." If you get out of it immediately, you look like you're acting.

2. **WHEN YOU SMILE AT THEM, GIVE THEM EVERYTHING YOU'VE GOT.** I saw Liza Minnelli one time. When she got through singing a song, she was standing probably ten feet from the edge of the stage. When she finished, she walked toward the audience with her arms outstretched. They died. They just went, 'Oh my God, she loves us!' She was basking in all the acceptance they could give her, and they were just putty in her hands.

3. **LOOK AT THE AUDIENCE.** I've tried this: I would look at the audience like a typewriter keyboard, slowly going across and looking at everybody. Then I'd go up a row or two, and I'd go back. I'd try to look at everybody's face. I did that one night at the Universal Amphitheatre in Los Angeles when Chris Rich was there. He played Brock on the *Reba* TV show. He came back and said, "You were singing right to me!" I didn't even know he was there.

4. **LEARN TO WEAR COMFORTABLE SHOES AND CLOTHING.** It keeps your focus off how uncomfortable you are so that you can give more to the audience.

5. **GET THROUGH THE SONG.** I get through sad songs by looking at the exit signs. I think, "That's a red exit sign," so that I don't cry. Because, you know, you have to get through the song.

MAKE A SONG YOUR OWN

Judges often tell contestants, "You've got to make the song your own." But what does that mean? And how do you do it—especially when the artist who made the song a hit in the first place did it so well?

Below, you'll find several examples of songs that have been recorded with dramatically different arrangements. In many cases, both recordings have turned out to be hits. Listen to the first version, then the second, and you'll see how each artist managed to make the song his or her own.

SONG	LISTEN TO THIS VERSION:	THEN CHECK OUT THIS ONE:
AGAINST ALL ODDS	Phil Collins	Mariah Carey
ALL ALONG THE WATCHTOWER	Bob Dylan	Jimi Hendrix
BABY, NOW THAT I'VE FOUND YOU	The Foundations	Alison Krauss
BALTIMORE	Randy Newman	Nina Simone
BEST I EVER HAD	Vertical Horizon	Gary Allan
BLUE BAYOU	Roy Orbison	Linda Ronstadt
BLUE MOON OF KENTUCKY	Bill Monroe	Elvis Presley
BY THE TIME I GET TO PHOENIX	Glen Campbell	Isaac Hayes
BYE BYE LOVE	Everly Brothers	Ray Charles

SONG	LISTEN TO THIS VERSION:	THEN CHECK OUT THIS ONE:
DO YOU WANT TO DANCE	Bette Midler	The Ramones
DON'T LET ME BE MISUNDERSTOOD	The Animals	Nina Simone
EMOTION	Samantha Sang	Destiny's Child
GIRL, YOU'LL BE A WOMAN SOON	Neil Diamond	Urge Overkill
THE GREATEST LOVE OF ALL	George Benson	Whitney Houston
HAZY SHADE OF WINTER	Simon & Garfunkel	The Bangles
HEAVEN	Bryan Adams	DJ Sammy
HOW CAN I BE SURE	The Rascals	Dusty Springfield
HOW CAN YOU MEND A BROKEN HEART?	Bee Gees	Al Green
HURT	Nine Inch Nails	Johnny Cash
I FOUGHT THE LAW	Bobby Fuller Four	The Clash
I HEARD IT THROUGH THE GRAPEVINE	Marvin Gaye	Creedence Clearwater Revival
I WILL ALWAYS LOVE YOU	Dolly Parton	Whitney Houston
IT'S JUST A MATTER OF TIME	Brook Benton	Randy Travis

SONG	LISTEN TO THIS VERSION:	THEN CHECK OUT THIS ONE:
JUMP	Van Halen	Aztec Camera
LAST TRAIN TO CLARKSVILLE	The Monkees	Cassandra Wilson
LIFE IS A HIGHWAY	Tom Cochrane	Rascal Flatts
LISTEN TO YOUR HEART	Roxette	D.H.T.
MR. TAMBOURINE MAN	Bob Dylan	The Byrds
NOTHING COMPARES 2 U	Prince	Sinead O'Connor
OL' 55	Tom Waits	Eagles
ON BROADWAY	The Drifters	George Benson
OOPS! I DID IT AGAIN	Britney Spears	Richard Thompson
PROUD MARY	Creedence Clearwater Revival	Ike & Tina Turner
RESPECT	Otis Redding	Aretha Franklin
SHAMELESS	Billy Joel	Garth Brooks
SMELLS LIKE TEEN SPIRIT	Nirvana	Tori Amos
SOME HEARTS	Marshall Crenshaw	Carrie Underwood
STAND BY YOUR MAN	Tammy Wynette	Lyle Lovett
SUGAR SUGAR	The Archies	Wilson Pickett

SONG	LISTEN TO THIS VERSION:	THEN CHECK OUT THIS ONE:
TAINTED LOVE	Gloria Jones	Soft Cell
TAKE ME TO THE RIVER	Al Green	Talking Heads
TALKING OLD SOLDIERS	Elton John	Bettye LaVette
TRY A LITTLE TENDERNESS	Frank Sinatra	Otis Redding
TWIST AND SHOUT	The Isley Brothers	The Beatles
UMBRELLA	Rihanna	Marié Digby
WALK SOFTLY ON THIS HEART OF MINE	Bill Monroe	Kentucky HeadHunters
WE CAN WORK IT OUT	The Beatles	Stevie Wonder
THE WEIGHT	The Band	The Staple Singers
WITHOUT YOU	Harry Nilsson	Mariah Carey
YOU DON'T HAVE TO SAY YOU LOVE ME	Dusty Springfield	Shelby Lynne

CHAPTER 5

YOU WON! NOW WHAT?

You've just won your show. The music swells as the audience leaps to its feet, cheering wildly. Cannons blast confetti all around you. The other contestants, the show's staff, and your closest family and friends rush to surround you, hugging you, reaching to shake your hand. You don't know whether to laugh or cry, so you do a bit of both. The credits roll.

Congratulations—you've just won the ticket to climb Mount Everest.

WHAT HAPPENS AFTER THE CREDITS ROLL

Before the final episode of one *Nashville Star* season, Carrie Simons said to the three remaining finalists, "Remember, whichever one of you wins is not done when the cameras stop rolling. That's when the work begins."

You want to run to your family. You want to celebrate the moment. What you have to do instead is an hour's worth of interviews and photos that take place on the spot, before you can even think about going to the wrap party. Once you get to the party, you have to keep in the back of your mind that your radio tour starts at 7 AM—or earlier, if you're doing television morning shows.

"And no matter how hard you party," Carrie says, "I will track you down if you're not on the phone at 6:55 AM to do your radio tour because all these stations have been supporting you and the show, and now is your time to take it to the next level." After three hours of interviews, you might have time for a quick shower before the next round of appearances begins—perhaps on the local midday news, transmitted on a nationwide feed for other stations to pick up. From there, it's more meetings or maybe a trip to the recording studio so you can start cutting your album, if a record deal came attached to the contest. If you're on a really big show, like *Idol*, you might hit one of the late-night talk shows before a dinner meeting with some of the executives who'll be part of your team going forward.

WHEN DOORS OF OPPORTUNITY OPEN FOR YOU, YOU HAVE TO WALK THROUGH THEM RIGHT AWAY—BEFORE THEY SLAM ON YOUR FINGERS.

You didn't think you were going to get a day off, did you?

For Bo Bice, much of the time between the end of the *American Idol* season and the end of the *American Idol* tour passed in a blur. "Two minutes after I walked off the stage, three guys came up and said, 'Hi, welcome to RCA Records,'" Bo recalls. "I said, 'Well, I guess I got a record deal, so that's one thing I don't have to worry about now.'

"I walked around for a week or two just working in a daze, just doing the same things I had done for the past couple of months. Carrie and I were on the press runs for two weeks. Then I signed contracts for a week. I went back to California for a month to rehearse for the tour, and then I was gone on the tour for a month and a half.

"It was a good thing to be that busy—it was what I had always dreamed of. One day you're walking down the street, fired from a job and not knowing how you'll make your house payment. The next day everybody in America knows you, and you can't walk down the street. It's the weirdest, most surreal feeling. It's almost like waking up and being in a ghost town or a *Twilight Zone* episode—you feel like you're alone in the world but you're surrounded by people."

When doors of opportunity open for you, you have to walk through them right away—before they slam on your fingers. If you're a winner, or even a finalist, you need to build on your achievement. If you wait too long, that window's shut, probably for good.

If you're even one of the last four finalists on a national show airing on television, you've already built a bigger audience than most performers ever know. Seize the moment and build on it as much as you can, even *before* the end of the show. Find a person who'll guide you and help you figure out what to do if you win. That person could be somebody with the show, or it might be a manager, an attorney, an agent, or a publicist. He or she should help you decide whom to sign with, what offers to accept, and which ones to reject. Think about these questions in advance, and be prepared because you'll be making those decisions in a whirlwind.

KNOW YOUR STORY, AND LEARN HOW TO TELL IT

Some people say they're superstitious and don't want to assume they'll win—like the award-show nominees who won't write a thank-you list beforehand. But if you want to maximize your opportunity, you've got to be thinking about this beforehand. You need a Plan A, B, and C so that you know what you're doing. Your music should help guide your decisions, but unforeseeable circumstances can put you in a quandary. What if, for example, you agree to appear on the first talk show that approaches you, only to learn later that a more popular show is also interested but demands an exclusive appearance? You'll want to say "yes, yes, yes" to everything because suddenly you'll be inundated with the sorts of opportunities you've always dreamed about, but if you don't have a plan, you could miss out on even bigger opportunities.

So have a plan of attack. Identify your targets. Know your story, and give people a reason to want to talk with you. Start looking at what worked for you and what didn't. Analyze yourself—

ANALYZE YOURSELF—BE WILLING TO ASK YOURSELF THE HARD QUESTIONS SO THAT YOU CAN START THINKING ABOUT THE ANSWERS.

be willing to ask yourself the hard questions so that you can start thinking about the answers.

"What can I do to build on this momentum?" That should be the foremost question in your mind.

Create talking points for your talk-show appearances. You'll have at least two or three such obligations after you win. So have a specific vision and message you want to get out—not just "Oh, I feel so blessed that I won." What is your music? What is your message? Not many people get the kind of platform that the winner of a national contest does. Grab that opportunity and send your message out—again and again.

"People want to hear stories," says Chris Young. "Have an idea of the points you want to get across—here's my possible album release date, here's my first single, here's a funny story that I can use that happened in the studio."

When you meet the press, you can expect typical first-time questions like these:

★ **"WHAT IS YOUR MUSIC LIKE?"** Think in these terms: "Lynyrd Skynyrd meets White Stripes" or "a lazy, easygoing Nikka Costa"—something that listeners can quickly grasp.
★ **"WHERE ARE YOU FROM?"** Home is more than a place on the map. How can you make your answer entertaining or intriguing or emotional? What stories about your childhood or your hometown add context to the music you want to make?
★ **"HOW WAS YOUR EXPERIENCE ON THE CONTEST?"** Keep in mind any confidentiality agreements with the show, but do dig deep. Think of funny moments—a time when you became close with another contestant or your emotional response to meeting your musical hero on the show.
★ **"WAS IT HARD TO BEAT YOUR NEW BEST FRIEND?"** Be honest but tactful. Make your answer too sappy, and you'll sound insincere. You both signed up for a contest—it's show business, not show friends!

- **"WHAT'S NEXT?"** The only thing you know is that the song you just performed will likely be a single. So push it—push it hard!
- **"ANYTHING YOU WANT TO ADD?"** Absolutely—always. Engage your fans, and capture those e-mail addresses. "Yes sir/ma'am. My fans can go to my Web site and tell me what songs they liked, what looks they liked, what magazines they think I should be in, and who they think I should tour with." That's just an example—you are the one who has to know what message you want to send out. But have a plan; know what you're going to say and how you can take advantage of this opportunity.

Think six months ahead. What will you be doing? What would you *like* to be doing? Maybe you'll have a record out, maybe you'll be touring. Whom would you like to tour with? Maybe there's somebody in particular—Reba McEntire, Pink, Velvet Revolver, whoever. People will be listening, and if you send that message out, (a) you have something interesting to talk about, and (b) it might come true. If an artist is aware you want to tour with them, you just might be invited. It happens more than you realize.

Whom do you want to thank? For example, if your stylist helped you develop an image using clothes from a certain designer, you might be able to start developing a relationship with that designer by mentioning him or her. Or perhaps there's someone you've dreamed about singing a duet with. Think about the positive information that can help you build your career.

YOU WON THE CONTEST—DON'T LOSE YOUR VOICE

Now more than ever, it's essential that you take care of your voice. That voice got you where you are. You don't want to wear it out. Try to get as much sleep as you can—it won't be much, at least for the first few days. You'll have to do so much talking and so much singing after you win, more talking and singing than you'll ever be able to predict. Talk on the phone as little as possible. If you've got to communicate with friends and family, do as much of it as possible by e-mail. Talking on the phone actually takes more energy and is harder on your vocal cords than talking in person. For the week after you win, minimize chitchatting, even though you'll really want to. If you don't, your voice will give out. Opt for texting instead!

Take your vitamins and stay healthy—it's easy to get sick on such a hectic schedule. Sleep whenever you can. You'll want to celebrate your win, but consider postponing the celebration for a while. Instead, be developing your plan, finding or getting to know your manager, listening to songs, meeting with producers, and developing a relationship with the people at your record label.

WHAT DID YOU SIGN UP FOR?

Every contest is different when it comes to the commitments you make to the producers of the contest and the obligations you have to them once the contest is finished. As you progress further into the contest, be sure to read and reread your contract so you'll have a good idea what's to come. Also, the show will probably have a confidentiality agreement that says you can't talk to the press about certain things that happen behind the scenes of the contest. Read that to determine what you can and can't say so that you don't get into hot water.

Don't forget about taxes. Whatever prizes you win, taxes will be assessed. If you can't afford the taxes, turn down the prize, no matter how much fun it would be to have. People get excited when they win, but their excitement can turn to headaches a year later. Get with someone who has been in the business for some time to tell you what you should think about. Tax issues related to the music industry could fill a book; I can't stress enough the importance of finding a business manager, or at least an accountant, early in your career. Always think about the taxes: what you spend and what you earn today will affect you come next April 15.

The shows often have first rights of refusal when it comes to signing contestants to a record deal or other contract. That means they have the option of signing anyone they want, and no other company can sign any contestant until the show decides they don't want him or her. Sony Music Nashville signed both Buddy Jewell and Miranda Lambert off the first season of *Nashville Star.* On *Idol,* 19 Entertainment picks and chooses the acts it considers the most viable, and the others have to fend for themselves.

If you win on one of the big shows, the show's producers may continue to get a cut of your income and demand to own a piece of the rights to all the things that you do—endorsements, movies, TV shows. They may get a percentage and part ownership. When my company approached an *Idol* contestant about an animated TV show, we learned that 19 Entertainment would expect to own a piece of our show, so we had to think long and hard about whether we wanted to go down that path. Know your rights and obligations.

BO BICE: THERE'S NOTHING WRONG WITH ASKING QUESTIONS

After *American Idol* ended, more than anything I was asking a lot of questions. And I don't think I asked enough. I wouldn't take a single day of my life back, but I do wish I'd asked a few more questions. So many people think that if they ask this question, they won't get the job, or if they ask that question, somebody will get mad. But if you just ask questions all the time, all they can do is not give you an answer, slight you with the answer, or give you the truth.

SELECT THE RIGHT PRODUCER

I devote an entire chapter to producers later in the book, but let me briefly mention here a few key points about selecting a producer. No matter what route you take, you will need to make a record. Have someone help you assemble a list of producers whom you might want to work with. But most important, *do your homework*. That way, you—and not just your label—remain in control of your career. If you have no idea how to begin, try following these steps:

1. Identify the producers of your favorite records.
2. Notice whether one person has produced more than a few of your favorites.
3. Listen again, peeling away the parts of the recording like layers of an onion: Do you like the sound? The musicians? The vocal? The space? The mix? The songs?
4. Take notes so you can communicate about the kind of album you want to create.
5. Make notes about recordings you don't like and why.
6. If you hear a guitar lick you love or a drummer you can't live without, share these details during your meetings with producers.
7. If you find a producer you like and the two of you see eye-to-eye on most creative issues but not every one, don't let that worry you. Follow your gut.

If you're smart, you made notes during your time on the show about which songs worked best for you. Perhaps you'll consider recording one or more of those songs since you already have an audience for them. Also, have your team spread the word with music publishers so that you can build your repertoire of new songs that you want to record. Have new material in mind—you want songs already headed your way the day you win. You don't want to sacrifice quality, and quality takes time, so get right on it. Don't forget about your favorite album cuts from years ago—a great song has no expiration date.

"Normally, getting to know your label is a month-by-month process," says Chris Young. "That did not happen the way I did it. Basically, it was like, 'Here's your label. Who do you like as a producer? We've got Buddy Cannon coming in.'

"We went with Buddy because he's an awesome producer who has worked with Kenny Chesney, Reba McEntire, and John Michael Montgomery. I lucked into having a wonderful producer. We picked him the day after the show was over and immediately went into the studio and made the record."

KELLY CLARKSON: SURROUND YOURSELF WITH PEOPLE YOU TRUST

You have to surround yourself with people you trust. Most artists, like me, are control freaks. I'm just learning it myself, but I think the key to longevity is letting go and letting everyone around you do their jobs.

ASSEMBLE YOUR TEAM

Start assembling a team to help you with your career as quickly as possible. Carrie Simons says, "You need to find the right family member, friend, trusted fan club president, or someone at the label to be your right hand—figure out your schedule, remind you of meetings and interviews, think for you when you're too tired to think for yourself!"

Also get your Web site to the next level. That is your bread and butter for continuing with your fan base. You want it to reflect what you're trying to achieve. At the same time, you want to make sure you're thanking your fans for their support—that's what brought you to this next level.

Nashville booking agent Rod Essig of Creative Artist Agency (CAA) points to Kellie Pickler as an example of an *Idol* alum who made the most of her opportunity. "She probably did the best of any *Idol*, as far as one who finished fourth or fifth down the line," Rod says. "She kept her profile high, put out her first single quickly, and started playing dates with other country artists."

If winning the show committed you to a certain major-label record deal and you don't have a chance to negotiate, don't worry too much—you'll have a chance to renegotiate once you're successful. That first record is going to be what it's going to be. It's not the best deal, but it's probably not the worst deal, either. The show and the record label have all the leverage—you've put in some time, but they've put in the money—so they're going to make their money back before you start seeing any. Meanwhile, find one person at your label with whom you feel at ease and call that person every day. Nurture that relationship because your label will be an important part of your future the second you win that show.

When it comes to publishing deals, each contest is different. Songwriters and publishers get an equal share of royalties for each song. Some contests will want to assign 100 percent of your publisher's share to an affiliated publisher and will let you keep your writer's share. Some producers/networks will want a portion of your publisher's share for themselves. Some won't ask for anything. You'll sign a standard contract at the start, and you don't get to negotiate the terms.

If your win doesn't lock you into a management contract, then look at hiring a manager. We'll discuss that more in a later chapter, but a manager can help you prioritize and can keep you on schedule. 19 Entertainment, which produces *American Idol*, has a management division that represents former contestants.

START ASSEMBLING A TEAM TO HELP YOU WITH YOUR CAREER AS QUICKLY AS POSSIBLE.

"I think one of the best components of *Idol* is 19 Entertainment's immediate role in managing all the *Idols*," says Carrie Simons. "The team at 19 knows how to create stars and how to protect artists. They can take the reigns of the *Idol*'s career, make the important decisions for them, and lead them on the road to success. Obviously, some will like the guidance more than others, but they have a proven track record that few others can attain.

"Management is really important because they can work with the label, the television network, the tour promoters, and radio to help you succeed. They can also be the bad guy when you need one to say, 'My client's too tired to do that' or 'Can this be pushed to another day?' They will be on the front line for you every day."

Other shows may not have a management division, but their staffs will often offer recommendations and guidance. "The success of the winner breeds the success of the show," Carrie says. "*Nashville Star* doesn't have the same contractual obligation for management that *Idol* has. So you need to find someone who is or will be looking out for your best interests and isn't trying to take advantage of you. The smart thinker will utilize the resources he or she has acquired during the series to help make the best decisions. Use the producers and judges as resources to help select that right person with whom to align. After the season ends, the judges are allowed to discuss issues like this with the contestants, so take advantage of your fortunate position.

"Chris Young [who won *Nashville Star*'s fourth season] has an amazing manager who's very hands-on. His manager once said to me, 'If I don't make Chris a star, I've failed.' If you have someone like that in your corner, your chances of continued success improve dramatically. They will help you make decisions, offer guidance, and have the personal investment and passion to be your manager and so much more.

"The manager can be your mind so you can focus on the craft."

THE MANAGER CAN BE YOUR MIND SO YOU CAN FOCUS ON THE CRAFT.

Be sure you stay informed. Ask to be told about all letters of interest that come your way. At the least, you want to be able to have conversations about these things with your manager. If you notice that a film or TV show was interested in you and you loved the concept, you and only you would have the power to get your label, network, or management company to bend, negotiate, or waive ownership. After nurturing a deep and fulfilling friendship with an artist like Reba McEntire, I've watched her and her husband/manager, Narvel Blackstock, conduct business in the right way. They send response letters, they deliver thank-you notes, and they never burn bridges. Remember, this business ebbs and flows—you might have to walk over that same bridge one day!

DO YOU NEED TO KEEP READING?

If you've just won a talent show that gives your career a big-time push with a major-label record deal and all the trappings of stardom, congratulations. You probably don't need the rest of this book. Make sure you've got a great attorney and a manager that you trust, and they'll teach you more than any book ever could.

For every hundred thousand or so people who read this book, perhaps one will find himself or herself in that situation. Everyone else—whether turned away at the first audition or voted off in the second round of the finals—will face a longer road. But first, you'll need to ask yourself some difficult questions and give yourself some honest answers. We'll start that process next.

Photo courtesy of Modern Management/Stephen Navyac

SARA EVANS: DON'T GET COCKY

Do not get cocky. That's the number one rule. Do not get cocky because you will not last if you do, especially in country music. If you come out of the box and make it really fast and great things start happening and you start believing it's because of you and not because of the support of radio or the fans or just luck or God's blessing on you, then you're going to fall away. I've watched it over the ten years of my career. I've seen so many artists do that. That's my biggest advice: Don't get cocky, and don't take your position for granted.

CHAPTER 6

OKAY, YOU DIDN'T WIN— NOW WHAT?

TIME FOR A GUT CHECK

You did everything you could. You followed all the advice in the earlier chapters. You studied. You practiced. You paid attention and asked questions. You made a great impression, and you sang your butt off. You still didn't win.

That's okay. It's not the end of the world. It doesn't even have to be the end of your dream. But it is time to ask yourself a very serious question and to answer it honestly.

Are you sure this is what you want to do with your life?

While preparing for this book, I asked several of my friends what advice they would give to a young singer or musician who wanted to break into the music business. The piece of advice I heard most often? "Don't do it."

My friends were only half-joking. Mind you, these weren't people who had tried to make a music career for themselves, only to have their dreams shattered. These were people who'd "made it" in the industry—successful artists, songwriters, and executives.

Because they've succeeded, they know the demands that the music industry places on those who enter it, the personal and financial sacrifices that invariably get made. They've had their hearts broken; they've seen marriages destroyed; they've seen lives ruined. We've all heard parents joke about not letting their children marry musicians. Here's why:

Ronnie Dunn

The music business is only for people who absolutely cannot or will not do anything else. If you'd be more content starving for a music career than being rich doing anything else, then maybe—and I stress maybe*—you've got a shot.*

Remember my rule as a manager? If my prospective clients had a Plan B, I wouldn't work with them. If they'd thought through another option, I knew that being an artist was not their calling. This is a hard business, and you've got to commit everything you have to it.

Nearly every artist we interviewed said something along the same lines.

Dierks Bentley says his father often asked him about his fallback plans. "I read an article about Jewel," Dierks says, "and she said, 'I knew if I had a Plan B, Plan B would become Plan A.' I thought that was great, and I told my dad—but it didn't have the effect I thought it would."

Ronnie Dunn's dream also strained his relationship with his parents, especially when he dropped out of college. "Everyone on the outside will tell an artist, 'You need a Plan B.' But it can't be made easy. Insecurity and poverty are the greatest motivators on the planet.

"I remember being in college in Texas, going, 'I'm crazy to even think about this, making this plunge, are you kidding me?' There was this wall that went up between me and my parents and the other people who knew me. It was, like, 'There's Ron who went to college; remember him? He's playing in some bar now.'"

Rodney Crowell, who wrote "Please Remember Me" for Tim McGraw and "Making Memories of Us" for Keith Urban, in addition to having several big country hits of his own, has a young daughter who is a songwriter. He doesn't tell her to have a Plan B.

"I tell her, 'First, you must get rid of all escape hatches,'" he says. "For a career artist, there is no Plan B. If you have something to fall back on, that's what will happen. It's spiritual to me because I believe wholeheartedly there's a wealth of inspiration out there for the creative artists, and now and again inspiration is going to spot you and say, 'Oh, that's one of our go-to guys or girls. They keep the tools sharp. They make themselves worthy of inspiration. Let's give them a dollop.' The good songs come that way.

"So I think Plan B is the enemy of inspiration."

To be fair, one artist did stress the importance of a backup plan. Cyndi Thomson, who had a Number One country hit a few years back with a song called "What I Really Meant to Say," studied marketing and journalism in college. "My Plan B was not necessarily a job," she says, "It was a reality check: know that this might not happen and be okay with it.

YOU MUST GET RID OF ALL ESCAPE HATCHES.

"It's dangerous for the quirky artist type to think only, 'I'm going to make it. I'm going to make it. I'll do anything to make it.' I have friends right now who are married to men who live that life. They make no money, they're in their forties, and their wives are desperate for them to get a good job."

Those people before who told you, "Don't do it," they know that most people who ask about breaking into the music business don't really want it. They might like the *idea* of becoming an artist, but they see only the glamour, the best parts of a successful result. They don't see the struggle, the frustration, the rejection, and the failure—and they're not willing to hear it. If they can hear it and they're scared off, they'd have been gone in a few months anyway. So if you're serious about doing this, understand what's coming and be willing to do it anyway.

Keith Urban may have the best perspective on the matter: "I didn't really have a Plan B, and I didn't even consider what I was doing Plan A. I considered it just my life."

So let's ask that question again:

Are you absolutely *sure this is what you want to do with your life?*

Okay, then, let's get going.

"MAKE IT A BUSINESS, NOT JUST A PLAYTIME"

Whether you're ready to move to a city with a strong entertainment industry or you're still in high school, you can start preparing for your career by educating yourself. If you're college-age, several universities offer excellent music business programs, including Tennessee's Belmont University and Middle Tennessee State University; California's UCLA and USC's Thornton School of Music; New York University; and Berklee College of Music in Boston. Whatever your age, you're never too young to start learning about the music business and, just as important, the people who comprise it.

YOU'RE NEVER TOO YOUNG TO START LEARNING ABOUT THE MUSIC BUSINESS AND THE PEOPLE WHO COMPRISE IT.

"Be educated," Reba McEntire advises. "Learn what to do. Make it a business, not just a playtime.

"If I could go back and do it over, knowing what I know now, I would have taken more dance lessons. I would have taken more voice lessons. I would have read up on the business.

"Back then, we didn't have the autobiographies, the books on how to do things. Nowadays, kids are rich with information on the Internet. They can find any information they want on how so-and-so did it, and they can take the best parts from each artist."

In the past, aspiring singers and musicians scoured the liner notes of their favorite albums to learn the names of producers, sidemen, and backup singers, getting a thrill out of noting that Phil Ramone had produced both Billy Joel *and* Barbra Streisand or that Leland Sklar played bass on Jackson Browne's *Running on Empty* as well as Linda Ronstadt's *Cry Like a Rainstorm, Howl Like the Wind.* These days, that information and much, much more is available with a few keystrokes at your computer.

Do you love the way Justin Timberlake's "SexyBack" sounds? Producer Timbaland's Web site has a discography that shows his work with Nelly Furtado, Jay-Z, Ludacris, Beck, and the Pussycat Dolls. Do you admire the way the Dave Matthews Band has run its career? A quick search reveals that the band's management company, Red Light Management, also works with Alanis Morissette, O.A.R., The Decemberists, Third Day, and Underoath and has offices in New York, Los Angeles, Nashville, and Charlottesville, Virginia.

Whether you want to find out about club owners and voice teachers or the track record of a potential producer or publisher, the Internet is a tremendous resource. You can learn about the industry by regularly reading the sites for *Billboard* magazine or *Pollstar*, which concentrates on touring. If you're thinking about moving to Los Angeles, Austin, London, Atlanta, New York, or Nashville, you can find the entertainment and business sections of their local newspapers online. If you're in a band looking to expand your touring base outside your hometown, you can connect with bands with similar styles in other cities, ask them about the best places to play, and maybe even set up a series of shows together.

LEARN YOUR HISTORY; STUDY YOUR CRAFT

At the same time that you're learning about the business, you should also be learning the history of your craft. If you're a singer, don't limit yourself to what you hear on the radio or what you see on TV. Learn about greats like Frank Sinatra and Al Green or Billie Holiday and Nina Simone. If you're a guitarist, learn about James Burton, Mark Knopfler, Albert Lee, Michael Hedges, and Ry Cooder.

"If you're going to write, educate yourself on Jimmie Rodgers and Hank Williams—why their work works and how it influenced the next guy," Rodney Crowell says. "Then educate yourself about why Chuck Berry and Johnny Cash worked.

"Study the craft and read, educate yourself, read poetry. Figure out why Sylvia Plath is an important artist. Come to understand why, even though she was tortured and killed herself, her work is important. That's the kind of advice I give. It's not sexy advice at all, but it's advice about longevity. By the same token, a choreographer might advise you to study dance. That's equally valuable—I just come from the writing angle."

If you're staying in your hometown for the time being, listen to every record you possibly can. Analyze each one, pull apart a recording like you'd peel the layers of an onion, and ask yourself, "What do I like about this music?"

One easy exercise is to take some older music—whether it's jazz, R&B, pop, or country—and rework it into a style that suits you. Listen to what Robert Plant and Alison Krauss did on their recent album, *Raising Sand.* They took songs from the Everly Brothers, Tom Waits, Townes Van Zandt, even New Orleans rhythm and blues singer Benny Spellman, and transformed them into something different and special. If you're more a stylist than a songwriter, take a lesser known song, change the arrangements, and you have a practically brand-new amazing song—not that it's actually new, but it sounds new. It's an exercise that a lot of people don't do, and I've always wondered why. It's a great way to (a) get a demo, (b) bring an older song to life, and (c) showcase your talent if your talent tends more towards music than lyrics.

DISCIPLINE AND PERSISTENCE EVENTUALLY PAY OFF

If you're a songwriter, try to find another songwriter with a bit of talent and write songs with her. Write every day. Try to write something—even if it's just a line or a possible title—every single day. Keep a notebook with you to jot down ideas. You may never use most of them, but you never know when something you wrote down weeks or months ago suddenly inspires you—like Rodney Crowell's gods of inspiration saying, 'Here's one of our go-to guys.' Keeping a notebook of ideas also means that you'll have a place to start any time you sit down to write.

Once you have plenty of covers and a few great songs that show the world who you are as an artist, go to a club, a coffeehouse, church, school dance, or any dive or honky-tonk where you can perform and create a following. Play for free if you have to, or play for tips. At this point, you're looking more for experience than money.

"Learn your craft and drill, drill, drill," says Nancy Wilson of Heart. "Become so good that, basically, no one can say no to you in the end. Get experience by going out and playing. Keep writing—one good song is only one good song. Those are the hard times and the dues that I think any artist worth his or her salt needs to pay. We still pay it now, even though we've had our supposed success and the arc of our career has been long. We still have the same work ethic.

"Usually, when you're just approaching a career, you don't already have a lot of family concerns—children and things—to hold you back from throwing yourself completely into your work. For instance, if you're in a band and you rehearse, even if you have day jobs, you go the extra mile and you write and you bounce the songs off your friends. You get out there and get the gigs, and you play the gigs until somebody notices. That's most likely when somebody with an ear will get excited about you. If you put enough fishing lines in the water, you'll get a bite eventually. But most of the time, that can take years and years. You're rarely an overnight sensation."

Bev Lambert is convinced the right person eventually hears the singer who's following her calling.

"Even if we hadn't done *Nashville Star*, Miranda would have been discovered," Bev says. "We were committed to seeing her dream come true. I see kids even twelve or thirteen, and I tell them if they believe this is their calling and people are telling them it's their calling, then they need to sing at the local rodeo, the FFA barbecue, everywhere they can for anyone who will listen. If it's a talent show, a contest, whatever—the right person is going to step into that room. I know a singer who's doing shows for an RV convention: guess what—somebody's son will be in the business. Sing everywhere you can, as long as you can afford to do it. If this is your calling, work for it."

IF THIS IS YOUR CALLING, WORK FOR IT.

When Ronnie Dunn moved from Texas to Tulsa, Oklahoma, he thought the town's scene, led by the likes of Leon Russell and J.J. Cale, would welcome him with open arms. "I thought, 'I'm going to fall in the middle of this and away we go,'" he says.

"But it was just as hard to get to them as it was to get to anybody else. A friend of that bunch finally told me, 'You don't want to hear this, but you're going to have to go meet some players and start playing in bars.' I wanted someone to say, 'I'll call Leon and he'll come over and listen and say you're a star, then he'll go, "Let's go into the studio and cut some songs." But here she was telling me I had to play the bars.

"Sure enough, she was right. That hurts—you think it's going to be handed to you or you're going to get a break. That can happen, but it hardly ever does.

"Persistence is extremely important. At the end of the day, you have to want it bad enough to go through things that most people wouldn't. You can develop talent and discipline, you can learn to be a writer, but somewhere deep down, you have to have a talent for it.

"I advise my kids, before you step out into life, go sit on a mountain and stare into space and figure out what your passion is. Sit there until it comes to you, before other things like mortgages and marriages and babies get in the way and get you trapped. You have to find your passion first thing and, if it happens to be music or show business, go get it. Good luck to you."

Speaking of luck, here's a thought from Rodney Crowell: "Luck is your friend."

Rodney believes performers create their luck. They create it by not having a Plan B. They create it by studying their craft and their business. They create it by developing their work habits. They create it by fearlessly stepping into the unknown.

"If I were arriving in Nashville now, it would seem like the nets are out there," Rodney says. "People are fishing for good songs. The nets are in the clubs; they're everywhere. So you just get yourself in circulation and show up. Eventually, somebody somewhere hears a song you play. The business is a fishing industry with nets out for good songs because good songs make money."

AVOID THE PITFALLS OF THE BUSINESS

Doing your homework beforehand can help you avoid many of the nets that turn out to be traps.

When you're starting out, you want to meet people so bad that your desperation can make you do unwise things. Don't let your eagerness fool you into signing a long-term contract too quickly. You can sign contracts that will affect your life for a long, long time. If someone offers you a publishing deal, but they're offering little or no advance money, don't sign it in hopes of making connections in the industry—or, worse, just to be able to say that you have a publishing deal.

When I managed artists and worked at a record label, I frequently saw kids who had agreed to management deals with local venue owners that tied up their careers far too long. The venue owners would spend some money to put the young artist in a studio and maybe get them to Nashville, Los Angeles, or New York, but they'd have an over-reaching contract that would be extremely expensive to break.

DON'T LET YOUR EAGERNESS FOOL YOU INTO SIGNING A LONG-TERM CONTRACT TOO QUICKLY.

Sometimes, the artist is naïve, and the club owner is passionate but inexperienced. The venue owner recognizes the artist's talent but doesn't know exactly what to do with it outside of the club world. Both the artist and the club owner want to have more success, but the match may not be right for either of them. Sometimes, of course, it's not naïveté—some people are just ruthless business people.

"Bands need money," says Creative Artist Agency's Rod Essig, "so the first manager of any band is that club owner who has a lot of money and makes the band sign a five-year deal. Later, when a booking agency shows an interest in representing them, all of a sudden it's, 'Where did *this* guy come from?' 'Oh, he owns the bar back home and had a lot of money and we needed a bus.' We get a lot of that. That's where you have problems getting out of stuff because that guy is all about money."

You shouldn't let a club owner sign you to a long-term management contract unless they've actually managed someone before you. That's a big red flag. You can sign a minimal contract where you agree to pay back loans with interest for money spent on studio time, demos, or flights to Nashville, but don't give them points (percentages of your income) for the rest of your life. You always want to remember the people who helped you at the beginning of your career, and if you're able to pay them back for what they've invested in you, you should. But that doesn't mean they should get money from you for the rest of your life.

Also be wary of contracts with producers that obligate you to them for long periods, especially if they're not an established producer working in an industry town and currently making hit recordings. Paying somebody to record you is one thing—and, often, even that isn't necessary—but promising them future rights is another matter entirely, sometimes a very messy thing. "Nine times out of ten, those local production deals wind up being something you have to spend money with a lawyer trying to get yourself free of," Rodney Crowell says.

Sara Evans warns against paying someone to produce demo recordings in exchange for a promise of a future record deal. Sara and her parents had firsthand experience with that. "I was only nine years old, and we paid $10,000 to Fox Fire Records for a demo," Sara says. "It took me years of performing in clubs to pay that back, and absolutely nothing came of it!"

For the first few years, as you're trying to establish a toehold, you may feel that anybody who says he wants to help you and offers you a contract has to be better than what you're going through now. But if you're good enough, you're going to get more than one offer. And if it's a music-publishing deal, you're going to get an advance. There's no advance with a management deal, but managers will help you fund showcases and assist with travel costs and business expenses. When they really believe in you, they'll help you in every area of your career and become your partner even before you start earning money.

GET USED TO REJECTION

Performers crave approval, which can make them easy targets for unscrupulous businesspeople. Successful performers must learn to handle rejection. More than handle it, they must learn to expect it.

You must be prepared to receive rejection because it's rampant in this industry. There's no avoiding it. When you hear rejection, measure it against your inner voice. It could be a great tip for you to follow your gut after ignoring it for a while. On the other hand, it might motivate you to commit and to focus even more strongly on what you consider your strength because that one thing that turns people on or off—that thing they're either going to love or hate—*that* is the one thing that leads to success.

Rejection either helps you fine-tune your weaknesses or makes you start thinking about a Plan B. It's good to listen to that inner voice: for those who are meant for this life, rejection may spur them to practice their guitar five hours a day instead of just two; for those who aren't, rejection will nudge them towards different career choices.

Keith Urban, for example, was interviewing producers right after he was signed to Warner Bros. I joined him for some meetings. Every producer had a dramatically different style and personality. One actually told him he shouldn't play guitar, or any instruments, on his own record. He told Keith that just wasn't the way things were done in Nashville. I recall Keith telling me after that meeting, "I might as well cut off my right arm then."

SUCCESSFUL PERFORMERS MUST LEARN TO HANDLE REJECTION.

Keith left that meeting with stronger resolve because he realized that, if he didn't play, he wouldn't be making *his* music. That criticism and rejection of his musicianship, his "foreign" accent, and his tenor voice caused him a lot of pain, but it made him stronger; it made him realize he had to find the person who believed in him as a musician, as a songwriter, and as a front man because he wanted to create his music his way.

Rejection can be helpful or harmful, but it's a fact of life in this business. You've got to learn to deal with it; otherwise, you're going to be forever unhappy.

MEET THE RIGHT PEOPLE—BUT WHO ARE THEY?

People often say that the music business is a business of relationships—"It's not what you know, it's who you know." That's true to a certain extent, but you'll get more out of *whom* you know if you know *what* you need to know. If you focus more on connecting with the power players than you do on perfecting your craft, you'll come across as opportunistic. That can hurt your credibility. I see a lot of people so focused on networking that when they finally get the audience they've worked so hard for, their talent just isn't good enough—they'll sing at a party with all these people from the industry, and they crash and burn.

If your motives aren't in the right place, and your talent isn't strong enough to back up your pitch, you could destroy your reputation and have to start from zero all over again. I see it happen to artists quite often.

Also, if you've done your homework and identified the movers and the shakers in your part of the business, don't focus solely on the most powerful people. As you're building your network, be sure to include many people who are on the same rung of their career ladders as you are on yours—or maybe one rung above or one rung below. People usually rise through this industry in groups, and the more alliances you have, the more likely you are to know the person who can help you when you need it most.

THE MORE ALLIANCES YOU HAVE, THE MORE LIKELY YOU ARE TO KNOW THE PERSON WHO CAN HELP YOU WHEN YOU NEED IT MOST.

When Garth Brooks broke through in the late 1980s, he brought practically an entire cottage industry with him. Tony Arata and Kent Blazy suddenly became in-demand songwriters. John McBride, who provided Garth's soundsystem and worked as his production manager on some of his tours, went on to build one of Nashville's most successful recording studios. John's wife, Martina McBride, sold T-shirts and merchandise on one of Garth's tours and soon was his opening act. Trisha Yearwood sang harmony on his first two albums and quickly got her own record deal. Garth even hired some of the interns who worked for his manager. All those people were trying to start their careers when Garth moved to Nashville in 1987. Because they all helped each other when none of them had money, they all found success together.

"Get to know people at the same level you are," recommends producer Tony Brown, who twice signed former bandmate Vince Gill to record deals. "Get to know songwriters,

A&R people, and musicians at the same level you are. Those people are all around, ready and willing to help you out, thinking that if you get a big deal, you'll help them out. There are a lot of people in the same boat."

You can learn a lot from people just one or two levels above you. If your next step is working in local clubs, then go see the band already playing there and talk to them. If they're just one level above you, they'll likely be easier to approach than bands playing arenas. If that band draws two hundred people a night and you're only getting fifty, they're just a little ahead of you. Maybe they've met a few more people and can offer you helpful advice.

In any business, you want to spend time with people who challenge you to be your best on a daily basis. You want to be around people who are further along than you, but you don't need to meet Donald Trump straight out of high school. A lot of people dream so big that they're not realistic. Having a big dream is good, but having realistic goals is even better.

SHOULD YOU STAY OR SHOULD YOU GO?

You may hear that you have to move to the city where the labels are. Relocating to an industry town certainly puts you around more of the people with whom you want to develop relationships. You're not likely to become a famous R&B singer if you're living in rural Montana. But you can do a lot of work before ever leaving your hometown. That's the crazy thing about this business. There is no career track. You don't have to go to school or get a master's degree or become a junior partner. With most careers, there's a general path to the top, but with the music industry, there's nothing of the sort. Every artist finds his or her own way.

At a certain stage in the development of your craft, you do need to go where the activity and the industry are. *But don't move there before you are ready.* If your music or voice or songwriting is not far enough developed, you can move too soon. I'm talking about brand-new baby acts, people who have the dream but move too soon. All of a sudden, they're in dire financial straits in a new city, they've given up the following they had back home, and no one in the new town knows their talent, which isn't fully developed yet anyway. They're not far enough along to win fans and might even damage their reputation. Remember the adage: It takes only five *minutes* to ruin a reputation but five *years* to repair it.

Making the move to an industry town can be a matter of timing. Shelby Kennedy, who works as the director of writer-publisher relations at BMI in Nashville, points to young country singer Ashton Shepherd as an artist who'd developed her skills at home in Alabama to the point where Nashville found her. Ashton signed a recording contract with Universal Music Group Nashville's MCA label and released her first single in 2007 at age twenty-one.

AT A CERTAIN STAGE IN THE DEVELOPMENT OF YOUR CRAFT, YOU DO NEED TO GO WHERE THE ACTIVITY IS. ***BUT DON'T MOVE THERE BEFORE YOU ARE READY.***

"Ashton is a good example of somebody who arrived in Nashville fully baked," Shelby says. "A lot of people think the artist has to do showcases, has to do artist development, has to learn to dress, has to co-write. If Ashton had been in Nashville, I think she would have been messed up.

"I don't know how she developed into what she developed into, but she's got close to two hundred songs and she never co-wrote with anybody. She learned everything she knew on her own. She didn't know the Nashville 'formula' song or anything like that."

With Shelby's help, Ashton came to Nashville and met some publishers and record labels, eventually signing with MCA. "I told her, 'You're at the point where we've got to get you to the plate, and you've actually got a bag of bats,'" Shelby says.

Shelby and several others championed Ashton and her songs in Nashville. You'll need champions at every step of the way in your career—and they can come from anywhere. We'll talk about them more in the next chapter.

REASSESS YOUR SITUATION

Ask yourself these questions:

1. Peel the onion to determine what exactly you enjoyed about your contest experience. Singing? Hearing others sing? Receiving compliments on your wardrobe? Meeting new people? Remember it—and write it down.
2. What did you sing for your friends before, during, and after the auditions? How did they react? Were they the same songs you chose to sing for the "important" people? If not, why not?
3. Did you wish you could have played an instrument while you were singing? Did you wish you could have performed a song you wrote? If so, that wish is the very thing you need to do from now on.
4. Did your butterflies get the better of you and your voice? If so, attack performing with a new fire in your belly. Play and sing live every chance you get.
5. Do you remember what critiques the judges offered? If not, hear my grandmother: *You have two ears and one mouth. This means you listen more than you talk.*
6. Do you feel rejected? If so, decide right here, right now, whether you want to use that rejection to fuel your engine to continue down this path. Otherwise, find a new direction.

CHAPTER 7

BUILD A GOOD TEAM AND A STRONG FOUNDATION FOR YOUR CAREER

YOUR BEST FIRST PERSON

As you decide to get serious about your career, whether you move to a city with a thriving music scene or start in your hometown, you need to seek out experienced people in your field. You want to find someone who can give you some basic advice, maybe introduce you to a few people. If you ask around for advice about the best first person to meet when you're trying to launch your career, you'll get several recommendations. They'll likely include the following:

- **A MANAGER—**A dexterous person schooled in several aspects of the business can help you make decisions and cultivate a budding career while you create your music.
- **A MUSIC-INDUSTRY LAWYER—**Typically the best-connected figures in any industry town, lawyers can introduce you to key contacts while showing you the ropes of the business. They can also prevent you from signing a bad contract when you are eager to do anything to move your career forward.

- ★ **A RECORD-LABEL ARTIST & REPERTOIRE (A&R) REPRESENTATIVE—**This person gets paid to recognize and nurture new artists; A&R people are the gateways to record companies.
- ★ **A MUSIC PUBLISHER—**A good publisher will not only help a promising songwriter perfect his craft but will often provide you an early income stream.
- ★ **A BOOKING AGENT—**All young performers need paying gigs, and a booking agent works on their behalf to land them.
- ★ **A CLUB OWNER—**Club owners can provide a first break, an entrance into the industry, a place to play, advice, and sometimes money. The great thing is that every town has them. But avoid signing any long-term contract with a club owner until you find an experienced music attorney.

All of the above are excellent answers. If you are fortunate enough to have a good manager or booking agent in your corner early in your career, you definitely have a leg up on the competition. Those people can not only help you get your foot in the door, they can eventually play an essential role in your career. If your best first person winds up being somebody else—a music teacher, say, or an experienced local musician—that's fine, too. Chances are you won't choose your best first person; more likely, he or she will choose you.

WHEREVER YOU GO, WHETHER YOU'RE BUILDING AN AUDIENCE IN YOUR HOMETOWN OR MOVING TO A CITY WITH AN ESTABLISHED MUSIC INDUSTRY, SEEK THE COUNSEL OF PEOPLE WHO KNOW WHAT THEY'RE DOING.

Wherever you go, whether you're building an audience in your hometown or moving to a city with an established music industry, seek the counsel of people who know what they're doing. Look for successful people—or ones with big address-book files.

Having said that, let me clarify: beware of aiming too high too soon. Targeting only the most powerful people in the industry is playing a high-risk game. Sure, it could pay off big. More than likely, though, at least early on, you won't even register with a record-company head or a top producer unless you're accompanied by an introduction or a recommendation from someone they know and trust. If you badger these individuals too often or too early, you'll come off as a minor annoyance—the kind they've trained themselves to tune out. Worse, you'll look like a fool or an opportunist.

Don't skip steps in your career. Nobody becomes famous as quickly as it seems to people watching from the outside. It's true that when good things finally start to happen, they often happen very rapidly. But those things can only happen quickly because a lot of people have been setting building blocks in place for a long time.

Before you worry about contracts and fame, start developing your gift and your relationships. If you're too desperate to get to the deal, you make a nice, big target for people who want to take advantage of you. But if you're making friends—or even just good business acquaintances—not only will the contracts come in due time, but you'll have people who will watch your back and help you find the right people to seal the deal. Maybe those people will be managers, lawyers, agents, and record-label executives.

Out in the real world, though, your best first person to meet can come from anywhere.

FIND YOUR CHAMPION

All you need in the beginning is one person who believes in you unconditionally—your champion. You need someone to shout your name from the rooftops, to pass along your music, maybe even to float you a few bucks for groceries. That person's enthusiasm will be genuine, often unsought and generally—at least at first—unpaid.

People can discover you in any number of ways—some traditional, some not so much. If you stay alert for opportunities, you'll see them—but not on your timeline.

Though it's essential that you eventually find a professional who believes in you, your first champion may be someone only peripherally connected to the business. Stories abound in this industry about a high-school girl who hears a demo and plays it for her brother-in-law who runs an indie label, or a mother who tells her executive son about a young girl she heard at a local talent show. You never know when or where you will find that first champion. So keep an open mind, focus on your craft and build your audience—that's the place from which your champions will arise.

The music business is full of early adopters. The same way some people have to have the newest technology, the latest music player, the biggest television, most people in the music industry pride themselves on being the first among their friends to recognize new talent. If they can turn somebody else on to a new artist, it enhances their reputations and maybe their careers.

As a music supervisor, when I find a killer artist who's not signed, I'll forward her name to all my A&R friends. Every major instrument manufacturer has an artist-relations executive. Develop relationships with them because they talk to people in the industry. I talk to Gibson regularly because I want Gibson guitars in my movies, and we talk about music a lot. Most people who work for an instrument manufacturer are music lovers.

ALL YOU NEED IN THE BEGINNING IS ONE PERSON WHO BELIEVES IN YOU UNCONDITIONALLY—YOUR CHAMPION.

One possibility is to look for the junior A&R people at the record companies. If you've just moved to town, you don't want the Clive Davises and Joe Galantes of the world to see you until you're sure you're ready. Cultivate relationships with the younger executives who are also looking to prove their worth. Help them look good to their bosses and you've got a champion for life.

Another option is to befriend a young, aggressive marketer or publicist. If you create a buzz—whether it's in the media, online, or around town—and the buzz gets to the decision makers before you do, that's always good. Then they're searching for you rather than your begging them to come to your gig.

People want to follow the buzz, they want to follow the heat—they're heat-seeking missiles. If you're creating your own heat, they'll be on your trail. Especially if you have a specific vision for your music and you're a natural live performer. Having a marketing or publicity person as one of your first champions is a great thing if you've got the goods because they can help you create the buzz.

A respected club owner or a music teacher at a local university isn't that many people removed from the industry's most powerful players. So remember, your champion may come from any segment of the business, from any level.

For Dierks Bentley, that person was a drummer.

"You would think it would be a producer or something, but that's the way it works out sometimes," Dierks says. "It ends up being someone you wouldn't expect it to be."

When Dierks played Nashville bars early in his career, the musicians with whom he played often cancelled at the last minute when they got better-paying gigs. Dierks kept a long list with the phone numbers of musicians and often found himself scrambling to fill in for a guitar player and frequently playing with pickers he'd never met. Eventually, he worked his way to a drummer named Steve Misamore.

"I didn't know what he did during the daytime," Dierks says, "but about three or four months into a gig at a place called the Market Street Brewery, I gave him a copy of a CD that I'd made on my own because I wanted to work on some original songs for the show.

"It turned out he was a tape copier in the library at Sony Tree Publishing, and he knew everyone over there. He wanted to take the CD over and play it for Don Cook and Woody Bomar. So I went with my drummer one day to Sony Tree, and I was able to get what I'd wanted all along.

"I knew if I could get a publishing deal, I could get a steady paycheck and quit all the side jobs I was doing, get a foot in the door in the Nashville community and concentrate on my music 100 percent of the time. That's one of those things I wasn't trying to force to happen, and the music just found a way."

Dierks's champion was a musician, so his connection to the music industry is fairly clear. But help for Jake Owen, a country singer whose hits include "Startin' with Me" and "Yee Haw," came from a less obvious source—a banker.

"She was, like, an accounts manager at SunTrust on Music Row," Jake says. "I knew she dealt with people in the music business on a regular basis, so I intentionally took a CD with me. It just happened to work out exactly how I'd planned it in my mind.

"When I went into her office to sign up for my little account with the little money I had, she said she'd love to hear my music sometime. I said I had a CD of my songs in my pocket, so I gave it to her.

"Surprisingly, she thought they were good enough to give to a guy at Warner/Chappell Music. He called me out of the blue, like, three days later and asked if I had written the songs. I said yeah, so he called me into his office. That's really when I got my foot in the door in Nashville."

Credit: Scott D. Smith

DIERKS BENTLEY:
DOING THE TOWN THE RIGHT WAY

Dierks Bentley moved to Nashville in 1994, not long after he graduated high school. During his first years in town, he educated himself about the local music industry through a combination of jobs and clubs, meeting business people by day and musicians by night. Dierks released his debut album for Capitol Records in 2003, and his first two Capitol albums sold more than a million copies. He won the Country Music Association's Horizon Award in 2005. Dierks has topped the country charts with such singles as "What Was I Thinkin'," "Come a Little Closer," and "Free and Easy Down the Road I Go," along the way developing a reputation as one of country music's most business-savvy young artists.

Nashville is such a big town for musicians; it's pretty daunting. When I moved to town, I had no idea how to begin doing anything. I had no one to lean on to tell me how to get started. The first thing I did was go to the Country Music Association and get a job as an intern. I didn't know what it was, but the CMA sounded like a good place to get information about Nashville.

Even that internship was competitive, but I was able to get a spot in the Public Relations department. Getting an internship was a huge step for me. They were working on Fan Fair and Country Radio Seminar, lots of little stuff along the way. It was a chance to begin to figure out how the whole music business worked. There are two sides, the music and the business, and that took care of the business side for me, helping me figure that side out. The only other thing I knew was to go where the music was.

I knew I wasn't going to walk in and set the town on fire. My approach was to come and learn, learn, learn, and get better and better so that when I did finally make my move I had a leg to stand on. I started spending a lot of time downtown in the bars and clubs on lower Broadway. To me, the music was kind of split up into two parts: the part of me that wanted to play and sing any song—just put a band together and have a gig, which is a huge challenge in itself—and the part of me that wanted to be a songwriter. I split time between going to downtown bars and clubs, listening to standards and learning songs at home, and also going out to places like the Broken Spoke, Douglas Corner, the Hall of Fame Lounge and, eventually, the Bluebird Cafe. I was like a sponge for the first few years, just hanging out in the corners and listening, getting better at what I did before I tried to do anything in public.

The songwriting stuff came first. I was going to places like Douglas Corner to listen to people do their rounds. I finally got up the nerve to put my name in the hat. After about six months, I got pretty comfortable doing these writers' nights a few days a week. But I still didn't have a gig anywhere, I didn't have a band, I wasn't playing standards—I was just doing writers' nights.

Eventually I played the Bluebird, which was the thing I was always working toward. Once I did the first open-mic night at the Bluebird, I realized I could hang in there with the town's other writers. Then I wanted to get on the Bluebird's Sunday writers' night, and you have to audition for that. I waited in a very long line to audition for a Sunday Bluebird performance. Two weeks later, I got a notice in the mail saying I had passed the audition and the first available Sunday was four or five months later. It's crazy how much competition there was for that Sunday night thing.

My cousin Avery Auger played banjo, and he moved to town with a band called Creede. We ended up playing onstage together, and then we put together a bluegrass band with people I knew from the Station Inn, a local bluegrass club. We were

(cont.)

a bluegrass band, but we played a bunch of country songs. That's really where I started my first gigs. We'd do a wedding or crawfish boil, a backyard barbecue or a tailgate party. I was able to put a little band together for five hundred bucks and everyone would make a hundred dollars and have a good time.

I had my first standing gig on Wednesday nights at Springwater. I played for free Natural Light draught beer. The more I drank, the more I felt like I got paid. We had a tip jar, and friends would come down and support us, a little money here and there—not enough to support ourselves. It was a huge feeling of pride to be able to call home or see people around town and say, "Yeah I've got a gig on Wednesday nights at Springwater; come on out." I thought that was a big step, to have a home base where people could come out and see me play.

At the same time, I was working at TNN (The Nashville Network) during the days. I also had worked at Randstad Work Solutions, temping for about a year. One week I'd answer phones for the Gospel Music Association; the next I'd help Sony stuff Clint Daniels radio boxes that the label was sending out to promote a new single; sometimes I'd answer phones and pour coffee at Famous Music publishing company. Randstad was a good job. The only problem was every third week you'd go down there and there'd be no job; then you'd have to call home and ask for money, and all the questions would start again.

PROS—A GREAT PLACE TO START

Maybe you've just moved to an industry town—or maybe you're just scoping out the place on a visit. If you don't know where to start and you have any interest in songwriting, a performing rights organization (PRO) makes an excellent first visit.

Performing rights organizations (the United States has three—ASCAP, BMI, and SESAC) monitor public performances of music. They license radio stations, TV networks, cable channels, restaurants, clubs, and other music venues to use music, and they collect fees and distribute them to their songwriter members. Every professional songwriter eventually signs with one of these organizations, and each PRO distributes hundreds of millions of dollars in performance royalties each year.

IF YOU DON'T KNOW WHERE TO START, A PERFORMING RIGHTS ORGANIZATION (PRO) MAKES AN EXCELLENT FIRST VISIT.

BMI and SESAC have membership offices in New York, Los Angeles, Atlanta, Miami, and Nashville. ASCAP has offices in all those cities and one in Chicago, as well. All three maintain useful Web sites that include writer/publisher resources and information on how to affiliate.

PROs are a safe first stop, right after you get off the bus. Anyone can set up an appointment with a writer representative and receive a crash-course survey of the music industry and, perhaps, meet a future champion.

"Really, it's the first place young songwriters can go and not have to reach into their wallets," says Shelby Kennedy, a director of writer/publisher relations in Nashville. "We're almost like that map at a shopping mall. You know, *You are here.* Everybody has the place they want to go, but the directions are different according to where *here* is."

BE PERSISTENT—GET IN THE MIDDLE OF THINGS

Half the game is showing up. The other half is sticking around. As you begin to make contacts in the music business, you have to prove that you're serious about what you do. Be a sponge, and learn everything you can, everywhere you go. But be smart about where you spend your time.

- ★ If your strongest gift is songwriting, go where the songwriters go.
- ★ If musicianship is your ace in the hole, play with everyone you can, on every demo you can.

★ If your voice is your calling card, then sing in bars, sing on demos, sing in your local church choir. Sing your heart out!

Whatever your strengths, you must be persistent. If the people around you don't believe that you take your career seriously, they won't take you seriously either.

Remember the words of President Calvin Coolidge: "Nothing in the world can take the place of persistence. Talent will not; nothing is more common than unsuccessful men with talent. Genius will not; unrewarded genius is almost a proverb. Education will not; the world is full of educated derelicts. Persistence and determination are omnipotent. The slogan 'press on' has solved and always will solve the problems of the human race."

Or listen to Keith Urban. "I was willing to go the distance," he says. "Nashville, in particular, wants to see that you're committed, you're serious. When I got there, people told me it would take me five years. I said I didn't have five years, but darned if they weren't right. It took at least five years, maybe a little longer. That perseverance is very important."

PUT YOUR TEAM TOGETHER

Always look for people you can trust. "Try to find someone who has a track record, who's been there before, who has enough experience of his own to draw on," says manager Gary Borman, whose clients include Faith Hill, James Taylor, and Keith Urban. "Sometimes this isn't the manager. Sometimes it's the label person or an A&R person or a wife or a husband—it's anyone on the team who has that vision that the artist believes in and who is willing to provide leadership.

"I have been part of that team on many occasions—sometimes I've been the leader of the team, other times I've just fulfilled another role on the team.

"With the artists I've chosen, that is what brought us together—either my vision for them that they didn't have or an ability to look at what they'd done and say, 'You've got it, you've just not been able to use it, and what you've been doing has not been on target; with some minor adjustments, you'll be fine.'

"That was the case with Keith Urban and Dwight Yoakam. It was the right moment, the right situation, the marketplace was right, and they were the right people to take the ball and run with it. Because at the end of the day, all of us geniuses in the music business can say the right thing at the right time, but if the artist cannot develop, it doesn't matter."

If you have a good feeling about where your strengths lie, start building your team from there. If it's songwriting, search for publishers. If it's performance, search for an agent.

EXAMINE YOUR STRENGTHS AND WEAKNESSES

As you start assembling your team, get input about your strengths and weaknesses. It's always hard to identify your strengths, especially when you're young. Getting some outside perspective can help immeasurably.

"Start with truth and honesty," says David Malloy, who has produced chart-topping hits for the likes of Reba McEntire, Kenny Rogers, and Dolly Parton. "Be honest with yourself first of all, and examine your strengths and weaknesses.

"If you've got a weakness, don't run and hide from it; address it. A career goes on for a long time, and I've seen singers who've never touched an instrument teach themselves guitar. Down the road, they're playing guitar and singing.

"You're never at a point where you stop and go, 'I don't need to learn anything new now.'"

Another tip is to watch for reactions. Do you get a response when you're working a room, or when you sing a song with just a guitar? Look for those reactions.

"When you go out and play live, you get immediate feedback," says Don Was. Don played for more than a decade in Was (Not Was) before going on to produce hits like Bonnie Raitt's "Thing Called Love" and the B-52s' "Love Shack" and executive-produced the multi-platinum soundtrack for *Hope Floats.* "You see what works and what doesn't. If you can be objective about your stuff, take it in front of other people. When do people start moving around in their chairs and looking around the room, not paying attention? When are all eyes on you and the place is quiet? When do people clap in the middle of a song?

"When Was (Not Was) was on tour, it became clear that no matter where we played—from Japan to South America to Detroit—a few things always went over. And they all happened by accident. Like the night the trumpet player picked up three trumpets and played. He'd put down one and play harmony with the other two. No matter where we were, that worked. So you just know it, and it doesn't take long to figure it out."

WHOM TO LISTEN TO, WHOM NOT TO LISTEN TO

So whom should you listen to, and whom should you ignore?

You should listen to someone who has *some* kind of experience and background in the industry they're addressing. Your parents or your aunt or you best friend who goes bowling with you may give you advice, but they may be trying to tell you what you want to hear or trying to make you feel better after somebody's rejected you. Your family and friends will support you, and that's good, but that also colors their advice. Listen to someone who has a track record.

People in the business, if they're truly interested in your career, will sometimes give you advice that's hard for you to hear. You might agree with them or you might disagree with them, but once you realize they're in sync with most areas of your music, you do have to listen to them and consider whether you should take their advice, their rejection, or their approval to heart.

In the stories Jake Owen and Dierks Bentley told earlier in this chapter, their champions shared a common trait. In both cases, the people who wound up helping the singers didn't brag about their connections. They didn't even let Dierks and Jake know they had them. They just quietly went about their business making connections. If you're looking for ways to tell the real people from the fake ones, remember the old adage about the two types of people in the world—those who talk and those who do.

"Whoever you get in touch with, they have to be connected into something that's pretty real," Jake says. "A lot of people claim to be connected to stuff but aren't."

I quoted Calvin Coolidge earlier in the chapter, too. Here's good advice from another president, Ronald Reagan: "Trust, but verify." Reagan often used the phrase when discussing America's relationship with the Soviet Union, but it's good advice when it comes to business contacts. If somebody's making you promises, ask around. Find people who know them and their reputation. Journalists have a rule of thumb about verifying information from three sources. Apply a variant of that rule to anyone with whom you're considering doing business: find at least three people who know the person and who vouch for them.

Don't let your desire turn to desperation and make you gullible. On the other hand, don't let caution turn you cynical. Weigh all the input you receive, and measure it against what you know in your heart.

"Along the road with all the naysayers and all the brick walls comes the odd person who tells you something you need to hear," Keith Urban says. "It's all about which voices you want to tune into. If you keep tuning into the negative ones, that's what you'll hear, but stay connected to the positive ones because they also have merit.

"For me, it was a guy named Cliff Audretch, who was working at Sony Music. He started coming out to see me every night, so I said, 'Why don't you sign us to the label?' He said, 'I would, if I could do it on my own, but I need everyone else's support.'

"Then he told me something else: 'You're really unique, and it will be your greatest curse until it becomes your greatest blessing.' And for some reason, that just went straight to the heart of me. I started thinking, 'I am different, but it's okay. If I stay true to myself, it's going to work out. It just may take some time.'

"I think everyone is going to find their own way to navigate those waters. But it's so important to keep honest people around you—not yes-people or family members who are biased—genuine people who will give you good advice.

"And don't be afraid to ask people their real opinions—not the glossy ones, not the backslapping ones. Ask for specifics: 'How can I improve? What's working? What's not working?' And be willing to sift through their answers for the authenticity."

Credit: Max Vadukul

KEITH URBAN:
COMPROMISING VERSUS ADAPTING

When Keith Urban moved to Nashville from Australia in 1992, he wasn't quite like anything else in town. He had a different look, a different sound, a different vision for his music. He even had a different accent. Urban finally had a Top 20 country hit seven years after arriving in Nashville; his first Number One, "But for the Grace of God," took another two years. During the years in between, Keith learned the difference between adapting and compromising—an important lesson for any artist. He has since topped the country charts with hits like "Days Go By," "Somebody Like You," and "Stupid Boy." In 2005, the Country Music Association named Keith its Entertainer of the Year.

At one point early in my career, a lot of people told me, "If you just changed this or you just changed that, you'd be able to get your foot in the door." I started to become tempted with the idea of changing what I did, and I did that a couple of times.

I even thought of changing my name because when I first got to Nashville in 1992, the town was still sort of reeling from the Urban Cowboy scenario ten years before, so the whole "Urban" thing was an obstacle for me. I couldn't think of anything else, so it didn't work out. I was willing to do it; that's the interesting thing.

But I did start to change my music and change a bit of the way I looked and performed. And that didn't seem to make any difference. I think what happened then was that I wasn't authentic, so the lack of honesty and authenticity prohibited me from getting through the door, too.

My other problem was that I decided I'd do whatever they told me, I'd use whatever producer they suggested, I'd use whatever band they wanted. Then, I thought, if I got some success, I'd use my own band and write my own songs. But I watched a few other artists suffer by taking that approach because nobody wanted to mess with a successful formula. The worst thing that happened to those people is that they had success based on the record-company formula. So when the artists got to do their own record and write their own songs, the record label didn't support it. So I thought,

"Note to self: The object here is not actually to get a record deal but to get the right record deal."

I realized I could adapt, which is not the same thing as compromise. I could focus on some part of what I was doing that made sense to other people and not think about all the other stuff I was doing that didn't make sense to them.

I figured out what things I was doing that would work at the time. I focused and expanded on those. At the same time, I played all the time, anywhere I could—a songwriters' night, sitting in with people, hunting showcases. I just kept doing it.

I was fortunate enough to sign a publishing deal that gave me enough money to live on. It was a meager salary, but it was enough to live on so I could stay and keep supporting my showcases. I spent a lot of money showcasing, recording, and investing in myself. In fact, I was so about performing and guitar playing that I didn't have the songs that really connected with people. So I spent a lot of time writing with people in Nashville, trying to find my voice. That took a long time, as well. It was a place I needed to spend more of my energy.

I understand someone's almost inability to have any patience when they're young, and that's okay because that's part of the fire that's fueling the drive. In a lot of ways, that can't be tempered. But that searching phase is so important because the pain is absolutely the touchstone of growth. If you really want to do things on your own terms, it's going to take longer. It's going to be more painful, and the only way to get it is to try lots of things. It will be preceded by enormous amounts of failure, frustration, and disillusionment.

But I really hate that word "compromise." I don't think you have to compromise, but I think you can adapt. That just makes sense because it's the nature of the business when you're getting started.

CHAPTER 8

MANAGERS

WHO NEEDS A MANAGER?

Any artist who experiences even modest success will need a manager at some point. A manager can act as a righthand man (or woman) and often handles much of the business side of an artist's career so that the artist can focus on the creative side.

Finding the right manager is like finding the right spouse. Just as no married couple will have quite the same kind of relationship as another, no manager/artist relationship will be the same as any other. A manager's duties will vary from artist to artist and may even change over the course of an artist's career. A manager can help coordinate all the different areas of an artist's career—recording, touring, songwriting, merchandising, sponsorships, etc. She can make introductions to key industry figures. He can help secure contracts with record companies or music publishers. She can advise on business decisions, even make some of them. He can act as a go-between for the artist and others, sometimes acting as the hard-liner who plays the heavy so the artist doesn't have to. She can be a protector, a shield, a confidante, a business partner.

There is no degree necessary to become a personal manager. It's about honesty, dedication, smarts, loyalty, and the ability to see the big picture. Different managers have different strengths, so make sure you find one whose strengths match your own. Denise Stiff is brilliant and successful with an Alison Krauss-type of artist, where the career is not about hit songs but diversity—whether it's recording with Robert Plant or singing a duet with Brad Paisley or working on a film soundtrack. Clarence Spalding—who represents Brooks & Dunn, Pat Green, and Jason Aldean, among others—is great at mainstream radio. Some managers are great at handling the big things—the hit songs, the major endorsements. Others specialize in grassroots marketing. Each has his or her strengths and weaknesses, so choose carefully.

DIFFERENT MANAGERS HAVE DIFFERENT STRENGTHS, SO MAKE SURE YOU FIND ONE WHOSE STRENGTHS MATCH YOUR OWN.

Gary Borman, who has represented James Taylor, Faith Hill, and others, believes there's no set answer to the question of *when* an artist needs a manager, other than "as soon as the artist can find one."

Borman adds: "Obviously, the better and more qualified the manager, the better it is for the artist. The reverse of that is not to go with someone who's not qualified just because that person thinks you're great. It's sort of a Catch-22—should you go with Mr. Jones over there even though he lacks the qualifications if no one else is knocking at your door? That's where faith and belief come into play. You've got to hold out till the right manager comes along, but the sooner you can get a manager on your side, the better. You need someone to go out there and stir things up. And no one does that job better, in my opinion, than a manager."

Management deals typically last from one to five years (three is about average) and charge a commission of 10 to 15 percent of the artist's income (some may go as high as 25 percent—but *never* sign a 50 percent deal). If you're considering working with someone who has no previous management experience, you'd do well to limit the length of any contract you sign (and get a music attorney if you're discussing a contract of any significant length). Things are changing dramatically these days as record companies and other organizations experiment with new business models, including full-service music companies that encompass all career aspects. That's a whole new ball of wax. That situation is more like a partnership, like the merger of two companies rather than a person managing for a commission.

Carol Peters, a long-time industry veteran who has worked at record labels and currently manages Heart and Deana Carter, says: "Back in the day, I used to tell artists they really didn't need a manager, that they initially needed an attorney. The first way of becoming validated used to be that you got the record deal, you got the publishing deal, and you got an agent. But that's the old paradigm, and that doesn't apply anymore. I find myself more and more taking on young artists because if I'm not going to do it, who will? It's like, you've got real talent and there's just no way you have a snowflake's chance if I don't help you out."

How much can a manager help you out? Miles Copeland used to tell me that, with the Police, he drove the van and took money at the door for gigs. When I first co-managed Keith Urban in 1994, I helped a young CAA agent book gigs and took money at the door so we didn't have to split it with anybody else. At that point, every penny mattered. I did his publicity, marketing, and set up our photography sessions. After that, I grabbed a stapler and hung posters around town to create a buzz about his band's weekly gig at Jack's Guitar Bar, which began as a humble, semi-empty club and ended up with sold-out shows where we had to turn away people every week because of fire-code restrictions. I even co-signed his car loan because he was Australian and couldn't get one without a co-signer. Miles funded many of the expenses it takes to get to the point of making a profit.

When Gary Borman first started working with Faith Hill, he and Warner Bros. A&R executive Martha Sharp invited the man who would become her first producer to see her perform. ("He fell in love with her, literally and figuratively," he recalls.) "I thought she was one of the most sincere performers I'd ever seen," Gary says. "Her warmth, her sincerity, and her genuineness hit me. She was beautiful, she had that voice, and she had a certain degree of innocence that was really appealing.

"Faith hadn't yet figured out who she was as an artist. She had this huge voice, irresistible warmth, and powerful ambition. I thought that if we could harness this in song and capture it in image, she would captivate everyone else just as she had captivated those few of us.

"When we shot the album cover, I suggested that she wear jeans and a man's shirt, untucked, and be barefoot, because she's a Mississippi natural—she's beautiful and she's got all this warmth. Why not show it off? The first single, 'Wild One,' came out, and it was a big hit.

"It was finding what about Faith was special and just trying to magnify that and put it forward. It wasn't about genius styling. It wasn't about image making. I possess none of those skills. It was identifying what about her was special and making sure we presented that and didn't let it get diluted or lost in some sort of artificial concept."

GARY BORMAN: FROM DWIGHT YOAKAM TO FAITH HILL

An attorney friend of mine in Los Angeles said he had a client named Dwight Yoakam who was looking for a manager. Dwight lived in Los Angeles, and he'd been in *Rolling Stone* and on MTV, so I had some exposure to him. But I said, no, the last country music I had listened to was Gram Parsons and Emmylou Harris. I had left off with Poco, the Flying Burrito Brothers, and the Byrds, so I said I didn't think I was the right guy.

Later I was in a bar or a restaurant in Sun Valley, Idaho, and I heard this great music on the sound system. I asked a person who it was, and he said, "Dwight

Yoakam." So I went to the record store and bought Guitar, Cadillacs, Etc., Etc. I flipped out when I listened to it, so I called the attorney and asked if he was still looking. He was.

Dwight was recording his next record at Capitol Records studios in Los Angeles, so I met him and we sort of hit it off. I told him, "I'm not a country manager. I've been to Nashville and I know Warner Bros. Nashville chief Jim Ed Norman because I worked with him on a project. But I don't know anything about country music, and I'm probably the wrong guy. I came here out of curiosity because I think your music is incredible and I wanted to meet you."

Dwight said, "You're exactly what I'm looking for. I don't want anybody who knows about Nashville. I don't want anybody who has anything to do with Nashville. The fact that you managed the Violent Femmes and the Bee Gees—that's exactly what I want."

So we're doing Dwight and things are going well. He's all over the radio and selling lots of records and tickets. I guess having someone with a different perspective appealed to the people at Warner Bros. because Warner Bros. Nashville head Jim Ed Norman called me and said he'd just signed a girl and wanted me to consider working with her. I said, "You've got to be kidding me. This is a fluke." I told him I lived in Los Angeles and couldn't take on another country client, much less a female because females weren't happening at all at that time. But I had to go to Nashville for a meeting about Dwight, so I said I'd be happy to meet her if she was performing.

So I went and met Faith Hill and saw her sing. And that's when I became her manager.

YOUR FIRST MANAGER MIGHT BE YOU

Typically, artists have to be well into their career to attract a top-flight manager. Many aspiring artists manage themselves, especially with the reach that the Internet provides these days. Garth Brooks, who majored in marketing in college and has a brilliant business mind, could easily manage himself if he were just starting out. If you have that kind of business sense, go for it at the beginning. But start doing research on the artists you like; learn about the people they've been with over the years.

If you don't start building your team with a manager, you should be able to find other people to assume some of the responsibilities a manager would normally have. Search out junior managers at large management firms. Try to introduce your music to them; invite them to your gigs. If you're a strong performer, sometimes a junior agent at a booking agency—if he really believes in you—might help with some management-related duties.

Obviously, everyone needs a good accountant. If you're touring, you've got to make sure you cover your taxes so that it doesn't financially endanger your future. An accountant can offer you early advice on your career's financial side. I've said it before, but it bears repeating: as soon as you start making money, get an accountant.

If your strength is songwriting, I'll bet you can find a publisher who will help. Ree Guyer Buchanan, who runs Reynsong publishing company in Nashville, is a good example of this type of publisher. She acts somewhat like a manager developing artists. She's a publisher, and she pays her writers an advance. She's also developing them as artists, helping them with showcases, looking for guitar pulls, introducing them to the right people, and generating that word-of-mouth buzz.

Any of those people should be able to, at the very least, keep you from making the worst kind of mistakes. When I see unknown acts putting ads on bus benches and renting billboard space, I absolutely laugh at the waste of money. I'd like to know who's managing them because only an inexperienced manager would suggest they do that.

If you find someone you trust who doesn't have much experience, you have two options. You can sign with that person and hope the two of you grow together. You could also try to find a more limited role on your team for that person. If he's not experienced, he might be your personal assistant once you get a record deal. If she has touring experience, she could be your road manager. Don't over-promise in your eagerness, saying, "You can manage me, no matter what." At the beginning of their careers, young artists are so hopeful they'll often promise anything. Then, when reality sets in, they feel they're being disloyal if they can't fulfill their promises. Avoid a lot of heartache—it's better to under-promise.

Are you dealing with a first-time manager? Offer to pay back at a certain rate of return any money he invests. Perhaps you could work out a handshake deal where you'll try but won't guarantee to involve him at the next level of your career. If he has no track record, don't tie yourself to him for very long. If it works out, you can enter into a more formal, long-term deal later. Whatever happens, you must act ethically—if he's investing time and money into your career, he deserves to be repaid. He's not doing this for fun. The first people who believe in you, before the rest of the world does, should be appreciated.

MANY ASPIRING ARTISTS MANAGE THEMSELVES, ESPECIALLY WITH THE REACH THAT THE INTERNET PROVIDES, THESE DAYS.

Matt Nathanson, a singer/songwriter who released four independent albums before signing with Universal Records, went to college with his manager, Jordan Kurland. "He wanted to manage bands, and I wanted to be taken seriously," Matt says. "It worked perfectly." Jordan still manages Matt and has expanded his client roster to include acts like Feist and Death Cab for Cutie.

"He got the Death Cab thing because he was friendly with the Death Cab guys," Matt says, "always being at their shows as a fan. When Death Cab was looking for management, it just happened.

"If I look back at it, there's a natural progression, the way it all works. You can't force it. When the time is right to need a manager, a manager is going to show up. The connections and the relationships you've had are going to yield one. Inevitably, it just happens the way it's going to happen."

When Colbie Caillat's MySpace popularity grew beyond her ability to handle it, she and her father—a respected engineer and producer who had worked on Fleetwood Mac's *Rumours* and *Tusk* albums—started meeting with managers.

"One guy said he thought I should play shows locally for about a year and get used to playing in front of people," Colbie says. "That was a good idea because performing was new to me at the time, but since my songs had been up on MySpace for so long, we didn't have time to do that. We had to get the music out while people were still interested. People had been listening to my songs for a year and a half, and I had no demos, nothing."

Colbie eventually settled on Chad Jensen from The Fitzgerald Hartley Co., a company that also represents LeAnn Rimes, Brad Paisley, Richard Thompson, the Robert Cray Band, and Vince Gill.

"At the beginning, Chad told me all these things he predicted for my future," Colbie says. "He'd see me at shows and tell me what I needed to work on. He'd say I needed to get a bigger band and have more rehearsals and play live more. I think it was his attitude, really. He doesn't let anyone take advantage of me. He puts me in front of everyone, and he's not a wimp. You want your manager to be in charge."

When the time finally comes to pick your manager, Colbie says you have to trust your instincts. "I know that's not much advice," she says, "but go with your gut. Depending on the career you want, you want your manager to have the same feelings. You don't want to have to tell him; you want to let him speak and see what he has to say, so you know that he's not full of it."

THE BIGGER THE ACT, THE BIGGER THE MANAGER

When you're a baby artist, busy managers usually won't have time for you. Sometimes, you'll have to rely on people who are at the same stage of their careers as you are in yours. When that happens, both of you need to be up front. You can't promise much because you don't know what you'll need in the future when things start to bust open. Under-promising and being up front and simple is the best route to take.

AS YOU'RE LOOKING FOR MANAGERS, LOOK AT THE CAREERS OF THE ARTISTS YOU ADMIRE.

When you have people who believe in you and you believe in them but neither one of you has a track record, tell them: "I want to find a role for you. I can't promise what it will be because this business is unpredictable. But if you have strengths that work in my future, you know I'm going to be there to fight for you. If you don't have those strengths, I'm going to have to protect my interests as I grow."

It's not uncommon for acts to change managers several times over the course of their careers. Say you break in Europe, but your manager doesn't have a worldwide office—you need a company that does, or at least one that can align with another firm that has that expertise. Perhaps you're starting to make money because your music is being licensed for television shows and commercials—your manager needs to have, or needs to develop, contacts in those worlds. You need a manager who has the expertise you need wherever your art takes you.

In the very beginning, if you're talented enough to attract a successful manager, you need to be realistic. You're in a situation of supply and demand. When you're earning a lot of money, you can demand more attention. But when you're not earning much money—in fact, early on, you'll probably *cost* your manager money—be humble. Find out who your point person is because that's the person who's going to be working with you most. That day-to-day person is key because that's the person who'll be proactive, hustling every day, working tirelessly. The big dog at the company may get involved every so often, to help with a key deal or award shows. In that sense, a big company is great because you and your point person can grow together.

As you're looking for managers, look at the careers of the artists you admire. See who manages them. Call those managers, or if you have an agent, your agent may be able to help you get a meeting. Take recommendations from people you respect. I would, however, be wary of managers recommended to you by your record label. Some great partnerships have come from that sort of thing—like Faith Hill and Gary Borman—but when a label suggests only one manager, it could lead to conflicts in the future. Listen to your label, but also search out additional recommendations from outside sources.

WHAT THE BIG GUYS LOOK FOR

If I take a meeting with a potential client, I've got some level of interest in that person's music. When I meet with her for the first time, I watch her body language, her level of confidence, how she works the room. Does her charisma fill up the room, or is she as shy as a wallflower? (We've all seen those people, and they're really hard to market.)

I like when artists ask me lots of questions because then I know they're dead serious about their careers. And I notice what kind of questions they ask. Some artists are more concerned with media: "If you're my manager, how many magazine covers can you get me on?" Other artists are serious about tours. Just the kinds of questions they ask tell me what their priorities are.

I want to see whether they can perform acoustically or *a cappella* right there in the room. If I'm going to get a record deal for someone, they're going to have to be able to do that. I'll ask them beforehand to bring a guitar to the meeting. (See how all that audition training we talked about earlier comes in handy?)

I also note how well they're able to describe their art and their priorities; I want to know how proactive they've been on their own. If they're already making their own videos and booking their own gigs, that's impressive. Some artists make their music and expect the world to do everything else for them. For the ones who are the most successful, though, it's their business, their life, their baby. As a manager, I helped make sure the plan got activated, but I looked for an artist with a strong vision. From my experience, the people who have a vision for their art and can communicate it are the ones who are the most successful.

The first time I saw Keith Urban was at a guitar pull at the Bluebird Café in Nashville. He was with three other songwriters, but he was the only one with an electric guitar and a mini amp. He sang "Tangled Up in Love," "Ghost in This Guitar," and "Walkin' the Country," and he was having fun. When he was playing and singing, I could tell that was where he was the happiest. It was where he belonged.

I immediately knew right then and there that I had to manage him. I called my partner, Miles Copeland, and said, "I've found an artist I'm 100 percent sure about." Miles flew in to Nashville, and Keith and the other two members of his band—bassist Jerry Flowers and drummer Peter Clarke—came in with their instruments and amps and did a mini-concert in my office. Miles knew that these guys were stars, that Keith was a star. We believed in them without a doubt and started investing time, energy, and money in them. At that point, Keith had tried to land a Nashville record deal for a few years but hadn't made much progress. He had an amazing publishing company, Ten Ten Music Group, and was doing the necessary homework for a new artist. Now he needed to find or write the songs that would attract the right label.

Keith was so likeable, but he was most confident when he was playing music. Without a guitar, he didn't really feel at home. Music really is how you communicate with Keith. You listen to his music, and you know where to start. The guy is a live performer.

I went on the road with Keith's band and watched them win people over from the stage. Keith loved the way Miles had built bands like the Police and R.E.M. over time. Those bands were also great live performers, and that's what they were about—winning one fan at a time (which is a slow yet sure way to build a strong and loyal fan base).

THE PEOPLE WHO HAVE A VISION FOR THEIR ART AND CAN COMMUNICATE IT ARE THE ONES WHO ARE THE MOST SUCCESSFUL.

When we had four demos we felt gave us a strong calling card, Miles and I met with Jim Ed Norman at Warner Bros. Records and Keith, Jerry, and Peter scored their first American record deal. After much trial and error, the music Keith wanted to release was not a style of music Jim Ed felt his label could get on country radio. Asking off a big label like Warner Bros. takes a lot of courage, but if you have a vision, you have to let it guide you. Keith's courage gave me the resolve to approach longtime fan Ansel Davis at Capitol Nashville about Capital signing the guys. I'll never forget our lunch, when I asked Ansel if he loved this band, he replied with a resounding *yes.* Then he said, "I'll tell you the same thing I told Keith. I don't know if we can make him a star or make him rich, but I'll get the world to hear his music, or I'll die trying. If Capital can have them, Scott Hendricks and I will make sure the record is out in six months." I knew then that Keith had found a safe home.

It's all about timing. Keith's current team, headed by Gary Borman, helped him soar to new heights. Watching what Gary, Keith, and their team have accomplished over the past seven years has been incredibly fulfilling for Miles and me. It's the dream we all had in the early years, but now it's Keith's hard-earned reality.

After spending thirty years in the business, Gary says he now looks for different things in potential clients than he once did. "I look for three factors," he says.

"First and foremost, does that person's music make me excited? Does it make me want to get involved? Does it push that little button in me that says, 'Oh my God, this is undeniable! I love this, I believe in this, and I think other people will love it, too'? Do I want to play it for my friends and help make it accessible? That happens so rarely that I don't have to worry about it too much.

"Second, I have to like the person behind the music. I've got to think she's a good person with whom I want to have that kind of intimate involvement. It's like a best friend. It's like a marriage. I've got to make sure I want that person in my life, and that person has to make sure they want me in their life. To me, that's always been a criterion.

"Then there's the business side. Do I believe this is a good business? Is this a good use of my time? Is it a good investment?

"If it passes those three tests, I'm in. With me, that's not so easy these days—not because I'm so desirable but because I've become so selective and because I can.

"As you go back further in my career, those requirements were less essential. In other words, in the very beginning, if they could hold a tune, I didn't care if they were a mass murderer and I didn't want them to know where I lived; I'd still manage them."

TIPS FOR MEETING WITH A MANAGER—OR ANYONE ELSE, FOR THAT MATTER

- ★ Positive body language exudes confidence. Positive gestures include maintaining eye contact (but not staring), keeping arms and legs open rather than crossed, nodding occasionally when another person is talking, leaning slightly towards another person. Such actions—when done naturally, of course, not forced or awkwardly—can help a person appear relaxed, personable, and friendly.
- ★ Negative body language includes looking down at the floor, not looking someone in the eye, slumping shoulders, biting nails. One or two of those traits is one thing,

but too many nervous habits suggest a person might be pursuing the wrong dream. If he gets nervous just meeting a manager or an A&R person, imagine what he'll be like showcasing for a record label's entire staff or performing on TV in front of a live national audience.

★ A sense of humor is always helpful, as is the ability to verbalize. A great conversationalist is ahead of the pack, and that can make a lot of difference.
★ Practice the meeting beforehand. Write down your questions and bring that paper to the meeting. It will be helpful for you, and it will inform the manager of your priorities.
★ Be confident and learn to express your vision for yourself, your music, and your career. If a manager senses too much ambivalence, she'll likely run for the hills.
★ If you play, bring a guitar and decide beforehand on two songs you will play. If you don't play but you have a demo, bring that instead. Remember, less is more: play one or two strong songs instead of several average ones. If you have a band, bring them to the meeting—but be sure to let the manager know in advance.
★ If you have success stories—MySpace, YouTube, regional ticket sales, etc.—bring examples of the success on which you hope to build. It's good information and will help you secure a successful manager.

CHECKS AND BALANCES: GOOD FOR GOVERNMENT, GOOD FOR MANAGEMENT

As in any industry, there are managers—they're few, thankfully—who are unethical. Sometimes it's subtle; other times it's obvious and financially devastating. Some people will skim from the top or not let you know about *x*, *y*, or *z*. To protect yourself, you really need to create a team that incorporates checks and balances. Your lawyer should not also be your manager. Your manager should not also be your accountant.

For example, you need two people making sure your taxes are paid correctly. This is a very complex business: you have to pay taxes across the nation, and every state has a different tax setup. When you tour, you have to consider the taxes in each state individually.

If you're dealing with a management company, insist on a key-man clause in your contract. A key-man clause names a particular person or persons whose participation in your career is paramount. It makes sure the people you trust the most are in your contract as long as they're part of your career. That's one way to protect yourself if those people either leave the company or lose their focus and start chasing the act that's making the most money rather than paying attention to you. The key-man clause gives you a little protection if there's someone at the company in whom you really believe.

AT ANY GIVEN TIME, YOU WILL HAVE ONLY ONE MANAGER, BUT YOUR MANAGER MAY HAVE SEVERAL CLIENTS.

As you're negotiating your contract with a manager, be sure you understand the circumstances under which either of you can end the relationship if things don't work out between you. Be sure you understand the scope of the manager's authority to do business on your behalf—in some situations, a manager may ask for power of attorney to sign contracts. Make sure the limits of those powers are written into the contract. Decide—and put into the contract—how your manager will be paid on work he has generated for you after the management agreement has been terminated. It's only fair for the manager to be paid for the work he's done, but the last thing you want to have happen is to still be paying him 15 percent of everything you make when you're paying a new manager that as well.

Finally, remember this: At any given time, you will have only one manager, but your manager may have several clients. You are the engine of this train, and you will see the same amount of success as the amount of coal you put into the engine.

Miles Copeland and Anastasia Brown in the studio

MILES COPELAND: BE EASY TO SAY YES TO

If I had to reduce everything to the simplest kind of advice I could offer anybody, it'd be this: Make the offer easy to say yes to.

Whatever you're doing in life, whether you're building a house, buying a car, or asking for a record deal—it all comes down to whether you can afford to do something and how long you can sustain being able to do it.

The fundamental reason most people don't get signed is that either (a) they don't have the talent to get anybody excited or (b) it just isn't cost effective to get into business with them. Put those two together, a guy walks in with no talent and he's expensive—he ain't got a hope.

You've got to make it easy for your partners to want to do business with you. If an artist walks into a record company and tells them he's great and the record company agrees he's great but then he tells them that he's got a ten-piece band who all need a $2,000-a-week salary or they won't work, they're all married so they tour only three weeks a year, and his record will cost a million dollars to make . . . Pretty soon, the record company looks at a four-million-dollar investment and decides they can't take the shot. But if the guy walks in and says, "I can make this record for 52 cents and I don't need an advance. I'll deliver the record to you, and all you have to do is market it," that's an easy yes.

In other words, the artist who makes it easy to say "yes" is the artist who's going to have the easiest time. So many artists don't understand that. Too many acts walk in and think they sign a record deal and they've made it. They think it's the record company's job to make them happy, and they think they just have to spend money.

It's remarkable in this day and age with the technology that exists that you can make very high-quality stuff for peanuts. A creative person with a $1,200 camera and a couple of $10 tapes can make a video that, as long as the idea is good and the music is good and he uses his creativity, can outdo thousands of people who think they have to spend thousands and thousands of dollars. The artist who makes it easy to get in the game is the one who has a shot.

That reality is going to be truer and truer as record companies face the fact that they can't make the same kind of money they once did. People are buying singles on iTunes instead of albums. Record stores are decreasing. The market is decreasing by 6 percent a year. The money is just not there anymore. The guy who knows how to spend a dollar wisely is going to succeed.

Of course, you have to have talent, as well. But talent without the possibility of affordability is a waste. The most brilliant artist who is too costly to bring to the market isn't going to succeed. Look at the Concorde, the most brilliant airplane ever created—it just wasn't cost effective, so it eventually died.

If you sign an act and six months later you're down half a million dollars and then you're down a million, you start looking for ways to pull the plug. If you think of the number of artists who made only one album and then had the plug pulled, that's usually the reason. It just didn't make sense for the record company to proceed.

I had a group called Animal Logic—Stanley Clarke on bass, my brother Stewart on drums, and a singer named Deborah Holland. We had a lot of hopes for the band. They signed to a record label for quite a big advance. We put the first single out and got a little buzz, but nothing really happened on the second single. We were getting to the point of going with the third single, and the label said, 'We've had two failures. The third one, we think that's a hit song, but suppose that one fails, then we have to go with the next record.' The deal on the next record was like a million dollars, so if the label failed with the third single, it'd cost them too much. So they didn't put out the third single. Now, if the advance on the next album had been zero, the label would've gone with the third single. That might have been the single that broke the act; then we would've had a major hit on our hands. But because the label's accountant looked at it and decided they could be digging a deeper hole with no way out but to pay a million dollars, bailing was the safest option. My cleverness at getting a big advance killed the group. The *yes* to the situation was just too big a leap for anyone to take, so the answer was *no*.

CHAPTER 9

BOOKING AGENTS

WHAT IS A BOOKING AGENT, AND WHY DO I NEED ONE?

Booking agents, sometimes also called talent agents, secure performances for acts. Managers, as we noted in the previous chapter, can temporarily help with this before the whole team is in place, if a team is formed, but a booking agent makes it his or her specialty.

Agents are an important part of the puzzle—a good one helps you grow your fan base, takes a long-term approach to career development, and impacts your bottom line more than anyone else on your team. Only the best-selling artists ever see significant royalties from major record labels. Only some acts write their own material and receive publishing income. But almost every act will tour—and that's where booking agents come in.

Agents can help you secure and negotiate gigs—they have relationships with promoters and club owners; they know the kinds of places you should and should not play. There are regional agencies and international agencies; depending on the stage of your career, you'll need one or the other—or both. Regional agencies can be great for helping you establish a local following and reputation. As you get more popular, big booking agencies can bring you more opportunities, like sponsorships or endorsements. Agents will look for commercial, television, and film opportunities—they often have their hands in many areas. They can also pair you with other artists for tours. Agencies tend to stay within their own rosters, so no matter how small you are, if your agency believes in you enough to sign you, they'll try to hook you up with other artists they represent once you have a following or a hit single.

A GOOD AGENT HELPS YOU GROW YOUR FAN BASE, TAKES A LONG-TERM APPROACH TO CAREER DEVELOPMENT, AND IMPACTS YOUR BOTTOM LINE.

For example, if you have a good following in ten states that happen to coincide with a region where a bigger artist draws poorly, you may get to open for that portion of a big tour. That gives you one more story to share: "I opened for Artist X." You don't have to mention that you opened for that artist in ten cities, just that you opened for her—that's your story.

"I love putting artists together with someone else," says Rod Essig. "It's like putting a golfer together with a better golfer. I love making them compete because they come out stronger than ever."

Agents negotiate your fees and your contracts. They'll help you develop your touring strategy. They'll also help you tour more efficiently by scheduling your dates so that your route makes as much sense as possible. Ideally, you'd rather not have to drive from Ohio to Illinois then back to Indiana and over to Missouri—good booking agents will do their best to route you in a way that makes sense.

They'll also get as many hard costs covered for you as possible. For instance, if you live in Boston and your agent books a Chicago date, he might negotiate a dinner per diem and travel costs to get you there. Agents also cover for you in the event of a weather problem or some kind of crisis that keeps you from getting to your gig. They make sure those sorts of things are covered in your contract rider, the part of your contract that deals with your requirements for the show, from production needs to band meals.

CONTRACT RIDERS—THE REASONING BEHIND THE RIDICULOUSNESS

A contract rider is an addendum that specifies your technical needs for a show. The rider names everything you need, from sound and lighting requirements to dressing rooms and meals to making sure you have water onstage. The riders are always negotiated, and some venues will give you more than others. Most clubs have monitors and microphones. Some will have the lights you'd like. Other clubs don't have a green room or a changing room, and you'll find yourself in your van or the bathroom changing your clothes and brushing your hair.

Some riders have requirements that have nothing to do with the production itself. In 2006, Barbra Streisand's tour rider required a police K9 inspection prior to sound check and metal detectors at every venue entrance. A 2003 rider for the rock band Coldplay, for example, insisted on eight stamped, local postcards.

The most famous contract rider requirement is probably Van Halen's "no brown M&Ms" rule—it sounds like a legend, but it's actually true. What's exaggerated is the level of destruction the band caused when that rule was broken. The rule wasn't an example of rock-star outlandishness—it served a real purpose. It was sort of the contract's canary in the coal mine: if the brown M&Ms had been removed from the bowl, the band's crew could be reasonably sure that promoters had attended to larger, more essential matters as well. In David Lee Roth's autobiography, the singer recounts a university show where lackadaisical promoters booked the show without noting the production's weight requirements—the band's staging sank into the floor of the gymnasium where the show was held, causing $80,000 in damage. Sure enough, Roth says, the backstage candy bowl that night had brown M&Ms in it.

(cont.)

The Smoking Gun Web site (www.thesmokinggun.com) has an impressive collection of contract riders. If you go there, don't just read the funny parts—the complete riders can be an education in themselves.

At the beginning of your career, you're going to have to eat humble pie when it comes to your requirements. You won't be able to negotiate much more than the basics into your rider. As your career grows, so will that rider. But don't make somebody remove all the brown M&Ms just because you can.

Agents negotiate with a goal of keeping your profit margins as large as possible. Like managers, agents work off a percentage commission—usually 10 to 15 percent of your performance income—so it's in their best interest to get you as much income as possible. The more you make, the more they make.

You need to nurture your relationship with your agent. Sometimes agents get so busy that all they can do is answer phones—there may be times when you feel your agent doesn't love you. Remember, even though you have only one agent, an agent may have twenty other clients. Artists often develop a what-have-you-done-for-me-lately attitude. But if an agent feels like the burden of an artist's career rests solely on the agent's shoulders, that agent's not feeling the give-and-take that any business relationship should have. If you're not doing enough for your own career, your agent may start to lose interest in you.

BE YOUR OWN BEST AGENT

You don't want a booking agent too soon. Getting a career started is hard work, and you don't know how long it will take. If you sign with an agent before you're in a position to generate bookings and demand income, one of you will get burned out. Someone will get blamed for it when, really, there is no blame.

"For some reason," says Rod Essig, "a lot of acts want to sign with somebody right away. In country music, as a rule, it's a singer/songwriter, and they've been working acoustically by themselves. They have to hire musicians to travel and go on the road.

"If you sign an artist, there's that whole process of putting together the songs and producing the songs. Somewhere a year and a half into the process, you have to tell the artist there's no reason to play Minneapolis when he has nothing to sell. By the time he gets a year and a half or two years into the relationship, he's all upset because he's not on the road working. He's bored. He's at home. He's not making any money. He feels like he's going to fail.

"So an agent is better off becoming friends with the artist and, once he's six months away from releasing a record, then signing him. Then the agent has a shot at all the excitement of getting the act on the road."

If you're an artist with a regional following and you make your money from performing live, you'll likely need an agent before an act that's more of a singer/songwriter. If you're that kind of regional touring artist, you might be best off signing with an agency that specializes in that area. (As I've said before, don't over-promise or sign long-term contracts at that early stage.) Once you've taken your career as far as you can in that region, your local booking agent might grow with you, or you might move to a larger agency. In some situations, the local agent can use his or her contacts with a popular regional artist to leverage a job with a larger agency that can benefit both the agent and the act.

Until you get to that point, pound the pavement. Find a club with a history of booking the kind of music you play, then call and say, "I'm kind of like an R.E.M. or a Pat Green" or some other act that will give the owner a reference point for your sound. You can make the call yourself, or one of your band members or close friends with a knack for sales can. But start sending the club owners and managers your music, reviews, press clippings, or merchandise numbers to prove that you have a following and that you can fill their clubs.

Don't go for a big venue at first. You might fill only 25 percent of the club, and that's a failure. It's harder to fill a venue than you might think, especially at the beginning of your career, and even if your friends tell you they're coming, they're probably not. It's always better to play a full, small venue than a half-empty bigger one, and having people lined up outside the door trying to get in to see you is one of the best advertisements you could possibly get. If you fill that small club, then that's a success under your belt. Even later in your career, venue size is very important because selling it out creates a story and promoters are more likely to book you when they realize you're a safe bet.

START WITH SMALL PROMISES

If you're working around your hometown and have a friend who has successfully booked you locally, you may have found one of the champions we discussed earlier. If both of you can rise through the ranks, that's great, but be careful not to lock yourself into promises you can't keep later.

ALWAYS GIVE PEOPLE INCENTIVES. IT HELPS YOU, AND IT MAKES THEM WORK HARDER.

If you want to formalize your working arrangement, you might consider doing something on a trial basis—say, six months. Don't agree to several years; don't give up a piece of your publishing; don't give this person a piece of your future. Don't promise a booking agent that he can book you now and manage you later. That's the sort of thing that scares off labels and might prevent you from finding a manager who can successfully handle your business at the next level.

Make small promises. And make sure the person who books you, no matter how small the gig, gets paid for the work he does. You don't want any guilty feelings, and you don't want to harm your reputation. You also want to be able to make a clean separation if and when the time comes.

At the beginning of your career, you may not get more than two or three hundred bucks for a gig. If someone is pounding the pavement for you and making hours of phone calls to arrange the gigs, a fifty-dollar commission isn't much money. If the commission on the gig is small but the agent has put in real effort, you could set up a deal in which she sells your merchandise and gets a cut of those sales, as well. Always give people incentives. It helps you, and it makes them work harder.

FIND AN AGENT

When the time comes to find an agent, look for someone who has passion for the music and for who you are as an artist. You want someone who believes in you, not any hype that might be building around you. Once again, take your time and don't rush into anything. An agent may tell you what you want to hear, but that's what agents do. They're salespeople, and they're always moving, making things happen, talking up this artist to that person and that artist to the other person. They're moving chess pieces.

Timing is everything, and you have to know your strengths and weaknesses. If you're a songwriter or a singer who's not touring, don't get an agent unless his strength is film and television and those are your areas of focus. The right agent can make a big difference—if your goals and your focus are in sync.

THE RIGHT AGENT CAN MAKE A BIG DIFFERENCE—IF YOUR GOALS AND YOUR FOCUS ARE IN SYNC.

"There are regional agencies that are good at clubs," Rod says, "and some that are good at colleges and some that are good at festivals. CAA pretty much won't take an act until it has a record deal or a reason for us to book it. We lose money on any band we book under $3,500. It just takes too much in phones, salaries, and paper. We do that for a lot of bands in the hope that they'll become stars, but if someone has a regional record out that's not making much noise nationally, we shy away from that. We'll let someone else do the grunt work. Hopefully, they'll grow and come to us down the line."

If you decide to start with a small agent, look at his client list. If you haven't heard of any of them, that's a red flag: he's probably not booking the kind of act you want to be. Or it could mean that you need to do some homework and find out about those acts before you sign the deal. Ultimately, though, the booking agent you want is someone who can make people excited about you.

"As far as I'm concerned, a good agent is a guy who's going to cut his wrist and bleed and talk about you every day," Rod says. "We all have to agree on a new signing at our agency, but everyone gets one passion act. That act is someone they're friends with or an artist who they watched grow. Then you've still got to sell everyone in order to book that act—why should this act be on a tour as opposed to someone else? You still have to make that sale within the house."

MOVING ON UP—TO THE BIG AGENCIES

Once you've paid some dues and gotten your own gigs, you eventually get to the point where you can't do both your music and your bookings, especially when you have followings in more than one city. At that point, either look in your own backyard or start looking in New York, Los Angeles, Nashville, Austin, Atlanta, London—every music town has regional or international agencies. Track those people down. Again, observe the rule of three: Make sure you find at least three people who vouch for the agency or agent. Check out the company's reputation. If you wind up with someone who's not on the up and up, that association will hurt you.

Your next step might be a junior agent at a big agency like William Morris, Monterey Peninsula, CAA, or for country music, Buddy Lee Attractions. Those agencies have partners who take care of the huge artists, so they'll likely not spend much time with you. But those junior agents are looking to help break the next big thing. They have as much to prove as you do. Sometimes it's better to work with a junior agent at a big agency so you can grow together. And you'll have other artists to tour with. That's an advantage of a big agency versus a local agent.

If you go with a big agency, you'll have to sign a contract. Put a key-man clause in there—name two people, like the junior agent who found you and his boss. That way, if one of those people leaves the company and no one's interested in you, the agency will find someone else to work with you or you'll be able to leave and go elsewhere.

CULTIVATE A SUCCESSFUL RELATIONSHIP

Be proactive in your relationship with your agent. Read the trades and find out what opportunities are available. If you read about a tour or a music-driven film going into production that's perfect for you but you don't know how to go about getting it, ask your agent whom you should call. You might say, "Can you give me a contact working on this TV show so I can submit my music?" If the agent gives you the name and address of the show's music supervisor, send a handwritten note saying how much you love their TV show, that you think your song is perfect for it, and give the reasons.

Meanwhile, the agency can pursue the network, and you guys tag-team them. You do that as a tag team for two reasons: (1) it takes a team, and (2) you won't leave the agency with the impression that you expect them to do all your work. Keep in mind that the bigger your star shines, the less time you'll have to do this sort of thing, but this kind of proactive work is required to get to that point.

Miles Copeland and I had a theory: we wanted to keep so much activity going on that the label, the agency, and everyone else felt like they had to work harder just to keep up with us. So when we met, we were able to share our accomplishments equally. You get a team mentality going, and then no one is pointing fingers or asking what you've done for them lately. It takes all those people working that hard to make a big career happen. So be proactive and nurture those relationships.

> BE PROACTIVE IN YOUR RELATIONSHIP WITH YOUR AGENT.

Showing your agent that you're proactive and showing your appreciation are both important. If you feel like you need a little more love from your agent, remember what your grandmother probably told you: "You can catch more flies with honey than with vinegar." That's the case with every career, every industry, and every way of life. I see so many people get frustrated when they don't have enough activity in their careers. Taking out your frustration on the people who are going to bat for you (and, incidentally, not making much money from you yet) is the last thing you want to do. Be cautious with your words, and if you have frustrations, go to your mom or your buddy. Don't take it out on your agent.

Finally, in the last few years, we in the industry have noticed a phenomenon some call "*Idol*'s Perfect Storm"—name recognition without performance payout. The show's finalists—there are more than sixty of them now—may have millions of fans, but most don't have the hits to sustain a headlining show. If you're an act whose celebrity outstrips your discography, you have two options: you can either take as much cash as possible without concern about whether the promoter makes a profit or takes a bath, or you can scale back your arena dreams, give yourself some time to have a few hits, and ensure that everyone involved with you makes a profit. The artist might not pocket as much money in the second scenario, but she ensures that she hasn't burned any bridges she might need in the future. Endorsements, merchandise, film, and television are all areas that can produce serious cash flow quickly. Touring is one place where slow and steady growth and consistent profits for *all* wins the race!

CHAPTER 10

PRODUCERS

WHAT DO PRODUCERS DO?

Producers cast the sound and the style of a recording. They're responsible for hiring the musicians, choosing the studio, and selecting the microphones and the engineer. Whether or not you sing bluegrass with a Sheryl Crow vibe, your producer assembles the people who will help you create the sound you hear in your head.

Producers play an important role in the industry—so important that a producer is one of the few people other than artists and songwriters who win major industry awards, like Grammys. Managers don't receive awards for Best Album, but producers do. It's a very important position, so artists need to select carefully. If you don't have the right producer, you may not experience success until you find one.

Certain producers have created whole sounds in certain eras of popular music. Phil Spector's "Wall of Sound" hits of the early 1960s were so closely identified with him that he's better known than acts like the Crystals and the Ronettes that sang on Spector-produced records such as "Then He Kissed Me" and "Be My Baby." Timbaland has had much the same impact on pop radio of the past decade with his hip-hop-influenced productions of records by Ginuwine, Missy Elliott, Jay-Z, Justin Timberlake, 50 Cent, and others.

Look at the person closest to me, Tony Brown. He has been called the "founding father of the alternative country movement" by producing Rodney Crowell, Steve Earle, Nanci Griffith, Lyle Lovett, Kelly Willis, and Allison Moorer during the 1980s and 1990s. In fact, when Steve talks about those days, he refers to them as "the great credibility scare of the mid-1980s." Hundreds, maybe thousands, of artists, musicians, and producers came to Nashville because of those records. So a producer can even impact the entire industry.

IF YOU DON'T HAVE THE RIGHT PRODUCER, YOU MAY NOT EXPERIENCE SUCCESS UNTIL YOU FIND ONE.

Producers like T-Bone Burnett create new sounds every day. Look at the *O Brother, Where Art Thou?* soundtrack and then Robert Plant and Alison Krauss's recent *Raising Sand* album, both produced by T-Bone. They're somewhat similar, but also very different. T-Bone is a chameleon whose productions take on whatever sound the recording demands. Every record he makes changes the environment of the music industry.

A great producer can completely define—or redefine—an artist's sound. Johnny Cash had been dropped from the Nashville labels, his recording career all but over, when Rick Rubin got hold of him and stripped his music to something basic and revolutionary. Rick helped recreate Johnny's persona with the series of *American Recordings* albums they made together. With the *Nick of Time* album, Don Was helped transform Bonnie Raitt from a cult figure into a household name. That's how important that producer/artist combination is, and sometimes it's a moment in time that you can't recreate.

WHAT CAN A PRODUCER DO FOR YOU?

A producer can help get the best vocals out of you, which, for a singer, is the most important thing. Producers know about hundreds of different types of microphones, and they will experiment with them until they figure out how to capture the best vocal for each singer. They'll experiment with different keys, arrangements, and music so that they can make that vocal shine and present its unique qualities to the world.

Producers can also help with song selection. If you don't write, an experienced producer often has strong enough relationships to find you top-drawer songs during your career's embryonic phase. Brand-new producers may not have that kind of access, but their highly trained ears can offer you perspective on material that, as a young artist, you may not have developed yet. There's a huge difference between an average song and a great song. I always say, "You're three minutes away from success"—finding a great song can change your career status dramatically.

Producers are also important because artists need an objective ear around them while they're creating their art; otherwise, they can get absolutely lost in the woods and not see the forest for the trees. Prolific songwriters need someone to help them sort through the songs and separate the great ones from the bad and the merely good. I love country singer/songwriter Taylor Swift's story—she's still a teenager and she's writing hundreds of songs. One key job for her producer is helping Taylor pick the best songs for her at this stage of her career. But at any stage of their career, artists need that confident, experienced, objective ear to help them determine the best direction for their music.

The right combination of producer and artist can make all the difference in the world. If you're with a producer and you're not able to get that sound you hear in your head, that doesn't mean your producer is bad. Perhaps it's just not the right match. But when the right combination happens, it's magic. Like Shania Twain and Mutt Lange—they created that pop-country sound in the biggest way the music industry had ever seen with songs like "Any Man of Mine" and "You're Still the One."

Don Was and Ziggy Marley

DON WAS: EVERYTHING STARTS WITH THE SONG

The way to make the best recording is to write a decent song. A great song that's recorded into the microphone that's built into a laptop is a great song. And a bad song recorded at the best studio with $15,000 worth of session guys is still a bad song. Don't worry so much about the microphone—whether you're a kid in Iowa with Apple's GarageBand software or a producer in Hollywood with a $200,000 budget. Make sure you've got something worth saying and that it's being expressed in an eloquent fashion. I've heard great things recorded in GarageBand through the microphone in the laptop. GarageBand is awesome, but whether you plug in a Shure SM58 doesn't really matter. Don't get distracted by that stuff.

A dear friend of mine, a classical piano player in Detroit, had tremendous promise, but he kept taking his piano apart because the action wasn't quite right for him. He'd give a recital, and his M.O. was he'd split halfway through because the piano wasn't good enough. He's done all right for himself, running a bakery in Detroit, but he never had a career as a classical piano player because he got so hung up on the mechanics of the piano that he forgot to play the song.

Don't distract yourself from the issue at hand, which is being a communicative artist.

PRODUCTION COSTS

The cost of a producer varies dramatically, depending on the producer's experience, his track record, the genre of music, and the city where he is located. The average in Nashville right now is around $4,000 per side, with additional royalties—or "points" ranging from 2 to 5 percent—on all records sold. Some top Nashville producers charge as much as $5,000 per side. In the pop world, the number can rise as high as $25,000 per side. The producer's fee is in addition to the cost of studio time, equipment, and musicians.

If you're releasing your music independently and using a producer with no more experience than you have, you may have some more flexibility with the costs. You might be able to make arrangements to split the studio expenses and any hard costs involved—like paying the musicians. Then, after those costs are covered, you might split the income from CD sales with the band and the producer. It's all about negotiation, and it's a completely different situation at the beginning. As I've said before, though, be careful about locking yourself into long-term obligations to finance your early recordings. Don't promise points on future recordings; don't commit to recording the next album with the producer. And don't give away your publishing to pay for recording costs.

THE ARTISTS PRODUCERS WANT TO WORK WITH

When Nashville producer David Malloy, who has worked with Dolly Parton, Reba McEntire, Kenny Rogers, and *Dancing with the Stars*' Julianne Hough, considers whether or not to produce new acts, he says he looks as much for the artists' drive as he does their talent.

"Drive and work ethic are everything," David says. "I can't tell you how many times I've seen talented artists who are lazy. Lazy artists want to know where the bar is set. Once they establish that, they don't really want to get high over the bar; they just want to get over the bar. Once they get there, they'll go fishing or whatever.

"There is such an incredible amount of talent and so much competition that we always go back to the drive and the work ethic. I learned years ago that you might run across this talent and think it could be huge. When you get into it, though, you start to see the flaws. First, you think you can cover them up; you can put a Band-Aid on the flaw. But it doesn't work. Sooner or later, they have to want it in their hearts and their souls."

David much prefers to see artists whose creativity pushes them 24/7—the ones who never go anywhere without their guitars, the ones who constantly sing and rehearse.

"The very first thing I want to hear," he says, "is the voice coming out of a pair of speakers.

In the end, there has to be a charisma about the voice, something alluring, something that you have to hear again. I've heard a lot of technically great and emotionally great singers, but something in the tonal quality of their voice was not that memorable. Like in acting, where it's not always the pretty boy you remember, it's the guy with a face that's a little different. That's the first thing I try to hear.

"If I hear that, I want to meet them and rate their personality. From the second they walk in the door, I look to see how they have their shoulders, their posture, their face, their eyes, their smile—everything. Then I want to see if I feel the connection. Do I feel their confidence, the confidence of knowing they're secure and in a good spot?"

From there, David asks the artists questions about their musical development. He'll ask about their live performance history—if they sang in church, if they've played clubs. David says he sees little actual live stage experience, especially with the younger artists; since they often can't play clubs until they turn twenty-one, that leaves them few options outside of school.

David also inquires about the artists' musical interests. "I have a little thing called 'peeling the artichoke,'" he says. "All these artists grew up listening to the radio or watching TV. Some song or some artist really pushes a button and releases all the emotions they want to express. In that process, they picked up some of that artist's style or some of the delivery of the singer who had that hit. Over time, those records are like the leaves on the artichoke.

"When they come to see me, those singers have three or four artists in them. If they sing a ballad, they do it one way; if they sing an up-tempo, they do it another. They've got these different characters. The thing about country music, for the great superstars, there's only one character, period. That's the person they stand for, everything about them. I want one character who sings all the songs. The songs can be different because the common thread is the vocalist. The vocalist needs to come from the same place each time."

That doesn't mean the singers David wants should be set in their ways, nor should they be spineless, without any opinions of their own. "I want one who's got a lot of opinion but at the same time will listen and evaluate," he says. "I don't want artists who are totally close-minded, those who think they've got all the answers. They're not mature enough yet."

My husband, Tony, once told David something he's used as a standard ever since. He told David that whenever he's thinking about signing an artist, he asks himself whether he would invite the artist to his house if he were throwing a party. "He slipped me a golden nugget," David says. "It was true, and I've never forgotten it. It's one of the first things I think about."

DAVID MALLOY: FUNDAMENTAL ADVICE FROM A TOP PRODUCER

The rarest ingredient seems to be common sense. Use your freaking common sense. Use the do-unto-others thing. If you want people to love you and embrace you and adore you, then love them, embrace them, and be respectful. Don't look down on other people. Don't be condescending. If you come from those emotions, it will not click.

- ★ If you can't say something nice, don't say anything at all. You put that bad energy out, it's going to come back tenfold. All entertainment towns are small. You never know who you're talking to or who knows what.
- ★ This is an incredibly competitive business. If you ask a professional athlete if he feels bad about beating his best friend, he won't flinch when he says no. You don't backstab someone, but you do everything you can to be better than him. If you can't do that, don't even try this.
- ★ Sing with the microphone and wearing the headphones as much as you can. You can sing in your bedroom or at the top of your lungs in your car, but until you put the headphones on, you won't hear what's coming out of your mouth blasted back into your ears at the exact same time.

FINDING A PRODUCER

These days, a lot of young artists produce themselves. Computer software like GarageBand makes basic recording much easier and much cheaper than it's ever been. You can make simple recordings to get started. You can experiment on your own or with your band. Nobody's on the clock; no one's under pressure to produce hits. You can work and learn and try different things until you come up with something you love. At the very beginning, you might have to do everything on your own anyway because financially you have no other choice. And if you generate some interest, several thousand MySpace hits or YouTube views, then you're onto something.

IF YOU MEET A PRODUCER AND YOU'RE NOT FAMILIAR WITH HIS WORK, DO YOUR HOMEWORK AND BUY EVERY RECORD HE'S EVER PRODUCED.

But if there's no interest, no hits, no excitement anywhere, obviously what you've been doing by yourself isn't working. That's when you need to search out someone with more experience who believes in you or find an aspiring young producer and see whether she brings any great ideas for your music to the table.

Sometimes, you'll have a manager before you get to this stage of your career. Your manager will help you strike a deal and may even front the money for the sessions so you don't lock yourself into an extended contract with the producer. If you find your producer before you find your manager, and the producer has experience, then you'll have to sign a contract. If they don't have experience, though, don't sign—you're trying to make something of yourself on your own, and you don't want to tie yourself to one person this early in your career.

When you first start talking to producers, find out about their credentials. Know what recordings they've produced in the past. If you meet a producer and you're not familiar with his work, do your homework and buy every record he's ever produced. If I were a top producer like Don Was or James Stroud, I wouldn't be interested in an artist who had to ask me what I'd done.

If you're talking to a new and upcoming producer, ask what he's done and then do some research on your own. You can find most producers' credits with a few Internet searches or a visit to the All Music Guide Web site (*www.allmusic.com*). Listen to the music in which the producer has played a part. If he's co-produced or engineered sessions, ask what he did for those sessions, who got the sounds, who chose the musicians. Ask questions. You'll be able to tell if his answers are authentic. Then, if you can, track down some of the musicians on the sessions and ask about the session. How was the vibe? How well did the producer get along with people?

Session musicians are usually pretty easy to locate. Since they make their living playing music, they have to make themselves accessible. Go to your local musicians' union and get a copy of their directory. If you love the sound of a steel guitar on a certain record, you can track that person down and say, "I love what you did here and here, and, by the way, how was that person to work with?"

Also, when you're talking with producers, talk about the music you love, not just the music you plan to make. When you discuss music, see whether the producer listens to you—do you hear and think about music in similar ways? If she has a different perspective from you, do you understand it or agree with it?

"Be open and hear what people have to say," says Phil Ramone, a giant in the music production field who has produced albums for Billy Joel, Barbra Streisand, Rod Stewart, Paul Simon, and many, many others. "Sometimes it's best to come in and say, 'I sound like I do, but I love this record and I love this mix.' Sometimes, three or four songs will give a clue as to what you really love and give the engineer and producer the combination of ideas. That's sort of just a pinpoint of how you should start."

TO SIGN OR NOT TO SIGN—THE PRODUCTION DEAL

Sometimes, artists will sign to record labels, and the label executives will help them choose their producer. Other times, though, artists will affiliate with producers before getting their recording contract—often with the hope that the producer can help them secure the label deal.

I always advise people not to sign long-term production deals because the label will have so much say in who produces you. If you find a producer with experience, I would recommend a four- or five-side production deal. If you promise the producer he can produce your entire record when you get your deal and the label decides to go a different route, they must still pay the producer for the entire album. That's not in your best interest because it makes what you're doing even more expensive than it already is. Instead, promise the producer that you and he will finish the sides you've started once you've signed your record deal and promise the producer a portion of the album. If the label needs to find another producer, they still can. You can still use the sides recorded with the original producer as album cuts or possibly even singles. You haven't impaired your career, and you haven't been disloyal to the first person who believed in you. That's an appropriate way to handle business that's fair to everyone involved.

I ALWAYS ADVISE PEOPLE NOT TO SIGN LONG-TERM PRODUCTION DEALS BECAUSE THE LABEL WILL HAVE SO MUCH SAY IN WHO PRODUCES YOU.

As a songwriter and a producer, Gary Burr has seen both sides of the production deal. Gary's hits include Juice Newton's "Love's Been a Little Bit Hard on Me," Wynonna Judd's "To Be Loved by You," and Garth Brooks's "One Night a Day." He also wrote "Before Your Love" for Kelly Clarkson and Clay Aiken's "This Is the Night." And he's worked as a producer for Olivia Newton-John and other artists.

Gary's a well-connected figure in Nashville, the kind of name that gives a person some credibility just by association. He's signed aspiring artists to production deals. When he does so, he says, he has to fight against his nature as a songwriter. "As a writer who's had to sign a lot of deals, I tend to go overboard in the writer's favor because I never want to be one of those guys I used to have to sit across the desk from and go, 'I don't understand here—why do you need another kidney?'

"But I've had to realize that I have to protect myself, too. In the past, I've had handshake deals with people who have gone on to very lucrative careers. Through bad business decisions on my part or too lenient business decisions or too much value on friendship, I didn't retain a piece of those careers, which would've been nice. In the cocktail hours of my life, I could've been sipping margaritas in Mexico."

When Gary signs artists to production deals, he says, he wants to work with them long enough to see what develops. "It's not like it used to be, where you could just gather some songs and go in the studio and cut something," he says. "You want to take a year to a year and a half to write with them because everybody wants to write these days. You want to write with them to give them a chance to figure out who they want to be because their style isn't even formed yet; they're still larvae."

In exchange for Gary's work—his songwriting and production expertise, and the time and money he spends on the act—he expects the act to push for his continued involvement once a record deal gets signed.

"The best I can hope for is they'll do their best to keep me in the project," he says. "Because I know that if push comes to shove and I'm writing with somebody but the record wants this big-shot guy to produce, I'm biting my own nose if I say, 'Forget that deal.' At least I've got songs on the album.

"If the artist sits you down and says, 'They're offering me a deal; they want Dann Huff to produce, but you'll still have eight songs on the record,' what are you going to do? You're going to say thanks.

"Basically, you're signing people to, under the best of conditions between two nice human beings, a fairly unenforceable contract. All you can do is include clauses that at least pay you for your time."

That said, not every producer who'll sign you to a production deal is so nice. Some would even rather see an artist fail than succeed with someone else. So step very carefully in the world of production deals.

From the producer's perspective, Gary says, a fair deal guarantees the producer exclusive rights to work with the artist for eighteen months. The contract should include a clause saying the producer must use his best efforts to secure the artist a record deal and another clause saying the artist must use his or her best efforts to have the producer continue in that role once the recording contract has been secured.

"There's usually no money involved other than, by signing a kid like that, I'm assuming all the costs of writing with them, producing tracks, and setting them up with other writers. When they're done, they're going to have a demo reel of a bunch of songs they're going to be really proud of that could get them a record deal."

Gary says producers will often sign young artists to publishing deals at the same time they lock in the production deals. "Because of the way the industry is right now, with too many people downloading for free and not buying albums, labels need to hedge their bets," he says. "One way you hedge your bets is by taking fewer chances on young producers, so the odds of a midline producer making it through to doing the record are smaller than they used to be." By becoming both an artist's producer and the publisher, Gary says, "If the label does say, no, we want so-and-so to produce the record, you go, 'Great, I hope every song we wrote is a single because I own half the publishing on every song.' I think that's totally fair for what an artist gets."

DON'T RUSH INTO SIGNING A CONTRACT OR WRITING A BIG CHECK, EXPECTING THAT YOU'LL GET GREAT SONGS AND A RECORD DEAL.

Here's the kind of production/publishing deal Gary considers fair: "If you have an eighteen-month independent production deal, I could see having a two-year publishing deal with a one-year option. Frankly, after eighteen months, you still normally have a six-month grace period, in case you're in negotiations with anybody.

"During that time, you're going to be busy writing with me, so I deserve half the publishing because if I didn't get it, I wouldn't be writing with you. If I set you up to write with Bob DiPiero, I should get half of that because I made the phone call and in this business it's who you know. You want to write with Bob and not give me half the publishing? Go find Bob and talk to him at a writers' night and see how accessible he is."

As you see, production deals can have upsides, but they can also create situations that are extremely unfriendly to the artist. Always approach them with caution.

Julianne Hough and David Malloy

DAVID MALLOY: WORKING WITH JULIANNE HOUGH

Shortly after the 2007 season of ABC's Dancing with the Stars *ended, Julianne Hough, the dancer who had won that season and the previous one, signed a record deal with Mercury Nashville. Julianne is managed through a joint venture between Tim McGraw's manager, Scott Siman; Eagles manager Irving Azoff; and Azoffmusic Management's Jared Paul. David Malloy is producing her debut album.*

When you meet Julianne, she has an energy, a charisma, an X factor—there's just something about her. In a way, it kind of reminds me of when I worked with Dolly Parton. She has that magnetism.

Julianne had gone into the studio one time in Los Angeles. It was the first time she'd ever been on a mic in the studio. Irving sent the demo to Scott. Scott liked what he heard, and he had me listen to it. I felt the United States had accepted her as a dancer, but why should they accept her as a singer? There needed to be a song that gave her a reason to sing it.

I got with Tim Johnson and Will Robinson, two friends and great songwriters, and we wrote a song called "Will You Dance with Me." The song tied the music into the show. Everybody seemed to love it, and I thought we nailed something really special. All of a sudden, we were dreaming pretty big.

Julianne loved the song, management in Los Angeles loved it, and a couple days later, I was in a studio with her. She came in at 10:30 at night to the studio, and she'd already been in eight hours of dance rehearsals. She spent another hour and a half on the vocal in the studio. That was the first time we met.

She didn't have a label at that time, so it didn't get promoted at radio, but she released a download of the song. People loved it. Even now, if you go on YouTube, you can find video clips where people have taken that song and edited her dances to it.

(cont.)

Things had worked great to that point, so we decided to go forward and cut some more sides. Scott asked us to cut four or five more things. At this point, I had no idea how well Julianne could sing. All I'd heard her on were these two things, and they weren't rangy songs. I had no idea about her range or stamina or how she'd hold up. But we were looking for songs.

We went around to publishers in Nashville for two days, looking for songs. We went to four or five publishers each day. We found a few songs, and we went in and cut them. They were rangy, powerful, emotional songs, and I was thinking, "Here we go, let's see what happens." We go into the studio, and out comes this big, fantastic voice. I'm going, "Wow, this is the real deal here; this is for real." I thought if she'd never danced a lick but walked into an office with that voice, you'd go, "Yeah, I'm in." That's been a lot of the reaction we've had. When somebody comes from television, we all have an idea in our head about what to expect. We might go, "Yeah, it's good, it's great," but inside we don't think it. But with her it's great.

The songs came out really great. They laid a nice groundwork for a direction. She knew what she liked and what she didn't like. She's delightful, and she's charismatic.

WHEN PRODUCTION DEALS GO BAD

If you sign an overreaching contract with a producer—promising him, say, the producer's role on your next five albums—and your label doesn't want him to be the producer, someone has to pay him. That sort of thing can be pricey. That expense makes you hard to say yes to. Record companies don't have any shortage of artists they could sign—you don't want to be giving them reasons to say no.

Watch out for producers with far-reaching contracts and blurry credits. Don't rush into signing a contract or writing a big check, expecting that you'll get great songs and a record deal. Things just aren't done that way. These days, it's just too easy to check a person's credentials online. There's no excuse for letting your eagerness get in the way of good business practices.

Any reputable producer will be cautious with his promises, so if you're talking to somebody who's promising you the moon, warning bells should be ringing all over your head. If you meet someone after performing at a church function or convention party, and he wants to sign you up on the spot and promises that he can get you a record deal, then you've just met trouble. People who have worked in the music industry for more than a year will be more likely to say, "I don't know if it's going to happen in a year or ten years or at all, and it's going to be really hard." We'll question *your* perseverance.

Unless we're running a record company, we'll never promise you a record deal. A producer, publisher, or manager—even a junior A&R executive—would more likely say, "I believe in you, I think you've got something. I'll work at moving you from point A to point B, but I don't know how long it's going to take. I don't know if you have the music quite right yet, but I think there's something." We almost always undersell rather than oversell because we know how hard it is to deliver and how many things can go wrong. About 90 percent of aspiring artists fail, and everyone who sticks around knows that. We're extremely honest, and a lot of us are so frank about the difficulties that it's almost scary. So if somebody's promising you contracts they don't have the authority to sign themselves, that's a promise that's too good to be true.

If a producer wants to sign you, take your time getting to know her. I'm not talking about a year, but I am talking about a few months to do your research and see whether you gel with her musically. Are you speaking the same language? Are you in sync musically? She could be a great producer that you just don't get along with, or she could be someone you can't trust. A successful producer won't have a lot of time, but she shouldn't be hurrying you. If she starts to push you to sign a contract, walk away. Your career won't be over, and you probably just dodged a bullet.

Photo courtesy of Tony Brown

TONY BROWN: INSIDE THE HEAD OF A HIT MAN

Tony Brown has been one of Nashville's most successful producers and record executives for the past twenty years. He got his start playing piano for gospel groups like the Stamps and the Blackwoods and later for Elvis Presley and Emmylou Harris. As a record executive, he has signed acts including Alabama, Steve Earle, Vince Gill, Lyle Lovett, and Trisha Yearwood. He has produced hit country albums for Reba McEntire, George Strait, Wynonna Judd, and many others. His productions have sold more than 105 million albums and generated 106 Number One singles. He's also my husband, so I asked him for advice for an artist who's planning to move to an industry town. He had a lot to say specifically about Nashville and country singers since that's what he knows best—but the basics of what he says apply whether you're planning on going to Nashville, Los Angeles, New York, or somewhere else.

If I were a young artist trying to make it in the music business, the first thing I'd do is learn who the players are in town. For Nashville, *Music Row* magazine has an annual directory of publishers, A&R people, managers, and agents. It's called *In Charge*. I always tell my assistant to get those for me and for everyone who works with me. Buy those things just so you know who the A&R person is for RCA and Warner Bros. and so on. Get to know which A&R people like which kinds of music—if you're a really country country artist, then you sort of know which A&R people like that kind of stuff. Usually, if I've seen someone I liked but didn't have room to sign to my roster, I've suggested she see certain people because of the kind of artist she was. An artist has to come to town and sort of know whom she wants to see.

You've got to do your homework; come with some knowledge. Subscribe to *Music Row* and other music magazines and read, read, read. I've always been a junkie for those kinds of magazines—you learn a lot in those things. *Billboard*'s a good one, though a subscription's expensive. You can usually find a copy at a good bookstore or maybe even your local library. Billboard always has articles about every genre, videos, everything.

After Trisha Yearwood had been in town for a while, I started to notice that 90 percent of all female demos had her voice on them. She sang "She's in Love with the Boy" and "The Thunder Rolls" during a showcase at Douglas Corner, and I loved her, so I set up a meeting with her.

Trisha and I talked about music, and she was so savvy—she'd been watching Nashville for years. She knew the things she liked about Reba McEntire and other artists. She knew about different producers and musicians and studios. I told her I had about fifty songs in my desk that were pitched to Reba that she was singing the demos on.

A few weeks later, I called Trisha and said I was interested in talking to someone about her. I asked if I needed to talk to an attorney or her manager. She said, "Joe Galante's interested, too, but Mary Martin says she wants me to go make some demonstration tapes to see what I sound like." I said, "Tell her I've got fifty in my desk; I'll make copies for her. Where has she been—does she not listen to demos?" Trisha said, "I love you, that's great!" That one little thing—I got to sign Trisha because I did my homework.

If you're coming to pitch someone in A&R, come to make a good impression. Be prepared and know about the business. I always ask people to tell me their favorite record on the radio right now, just out of curiosity. I want to see what their musical taste is—see if they like Garth because he's an entertainer or Joe Nichols because he has a great voice or Lyle Lovett or a singer/songwriter kind of person.

Have one song that you know you sing well. Don't just play the latest hit. It amazes me how some people pick stuff to play for me. Pick a song—not two or three—pick one song that you know you can pull off because it's worked every time you've done it. Everyone has that kind of a song. If you can't play guitar, bring someone with you who can. I don't want you singing *a cappella*. Come prepared, and if you're asked to perform and you're not good at doing that, then prerecord it.

As for songs, I much prefer a song plugger pitching me because if it's a writer, I'll keep five songs I'm not going to cut just because I can't stand to hurt his feelings. But a plugger, that's their job. So I listen and I'm always thinking, "I can't use this, but who could?" Maybe I'll say this is really a good song, go play it for Byron Gallimore for Lee Ann Womack.

(cont.)

I like lyrics, and everybody in town knows I like lyrics. I like to see where the song is going, and I'm making my decision about the melody, the lyric, the song itself. By the chorus, if I think it's boring, I just stop. Why waste my time, especially if I've got to listen to five or six more? With this last George Strait record, I had two writers bring me twenty songs. They were writers I knew very well, and I wanted to scold them because, come on—don't bring that many songs.

If I'm interested in an artist, I always ask, "Do you write?" They always respond, "I'm learning; I'm going to be writing." And I go, "You know, I don't care if you write or not—actually I'd prefer you didn't because, if you don't, I can get some good Lori McKenna or Jeffrey Steele songs. If you do write, I've got to deal with your feelings about your own songs—if your own songs are not good enough, then that's another hurdle I have to deal with." But they always think I want them to say yes.

If I like the artist, I'll start digging into their head and see what kind of taste they have, if they're smart, if they follow up. Nine times out of ten, they don't follow up. I'll tell them to go through their favorite albums and find five songs that were not singles that they really like and put them on a CD so I can see their taste in artists. Often, a couple of months will go by and I won't hear from them. Then the person who pitched them will call and say, "What did you think about Billy?" I'll say I told him to go do this and he hasn't done it, and I was just waiting to hear from him. And then a week later, I'll get the CD. So already they have one bad mark against them because, to me, if you're going to run with the big dogs, you've got to get off the porch.

That's what I love about Kenny Chesney—this guy wanted it so bad, and he finally got it. I don't think I'd ever have believed he'd be the biggest artist in the format like he is now. Kenny isn't a stylist at all; he just sort of sings on pitch and he knows good songs and he learned how to max out his vocals. Now when I hear him, his voice sounds like radio. He really worked hard for it. I never in a million years would have believed it.

When I did the *Duets* album with Reba, her business ethic is so incredible she stayed on top of everybody. And about eight out of twelve of the artists who sang with her came in prepared. The three or four who came in unprepared, Reba just showed them up. Not on purpose, but just because she's always there, always prepared. Chesney walked in and nailed it to the wall. I'd never worked with Chesney, so I wondered what he'd be like, but he was really good.

If an A&R person at a label really likes you and they want to do demos on you, the label will pay to do that. The label will find a way to recoup it. It's amazing to me the number of talented people who are pretty big-sized artists who cut demos back in their hometown and paid for them. They had someone finance it, and they had to sign something that said if they got a deal, these people would get to participate in some form or fashion. Joe Nichols had so many strings attached to him, the label spent five years getting him out of deals with people who were connected to him. And it was always these "backers." People will say, "We've got a backer." I don't want to hear that.

Find a way to come to town unattached and live as frugally as you can. Record companies don't want you to have strings attached because once the label owns the master recordings, they don't want to find out there's a third party involved because someone has innocently signed a contract saying this person owns 30 percent of any masters.

It's okay to spend some money to make a demo; just don't sign away any part of your future. Find a friend who can do it with computer software or something, or someone who would do it with you on spec—that happens all the time. Some people will help you make a demo for free, hoping that when you play it for me, I might go, "Who's playing guitar on that?"

Always nurture those relationships both inside and outside your circle. This business is all about knowing different people and forming relationships. There are really no set rules; the main thing is to use common sense.

CHAPTER 11

PUBLISHERS

WHAT DOES A PUBLISHER DO?

Songwriters earn their income from five main sources: mechanical royalties, performance royalties, synchronization licenses, print licenses, and foreign licenses. Mechanical royalties, often called simply "mechanicals," come from the sale of physical products such as CDs. Performance royalties come from public performances such as radio, live shows, and the music played in bars and restaurants. Synchronization licenses cover the use of music in films and television, when music is "synchronized" with visual images. Print licenses cover the sale of sheet music. Foreign licenses encompass the above four income sources when licensed for use in foreign countries.

Writers and publishers both receive income for the use of songs. Many writers split their royalties with outside music publishers, but if you are the publisher as well as the writer, you get 100 percent of all the income your songs generate.

You'll often hear people advise songwriters to hold on to their publishing rights as long as possible. That's a good rule of thumb, but most songwriters, at some point, decide to sell the publisher's portion of their copyright in exchange for the services a publisher can offer them. It's not necessarily a bad thing to give up some of your rights—the trick is knowing when to do it.

There's no set answer, of course. If you'll be splitting the money 50/50 with the publisher, one of the questions to consider is whether a publisher can collect more than twice as much money as you can by yourself. The math's pretty easy then—half of a whole bunch is better than all of a little. And publishers can sometimes greatly increase the value of your songs—by getting other artists to record them or by placing them in films, television shows, and commercials.

FINDING THE RIGHT PUBLISHER WHO BELIEVES IN YOU AND YOUR MUSIC EARLY ON IS LIKE FINDING A LIFE PRESERVER —IT CAN HELP YOU STAY AFLOAT.

Publishers do more than that, though. They also administer a songwriter's catalog, handling the paperwork and collecting the royalties. That leaves the songwriter more time to do what she does best—spend more time writing and less time making sure she's getting properly paid. The publisher takes care of that.

A songwriter's most valuable potential asset is his song catalog. But "potential" doesn't pay the bills. That's another place where publishers come in. Any publishing deal worth signing will include an advance—money paid up front against the possibility of future royalties. Advances are usually recoupable, which means that the publisher keeps the writer's share of any royalty until the advance is repaid. They are also usually nonrefundable, which means that if the songwriter's work doesn't generate enough income for the publisher to recoup, the songwriter does not have to repay the advance.

Finding the right publisher who believes in you and your music early on is like finding a life preserver—it can help you stay afloat. Many songwriters have found that an early publishing deal gives them enough money to keep from having to work outside the music industry. I can't count the number of times a waiter or a valet has given me a CD—it's not something to be ashamed of; we've all done it at one time or another. A publishing deal may allow them to write or perform full-time. It also gives them entrance into the industry and a team to work their songs. Others can afford to hold out until their career success puts them in a better negotiating position, and they make more money when they eventually sign their publishing deal. If you're able to keep your publishing during your lean years, fantastic! If not, keep the big picture in mind, minimize the length of the contract, and benefit from being part of a team.

Publishers can also pave the way to a recording career. Michael Pizzuto, the head of creative and A&R for Stage Three Music in Los Angeles, tells of an artist named Jesca Hoop whom Stage Three president Lionel Conway signed as a songwriter.

"She had nothing but a song or two," Michael says, "but it was so special we signed her and gave her an advance, something to live off, and helped develop her.

"Lionel gave a very rough demo of one of Jesca's songs to Nic Harcourt at KCRW in Los Angeles, and Nic started playing the song and it became one of the station's most requested songs at the time, three years ago.

"Then I came into the picture and started making the label community aware of her. I brought A&R guys down to the shows, and before you knew it, she had become a buzz in Los Angeles. It was all publisher-driven. That resulted in a label deal with Columbia Records." Michael also placed one of Hoop's songs in a movie. Not only did she receive money as the songwriter, but because she wasn't signed to a record label, she owned her recording, so she made money on that side, too.

As with managers, agents, and producers, different publishers have different strengths. In Nashville, for example, publishers often focus on getting artists to record songs by their songwriters. Because Los Angeles is the heart of America's film and television industry, music publishers there concentrate more on placing songs in movies and TV shows—sync licenses. Getting music into commercials figures more prominently in New York, where much of the country's advertising industry is located.

"Songs live forever," Michael says. "Say you sign a band with a writer or two and the band breaks up. You still have the songs. You can still exploit them and get them covered by other artists. You can still get sync opportunities with them."

FIND THE RIGHT PUBLISHER

The importance of a publisher for an artist/writer grows each year, as direct access to record label executives gets harder and new-artist signings decrease. Today, publishers develop a lot of new talent the way labels once did, serving as a *de facto* A&R arm of the labels. During the 1970s, music towns were more open and accessible. Since the 1990s, though, labels have become less willing to spend development dollars; publishers assume that role while recording demos and casting co-write sessions.

If you're considering signing a deal with a music publisher, don't forget the advice we've talked about before. Any time you sign a contract, have a music attorney representing you. And just as you would with a manager or a producer, get to know the publisher well before assigning your copyrights to the company. Since a publisher can cultivate your talent, the more honest the dialogue you have with her, the better decision you'll make for your career.

As with any industry, some people will sit back and take your money and others will work for it. As you separate the good eggs from the bad, you need to find the right fit for you. Once again, you must dig deep and determine your strengths and your needs.

Make sure the publisher's interests match your interests. Do you want others to record your songs? Make sure the publisher has song pluggers, whose job it is to pitch songs to artists and producers. Is your music edgy and alternative, good for TV and films? Find a publisher who excels in that area. Are you interested in becoming an artist? Make sure your publisher has a track record of developing talent and is willing to hold songs for your future record deal instead of pitching them to other artists.

"If you have a sense that your path in the world is to be an artist and to express your sensibilities as articulately and dramatically as you can, it behooves you to align yourself with somebody who nurtures that," Rodney Crowell says. "If someone is nurturing you toward the more broad-stroke approach that may work for everybody, it's going to be at the expense of your individual gifts.

"The good publishers nurture the individual creativity," Rodney adds. "If a young songwriter needs direction and help, a good publisher knows how to spot that sensibility, spot that talent, and nurture it for the uniqueness that it is."

Publishers can do more than act as a bank and an exploiter of your songs to other acts.

As Mark Knopfler's publisher, David Conrad, former senior vice president of Almo Irving Music (Rondor Music Publishing), introduced the Dire Straits leader to a new fan base and a source of creative infusion. David found five songs in Mark's catalog he thought would translate well to the country format. He took those rock album cuts—songs like "Water of Love," "Setting Me Up," and "When It Comes to You"—and without even asking for Mark's approval, cut them as country demos. Before Mark knew it, he had country covers from the Judds, Waylon Jennings, and John Anderson. Those covers aroused Mark's curiosity about Nashville, so he came to town to record and left with a new band, as well as an engineer and producer (Chuck Ainlay). He also formed a bond with fellow guitarist Chet Atkins that resulted in their recording the Grammy-winning album *Neck and Neck* together.

Wyatt Easterling and I did the same thing for Sting when we worked for Miles Copeland. As head of our publishing company, Wyatt wanted to exploit Sting's copyrights in the country genre. Wyatt got Tammy Wynette to record "Every Breath You Take" with Sting for her 1994 duets album, *Without Walls.* The song never sounded so country, and it generated additional revenue for Sting. We duplicated that success when I signed Waylon Jennings to Ark 21 and suggested he record Sting's "She's Too Good to Me." Then Sting challenged us to get "I'm So Happy I Can't Stop Crying" cut by a country artist. Wyatt and I jumped at the chance. In the end, Toby Keith stepped up to the plate—it became a hit on the country charts, secured Toby's first Country Music Association awards-show performance, and broadened the song's appeal and financial value.

Photo courtesy of Anastasia Brown

Anastasia Brown, Sting, and Waylon Jennings on a break during a recording session for "She's Too Good For Me"

David also is a fan of Emmylou Harris. "She didn't need me, but she did need a publisher," David says. "I had always encouraged her to write more, so one day she walked in my office and said, 'I'm ready to apply myself, and I want to do it with you.'

"I always shot from the hip and was always honest. If the verse was weak, I said so. There were times when we went round and round. Sometimes, she'd stomp out like she was never coming back, but the next day she'd come running, saying, *Listen to this!* My questioning her caused her to question whether the song could be better."

So besides giving you money to live, good publishers can develop your talent, expose you and your music to the industry, offer a sounding board, provide a creative environment in which to write, share enthusiasm and encouragement, and ultimately create a safe harbor for you. The experienced publisher can tell you when you are working on a competitive level and then get that work to the world.

DAVID CONRAD: DO'S AND DON'TS WHEN FISHING FOR A PUBLISHER

David Conrad has long been one of the most trusted and admired publishers for rock, alternative, R&B, and country songwriters. He has published writers like Mark Knopfler, Emmylou Harris, Patty Griffin, Paul Kennerly, Will Jennings, Annie Roboff, Mike Reid, Nanci Griffith, and Gillian Welch. He's worked with rock legends and developed new artists. He has some insightful suggestions for meeting with publishers.

1. Do your homework. Know the publisher's writers, the history of the company, and the style of music toward which it gravitates.
2. Bring two or three demos to play and leave behind. That's your calling card.
3. Bring a guitar. You may have written a new song that you haven't demoed or that you can communicate best by singing live. Bring the tools to help you shine.
4. Don't roar into a meeting making demands early on. Confidence mixed with humility goes a long way.
5. Ask these questions: "What do you need in a songwriter?" and "What do you expect from a songwriter?"

6. Another good question to ask is, "What can we do to help each other?"
7. Two other key questions: "How many writers do you have?" and "How many professional managers (song pluggers) do you have?"
8. Listen! If you are offered constructive criticism, don't argue or defend yourself. Remember what's said, and consider how it can help you improve your song.

THE INS AND OUTS OF PUBLISHING CONTRACTS

A far-reaching publishing deal allows the writer to keep the writer's share of royalties while, for a good advance, the publisher owns the publisher's share forever. Another route, one sometimes favored by successful songwriters, is an administration deal, where the writer receives a much smaller advance and the publisher administers the copyrights, meaning they handle the paperwork and collect the royalties to give to the writer. The downside to doing an administration deal is that no one at the publishing company is pushing your songs. They're just hoping you'll record your own songs; then they'll track down your money. So if you're a songwriter first and a singer second, you'll have no one exploiting your music for you. But if you're a singer/songwriter who records your own material and doesn't get a lot of outside cuts, then an administration deal can be a great way to go. You're not splitting the money; you're giving the publisher 15 percent to do the administration. You get to keep all your publishing rights, but you're not getting much money up front.

A few chapters ago, we told the story of Jake Owen, a country singer who got his break by giving one of his CDs to a banker in Nashville, who in turn passed it along to a music publisher. That publisher eventually offered Jake a publishing deal, but he ended up turning it down.

"I was about a day away from walking into this guy's office and signing a normal new-writer deal," Jake says. "I think it was for eighteen months, about $18,000 a year, and eighteen songs. I figured it was a way for me to get money.

"I started looking over the deal—and maybe I'm jaded because I hadn't had a deal before—but I thought about all the time I'd put into my songs, writing them myself. I felt like the way the deal was structured, it wasn't going to work for me because it wasn't worth the time and effort I'd put into it just for getting my foot in the door that way. I didn't need some guy to steal my creativity by underpaying me for it."

A few months later, Jake found himself on the receiving end of a much better offer. "I went from almost signing an $18,000 publishing deal to, four months later, signing one for well over half a million dollars," he says.

"You have to respect what you do," Jake adds. "It's so easy for people to let their guard down and let people take advantage of them because they want to succeed so badly. I see it time and time again in Nashville. People who are just as talented or more talented than I am get to the point where they want something so bad, they'll do anything for it. You have to keep your head about you."

Jake's story doesn't mean that all new-writer publishing deals are bad—though, clearly, the shorter track record writers have, the less negotiating leverage they have. First-time publishing deals are almost always weighted in favor of publishers simply because the publishers assume the most financial risk—writers who don't recoup their advances don't have to repay publishers, so publishers never have a guarantee they'll see returns on the money they invest in writers. First-time deals have kept many young writers from starving. Later, when they became successful, they have negotiated more favorable deals for themselves.

"You can't expect to walk into this business and demand the same things that someone who has been doing it for a long time and has a track record can," says Gary Burr. "When I got my first cut, I got none of the publishing. The publisher took it all. And I'd do it again because it gave me a career.

"On the next song, I got to keep half of the publishing, and then the next song I got to keep three-quarters. From that point on, I gave up half the publishing, but I was paid to give it up. That's when I got a publishing deal, and giving away 50 percent of the publishing seemed like a fair trade because I had a string of hits. By the time I signed the deal, I wasn't signing for pennies, I was signing a deal for something I could look at and say, 'You know, it's worth half the publishing to have infrastructure around me.'"

For Rodney Crowell, a big payment up front presented its own problems. "I made a publishing deal where I got a super amount of money in advance," he says. "That had to be collateralized against all money coming in. In other words, after I took all that money in advance, the deal was structured so the publisher recouped it all before I saw any more. In my case, I got a divorce, and, suddenly, that huge amount of money is half of what it was. But I still have a manager and a business manager. I had to go about earning all that money back—100 percent of it, not half of it—and there's a lot of pressure. If you're a guy like me, when somebody gives you money, you feel beholden to them.

"Back-end money lasts longer than front-end money. It's been my experience every time when I'm in a position to do some work and it hasn't been front-loaded with money, I make more money in the back-end. I'm freer, and my creative path is a lot freer.

"I'd advise young artists to be careful about the amounts of money they take in advance. You've got to pay it back."

If you've already started building your team, your manager or your agent often will be able to offer sound advice when deciding on publishing deals. They'll help steer you away from bad deals since it's in their best interests for you to make the most money possible. "If something is bad in a group, it'll weed itself out," says BMI's Shelby Kennedy. "If you have five people working for you, I guarantee you that you don't have five snakes working for you."

However, if you don't have any other team members in place and you're not sure whether or not you should sign a deal that's being offered to you, don't be afraid to ask another songwriter for advice, especially one who writes for the same publisher. "We're all on each other's side," says Gary. "It's us against the world. Don't be afraid to use that resource. Call up some writer and say, 'I'm a young writer and I'm thinking of signing to this publishing company. You work for them; what can you tell me?' You're on the writer team, so he's not going to be betraying any confidences. He wants you to have a good deal so everybody stops doing bad deals."

THE WIDE WORLD OF SYNC

If you've ever heard a song in a movie, on a TV show like *Grey's Anatomy*, or in an iPod commercial, that song needs a sync license. Thanks to shows like *Miami Vice*, *The OC*, and *The Sopranos*, music is more popular than ever on television. And just ask acts like Jet or Feist how much having music in an Apple iPod commercial can mean to someone's career.

"A few years ago, getting your music into a commercial was so lowbrow," Michael Pizzuto says. "Now it's like the new radio.

"The stigma of putting your song in a commercial is, for the most part, no longer a stigma. It depends on what you want to be associated with. Everyone wants to be associated with the coolest, hippest thing, which is Apple and iPod. Target's gotten really cool. When I mention Target to some of our artists, maybe ten years ago they would have said, 'Nah,' but now it's 'That would be great.'

SYNC LICENSES ARE BECOMING AN EXTREMELY IMPORTANT WAY FOR PUBLISHERS TO EXPLOIT THEIR COPYRIGHTS.

"There are still those artists who hold their music so sacred they won't put them into commercials, and those are just the real big ones who don't need the money as much."

One of Stage Three's acts, a Brazilian band called CSS, had their song "Music Is My Hot, Hot Sex" used in a commercial for Apple's iPod Touch in the fall of 2007. "Within two weeks, they went from selling three hundred CDs a week to selling between 1,500 and 2,000," Michael says. "The song climbed to Number Fifteen in song downloads and Number Five in ringtone sales within two weeks. They worked their way into the pop charts, and this was pretty much an unknown band."

Michael points to an artist named Matt Nathanson as someone who has benefited from having his music licensed to television shows. "He's an artist who's done grassroots all the way through," Michael says. "It's all about the live experience for him. Even before his latest record, *Some Mad Hope*, we'd gotten a lot of syncs for him, but with that record, it went through the roof. We got dozens of syncs for him on great shows like *Men in Trees* and *Private Practice*."

With steadily declining CD sales in recent years—which has meant lower mechanical royalty payments—sync licenses are becoming an extremely important way for publishers to exploit their copyrights. "Sync is much bigger now than even a few years ago," Michael says. "It's huge. It's much of what my day is. I think the new record executive, the future A&R guy, is going to have to be aware of what's going on in the sync world. It's funny how many A&R guys from record companies call me, asking for tips on how to get their bands into TV shows and films. I tell them, 'Get the film and TV directory and start making calls; start taking these people out to lunch. Your bands will love you.'"

DON WAS: PERFORM LIVE ALL YOU CAN

Everybody, no matter what their artistic aspirations are, on some level, they're still there to entertain people. Bob Dylan is an entertainer. Byron and Keats were entertainers, too. You have to learn how to get up in front of an audience of people, keep their attention, and keep their mind off the fact that we're all mortal. I see bands showcase in Los Angeles, and they get up in front of these A&R guys and it's like, 'Get your checkbooks ready.' None of them have been in the trenches to understand what it really takes to sustain an audience's attention. It's not that hard, but you've got to get out there and keep doing it to see what works.

When all else fails, I think of Robert Johnson, who used to blow into town on the back of a train. He'd go to a barber shop and stand outside all day, singing songs and promoting that night's show at some roadhouse. That's what you've got to do: Get in front of people. Play all the time. Figure out what works, and discard the stuff that doesn't. I believe that anyone who can do that in front of people and stick to it will develop an audience and see everything else fall into place. If you can't do that, you're screwed anyway.

CHAPTER 12

RECORD LABELS/A&R

WHAT IS AN A&R PERSON?

A&R stands for Artists & Repertoire. A label's A&R staff is responsible for scouting and signing talent, then developing the artists that record for the label. Years ago, A&R people would take artists with extremely raw talent and help them develop their craft. Some A&R people still do that, but it has become rarer. The development process tends to fall on the shoulders of early believers, whether it's a manager, a producer, or a publisher.

A really great A&R person is out on the club scene watching what's going on, like a scout for a pro sports team who watches promising college prospects. They listen to demo tapes and mp3s; they scour sites like MySpace and PureVolume© for unsigned talent. A hungry, driven A&R person may travel all over the country looking for talent. You might not even know an A&R person is the room; he might watch you a couple of times and then, if he thinks you're good, he'll introduce himself.

If you've signed to a label, an A&R person there will help guide your creative path. That will include helping you find songs and evaluating the songs you write (that's the

"Repertoire" part of "Artists & Repertoire"). She'll help set a recording budget, with input from the label's business affairs department; then she'll help you pick a producer (at some labels the head of A&R might even *be* your producer). If you don't have a manager, she might even help you find one. If you've always wanted to sing a duet with a certain artist, she can help you make that happen, when the time is right. But first things first: you have homework to do before you're ready for a record deal.

IF YOU'VE SIGNED TO A LABEL, AN A&R PERSON THERE WILL HELP GUIDE YOUR CREATIVE PATH.

"Labels are not developing acts like they used to," says Reen Nalli, outside consultant and A&R executive for Universal Music Group. "There are talented people at labels who will sign you once you are developed, offer a big advance, and throw your music against the wall to see if it sticks. But I still believe that true, real artistry has nothing to do with business. It's spiritual.

"I have never been able to secure an act through an attorney, as they tend to move toward bidding wars, which aren't something I normally get involved in. The case of India.Arie is a perfect example. A friend of mine at ASCAP named Mike Doyle told me about India and the Earth Seed movement in Atlanta. India was writing and gigging, and it took me six months to get a meeting with her. We agreed on a handshake to work together. I spent some seed money developing her, finding the right producer, and helping her hone her craft. Then the time was right for her to go to the next level, and that's when the attorneys got involved.

"Young acts tend to feel rushed to sign a deal with a record company. I don't believe in that. Until music is honed correctly, time is not an issue. Blue October had been playing live for a while when a young agent from a small, regional agency mentioned them to me. He said that people in the audience were crying at their gigs. I chased them down, and the rest is history." Blue October's *Foiled* album went platinum in 2007 on the strength of singles like "Hate Me" and "Into the Ocean."

You have work to do on your own before you're ready for a record label to sign you. You're much more appealing to an A&R person if you bring something more to the table than just good looks and a great voice. Have you played out enough to bring a built-in audience with you? Have you surrounded yourself with a team of respected professionals? Do you have a musical vision that's unique yet still commercial? Have you created a story and a following on MySpace or YouTube? Do you come with a catalog full of songs that he loves? Have you convinced him through your actions leading up to your signing with his label that you have a work ethic that just won't quit? All of those things make you more attractive to an A&R person.

"These people who come to town and say, 'I need a producer, produce me; what songs do you want me to cut?'—I'm never going to sign that artist," says Scott Borchetta, who started Big Machine Records with singers Taylor Swift and Jack Ingram after spending years creating a reputation as one of the top radio-promotion men in the country music business. "I don't care if they're the most beautiful things I've ever seen and they're a great singer."

YOU'RE MUCH MORE APPEALING TO AN A&R PERSON IF YOU BRING SOMETHING MORE TO THE TABLE THAN JUST GOOD LOOKS AND A GREAT VOICE.

What does Scott look for in an artist he's interesting in signing?

"I look for individuality and natural charisma," he says. "I look for more natural things than learned things. Are you well spoken? Do you know who you are? When I ask you who you are and what you stand for, how are you going to answer that? Within those few points, I can tell if we have a chance of working together. Because if people can't tell me that, if they don't have those attributes from the beginning, I can't give them to them. I'm not a Play-Doh© factory. I can't put a green glob in one side and have a green star come out the other side."

Scott points to one of his label's acts, Taylor Swift, as a great, young example of what he's looking for.

"She had amazing vision, she just needed someone to support it," Scott says. "The same thing applies to any important artist, whether it is Toby Keith or Reba McEntire.

"A lot of artists have such a desire to be famous, but there's not a huge love of the music. I always encourage everybody on the creative side to love the music first. If you do, it's going to show through. If you love it and you're talented, that's going to be one element of cutting through. But when I talk to guys or girls who really just want to be famous, that's a strike against them for me.

"Being famous sucks. Do you love doing this? If you love doing this, you're going to be able to handle fame because it's going to be built on a foundation of something that you really believe in and love doing. If you're just doing this to be famous, you're going to be very unhappy."

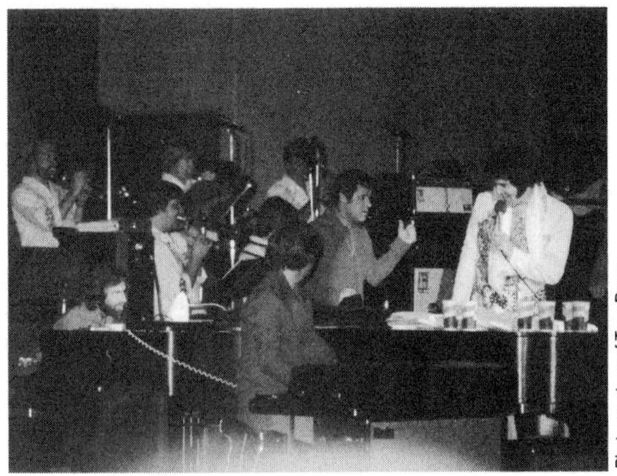

Photo courtesy of Tony Brown

Tony Brown in his early days playing piano for Elvis Presley

TONY BROWN: DEMOS

I was an A&R person during The Garth Years, as we call them, from 1989 to 1997. MCA was the number one label for, like, nine years in a row. So my profile was really big—I was producing George Strait, Reba McEntire, Vince Gill, Trisha Yearwood, Wynonna Judd, Marty Stuart, and Tracy Byrd. I had songs on the charts, a lot of young artists knew my name, and that meant I got some creative pitches and demos.

One time I got a Fender guitar case. I opened it, and the note inside read, "This is a good case for listening to this demo"—there was a demo taped in there. Another time somebody sent a demo stuck inside a bull scrotum. It had a little thing that said, El saco del toro . . . this is an authentic ball sack of a bull." And I was thinking, "This is so gross." But I reached inside, and I listened to the demo. It was so bad that I never even called the singer back.

People have thrown demos in my lap while I was in my convertible. One guy threw one to me, but it was so bad I tossed it in the trash. Later, he called the office, and my assistant said, "This is that guy who threw the demo in your convertible and he wants to know what you think." I said, "Tell him I pass." She said, "He wants to know if he can have it back." I said, "Tell him I threw it away." She said, "That was the only copy he had." I said, "Tell him he's stupid." That was so stupid, to give me his only copy.

Another person pulled up next to me and said he had some songs he wanted me to hear. I told him to toss me a CD. He said he didn't have it on tape, but could I pull over to a parking lot and listen to him sing it? And I said, "No! It's rush-hour traffic!"

Someone else tried to give me a demo at the Country Music Association awards one year, but I wouldn't take it because it would not have fit in my tux. I find a lot of demos under the wiper blades of my car. If they're at my car, I'll listen to it right then. But the wrong approach to giving someone a tape can affect the way you're going to be accepted. If I remember that you're the guy who tried to hand me a CD at the CMAs, it's not going to help you.

These days, with the Internet, I get flooded with mp3s when people find my e-mail address. Sometimes I'll actually listen to those. As long as it's easy, I'll listen to something from someone I've never heard of. But most of the time, I won't go out of my way to listen to something unless I know the person sending it—whether it's a musician, an engineer, or an attorney—and they've asked if they could send me something. I also like to have a picture and some kind of information about the artist so I know who I'm listening to.

THE A&R REP: YOUR LABEL LIAISON

After you sign a record deal, you need one person to act as a liaison between you and the label. That's your A&R person. Your manager will spend a lot of time dealing with the people in business affairs and the promotion and sales departments, but you need a contact that relates to your music. Your A&R person is your foot in the door at the label, and that's a relationship you need to nurture.

When you're a new artist at a label, the A&R person will be closely involved with the creation of your art. He'll be there as you make the record, offering suggestions and advice and representing the interests of the label. When you finish your album and turn it in, the A&R person's job is to convince everyone else at the label how important, how commercial, it is. If your A&R person is excited about the music you're making, that enthusiasm will have a ripple effect throughout the label, which can make a huge difference for you when the label releases your music.

YOUR A&R PERSON IS YOUR FOOT IN THE DOOR AT THE LABEL, AND THAT'S A RELATIONSHIP YOU NEED TO NURTURE.

Labels have two types of priority artists. Carrie Underwood is a priority artist because she's a household name, thanks to *American Idol.* Carrie's a slam-dunk. Any new album from her obviously will be a top priority for her label. You see the same sort of thing with pop artists like Beyoncé or Madonna—the big media machine cranks up, spending a lot of money, and suddenly their faces are everywhere.

Then there's the love priority. For years, Kenny Chesney was BMG's love priority. Kenny was around for nearly a decade before BMG established him as one of country's core acts and got him his first platinum record. But Kenny had an incredible work ethic, and he nurtured a strong relationship with his label. In turn, his label believed in him, even when other acts were having more success. He was label head Joe Galante's and vice president of A&R Renee Bell's passion project, and that dedication eventually paid off for Kenny and for the label. So it's very important that your A&R person loves to see you walking through the door rather than dreads your arrival. That person's attitude will carry over to everybody else on the staff, and it will directly affect how hard they work on your behalf.

The right A&R person will not only be helpful when your record is about to come out, but can also help while you're making the record. Even though he works for the label, a good A&R person can be an objective person to approach when you need advice. Don't be afraid to disagree with him and explain why you feel that you've got to do your music in some way that's different from what he or the label has in mind, or why you want to cut one song instead of another. However, you need to be prepared with good reasons for your opinions. Like Keith Urban said, don't compromise, but be willing to adapt—and be ready to explain the difference. The label executives know their market, and you know your music—so work as a team.

If you do your homework and learn about the other artists your label and your A&R person has signed and worked with, you should be able to get a good idea of how the label thinks and what kinds of acts have success there. If you're signed to Rounder Records, where Alison Krauss records, they're going to have a way of doing things that favors acoustic music and non-commercial radio artists. If you're signed to Sony BMG's country division, they're going to be thinking a lot more about mainstream radio hits. As a general rule, they're going to take you in the direction that they've taken other artists—not that they'll expect you to replicate their sound, but if they've done well with records at radio, they'll push you to make radio-friendly records. If their acts have found success with rigorous touring schedules, you can expect to be out on the road a lot. But—since there's a but in every scenario when you're talking about art—you could be the one artist who adds some depth or who changes the personality of the label.

DOING THE RECORD DEAL

A record deal is a goal—but it's not the final one. Too many acts make the mistake of looking only to the record deal and not beyond it. Once they get the deal, they think they've got it made. But it's like we said about winning *American Idol*—you've just won your ticket to climb Mount Everest.

Don't expect a record deal immediately, and don't panic if you get turned down by a label—or two or three. Pretty much every major record label in Nashville passed on Garth Brooks—some of them twice—when he came to town. Whether Garth figured out something he was doing wrong or one of the labels finally wised up, he eventually found a successful partnership with Capitol Records. If a label turns you down, listen to what they have to say, then adapt if necessary and try again.

Getting turned down by a record label is horrible for artists' egos, and it can lead them to make bad decisions. The desperation to get a record deal—a level which few aspiring artists ever reach—compels them to take offers that make it nearly impossible for them to make money off music sales, unless they're selling millions of copies. But that particular feat becomes more rare every year as the music industry undergoes seismic changes in its business structure.

Major record companies are geared towards blockbuster releases, and the new realities of the music business, where multi-platinum albums are fewer and further between than ever before, mean that new concepts and new business models are cropping up everywhere. The rules are changing quickly, but there are still a few things you should be sure to avoid.

IF A LABEL TURNS YOU DOWN, LISTEN TO WHAT THEY HAVE TO SAY, THEN ADAPT IF NECESSARY AND TRY AGAIN.

"Anytime somebody's charging you, saying, 'Sign here and bring money so we can go make your record,'" says Scott Borchetta, who runs Big Machine Records in Nashville, "any time you're paying, that's a big red flag. If you're being charged for everything, you're not being signed to a record-company contract in a traditional sense."

If the record company insists on managing you, publishing you, and having you pay to make the record, that's a big red flag. Recording contracts are changing these days, with the record company asking for pieces of touring, publishing, and merchandising income—these are often called "360 deals" because they cover the entire scope of the artist's income and career. These deals are relatively new, so it's more important than ever to have a music attorney representing you who is familiar with them and understands the nature of the beast.

"It's not easy to break an artist today, outside of doing it through television like *American Idol* and Disney do," says music lawyer John Mason, "so the record companies are looking to sign overall agreements, participate in all areas of income, and hope that the artists succeed through their own efforts.

"Record companies today want and are demanding an interest in everything—personal appearances, music publishing, records, merchandise. They want to give you an advance and cross-collateralize it.

"They're not saying they're going to make you a star—nobody's making you that promise. The contracts specifically say 'we're not guaranteeing you that we're going to make you a success;' you understand the business is bad. They all say we don't have to do anything. If you're lucky, you can negotiate something called a "pay or play" clause, which means if they don't do anything, you can leave, maybe you can leave and get paid."

Scott Borchetta co-manages Taylor Swift in addition to running the label for which she records. "But our agreement is that if she doesn't want me to do that anymore, I don't," he says. "I'm her record company first, but we built a management team around her so we could move as fast as we do." So far, the situation has worked—Taylor has sold 2 million copies of her debut album and even more downloads. "But if it gets to the point where she feels trapped, I can't have that conflict of interest," Scott says. "I'll tell her to go get somebody else."

When you think you're ready to sign with a major record label, you'll get a better deal if you come from a position of strength.

"Every deal and every negotiation in the business is based on leverage, how much power you have," John Mason says. "If you've been able to have success on your own, the deal you can make is going to be better."

When Matt Nathanson signed his deals, first with Universal and later with Vanguard, he had a history of selling his records independently, so his label knew that he had a loyal fan base from which to build. "I always came from a position of strength," he said, "Like, 'Look, I sell this many records by myself and I sell out all these venues; let's do a deal.' If they said no or gave me something I didn't want, I could always go back to what I was doing.

"Don't give up that edge because then they'll run all over you, and you'll end up talking about how naïve you were and what they did to you."

Contracts are changing so much that established artists often aren't entering into new recording contracts when their old ones expire, as they might have just a few years ago. "Instead," says John, "they're looking for new ways to exploit their intellectual properties."

John points to Toby Keith's relationship with the Universal Music Group a few years ago. "We could have renegotiated it, but my advice was to set up his own company, a distribution entity, and hire some promotion people, and that's what happened. They set up Show Dog Records."

If you don't have the leverage of a Matt Nathanson or Toby Keith to bring to your negotiation with the record label, you've got a tough decision you're going to have to make.

"If you're given that opportunity, you may have an onerous contract," John says. "You have to decide, 'Do I want to be a hairdresser for the rest of my life, or do I want a chance to get on TV and become a celebrity and work my way out of these initial contracts?'"

Credit: Hannah Elaine

Scott Borchetta and Taylor Swift

SCOTT BORCHETTA: SIGNING TAYLOR SWIFT

When Scott first heard about Taylor, he was working for DreamWorks' Nashville division, and the label was in the process of closing. The person who managed Taylor at the time sent Scott a package on the then fourteen-year-old singer.

"It was a great package," Scott recalls. "There was music and top-notch photos, and the bio was right. There was an Abercrombie & Fitch spread that Taylor had a full page in, and it just knocked me over the head."

Scott set up a meeting with Taylor and her manager. "Taylor was a little bit shy and obviously intimidated," Scott says. "I had her start playing and playing. I think she played ten songs, and I was just knocked out.

"I went to see her a couple nights later at the Bluebird Café, and she sat there with people like Robert Ellis Orrall and Michael Peterson and absolutely held her own. So I got to know her family and said, 'Here's the deal. I'm going to start my own label. If you'll wait, I promise you a record deal. That's all I can do.' They looked at me like I was nuts and left, but Taylor called me about ten days later and said she had made up her mind, she was waiting for me."

Big Machine released Taylor's album in the fall of 2006, when she was sixteen years old. By the time she turned eighteen, it had sold nearly 2 million copies.

IS A RECORD DEAL THE ONLY WAY TO GO?

While almost no albums sell 10 million copies any more, more people are releasing music than ever before. If your goal is to be an old-school star—the kind of celebrity who plays the Grammys and appears on the covers of magazines in grocery-store checkout lines, then you're still going to need a major-label record deal.

"If you're the Pussycat Dolls, you need to call Universal," says Don Was. "They know how to sell that. They're moving a certain kind of record. But it might be detrimental for an artist who's not a natural fit on the radio, and that's most people. The options are even smaller because only a few people control many of the stations. You don't even have the option of slipping someone a hundred bucks and hoping your record takes off in a region."

Major labels still have the ability to turn a commercial song into a big hit. Just look what it did for Chicago's Plain White T's and "Hey There Delilah." That song had kicked around for a couple years. The Plain White T's had already released the song on an album and a single. All their fans knew it and sang along with it during the band's shows. When the Plain White T's signed to Hollywood Records, they didn't plan on including "Delilah" on the band's major-label debut.

"We were thinking, 'Fans want a new record; they don't want to keep hearing 'Hey There Delilah,'" says singer Tom Higgenson, who wrote the song. But even if the band's fans knew the song, millions of others didn't—until Hollywood Records' radio promotion department got hold of it. Quickly, that two-year-old song that wouldn't die became one of the biggest summer hits of 2007.

"The song had never really gotten the chance that, apparently, it deserved," Higgenson says. "On the indie level, we could've written 'Yesterday' and it wouldn't have gotten any further than this song did. They just didn't have the mojo to take it to that next level.

"That was one of the reasons we wanted to sign with Hollywood: We knew that there was no ceiling. We knew that if we wrote good enough songs, they could become hits and the world could hear them."

More and more, though, performers at every level of the business—including the Plain White T's in their early days—are opting to release their music on small, independent labels or even release music themselves. The likelihood of celebrity is less, but the artists retain more control over the direction of their music and can build their fan base, sometimes even make a living, in a lower-pressure environment.

With the rise of 360 deals, John Mason has grown cynical about record companies' value to new artists. "They take interest in merchandising rights, but they don't do merchandising," he says. "They're not in the personal appearance business, and don't even get me started on publishing and what they don't do.

"I can't see what record companies have to offer to a new artist other than the money to make a record. I'd feel differently about a country artist signing with Joe Galante and Sony BMG in Nashville because their track record is very strong and they bring a lot to the table. They're breaking artists. But overall, particularly on the pop side and even the R&B side, the record companies aren't breaking acts anymore. Look at Carrie Underwood, one of the best-selling acts of the past few years—she came directly off *American Idol,* directly off big TV success where she found millions of fans.

"Another exception is Rascal Flatts. They've found their success with years and years of touring, but that's Disney and country radio together. Lyric Street Records, Disney's country label, stuck with them, but they toured and toured and worked extremely hard. And then what really launched them? A movie soundtrack." The group's version of "Life Is a Highway" appeared on the soundtrack for the animated movie *Cars* and in the film's closing credits.

"Since probably 2004 and maybe since 2002, TV is the medium to break record acts, and there's not a record company in the business outside of Disney that has that TV deal figured out. Disney has its own network."

DON WAS: HOW WAS (NOT WAS) GOT A RECORD DEAL

Before Don Was produced acts like Bonnie Raitt, Bob Dylan, Brian Wilson, and the Rolling Stones, he and David Was had an eclectic, dance-oriented rock band called Was (Not Was). The group had its biggest hits in the late 1980s with "Walk the Dinosaur" and "Spy in the House of

Love," but Was (Not Was) launched its recording career with "Wheel Me Out," a 12-inch single released on Ze Records in 1981. Here's how Don used a short-term contract to set up a better, long-term deal.

I was destitute in Detroit, really destitute, and my partner David Was was out in Los Angeles working as a freelance jazz critic for the now-defunct Los Angeles Herald Examiner, clearing maybe sixty bucks a week. This was in 1980. So we targeted a record company in New York called Ze Records. They specialized in alternative dance music and had acts like Kid Creole and the Coconuts and James White and the Blacks. It was a pretty groovy place, and we decided we wanted to be on this label.

So David called up the president of the label, Michael Zilkha, under the guise of being a writer for the Herald Examiner and did a half-hour interview. Around minute 27, he said, "By the way, there's this band from Detroit you've got to hear." He described the thing, and Michael Zilkha said to have the band send him a tape. David said, "I'll have the guy call you." And that' s how we got our first record deal.

I don't advocate passivity and waiting around until someone discovers you at Schwab's drugstore. You've got to do whatever you can do. It's a very competitive scene, and you've got to be creative.

We'd almost had another record deal once before that with Portrait Records, which, at the time, was part of CBS. The guy sent us a terrible contract, but I didn't care. It was for a 12-inch single, and I wanted to get to the album deal, so I signed it. We were getting a $5,000 advance for the 12-inch, but we didn't like the contract, so we got some high-powered lawyer in New York to renegotiate the thing. He dragged it out for months and certainly spent more than the $5,000 advance we were getting. We waited so long the record company folded. We could have had the record out, but we showed them! We were tough negotiators!

I wasn't going to repeat that mistake—so, this time, no lawyers. In fact, I told Ze to take the record for free, just put it out and we'd take the royalty on it. We didn't need an advance because I knew it would lead to an album deal, which it

(cont.)

did. Then we were in a position of strength. The single did well and they wanted to do an album, so we had negotiating position. It didn't matter what was in that first agreement. What mattered was what we'd require if they wanted us to release another record.

Don't get too hung up in these contracts and the legalisms. You're going to get screwed at the beginning, period. People are going to find a way to steal your money. But when you get to a position of strength, you can come back and revisit the terms that aren't really fair. But get to a position of strength first.

CHAPTER 13

OTHER MEMBERS OF YOUR SUPPORT TEAM

For the past few chapters, we've discussed some of the core members of the team you'll need in order to build a successful career. In this chapter, we'll look at some other team members that may come later or that may not interact with you on a day-to-day basis, the way managers and agents will.

MUSIC LAWYERS

Your lawyer may actually be the first member of your team you put in place. If you're lucky, though, you shouldn't need him or her on a daily or even weekly basis.

We've said this before, but it's worth mentioning again—make sure your lawyer specializes in the music industry. Even if you have a friend or family member who's a respected lawyer in contract law or another field, that's no substitute for knowledge of the specific intricacies of the music industry. You may think you're saving a few dollars with this shortcut, but you'll wind up paying for it elsewhere.

Joel Katz—who, as the Global Entertainment Law Practice chairman at Greenberg Traurig, is one of the most important attorneys in the music business—says, "I see people coming in here who say, 'Our family real-estate lawyer handled this contract.' I look at it, and it's a disaster. Just like I'm not out there handling a major real-estate transaction, a real-estate lawyer should not be handling a major entertainment transaction. If you're going to a dentist, hopefully you're not asking him to do cardiac surgery on you."

Even within the entertainment industry, lawyers specialize in certain areas. Some deal mostly in contracts, others in copyright law. Some lawyers specialize in music, some in film, some in television, and some in live performances. Joel's firm, Greenberg Traurig, has nearly ninety lawyers working in seven offices internationally in the entertainment branch of the firm.

Don't feel like you have to hire a Joel Katz right off the bat. When you're starting out, it's more important to have an attorney with enough time to deal with your issues. That could be someone on staff in a big firm, or maybe it's someone who has only a few clients but still has the knowledge you need. For an aspiring artist, the key factor is choosing a lawyer who cares about your needs and will give you the necessary face time.

MAKE SURE YOUR LAWYER SPECIALIZES IN THE MUSIC INDUSTRY.

Because so much of the music industry is built on contracts, music lawyers are often some of the best-connected people in the business. "Usually, the attorney is pretty wired and connected to managers, record companies, agencies, and publicists because they're dealing with them for their other clients," Joel says, "so they could help you in that world about which you're not knowledgeable." Attorneys can help you secure and negotiate your recording contract and your publishing contract. They might even introduce you to potential managers and help you interview them.

When you hire your lawyer, Joel says, the two of you need to outline precisely the lawyer's duties in writing. "That sounds basic," he says, "but many times attorneys are doing things for the clients that the clients don't know about, and they get a bill at the end of a month or two and get crazed.

"Young clients have less money to spend than superstars with millions of dollars to spend, and one thing they want to do is to keep that money. They need to make sure the engagement of the attorney is very clear as to what they want their attorney to do."

Additionally, Joel says, the artist and the attorney need to be clear about how the attorney will be paid, and the artist needs to make provisions for the payment.

"Some lawyers will spec time, where they bill you for the time but don't expect it to be paid until the transaction is closed," he says. "Some lawyers will take a percentage of income for a period of years when you sign a contract with them. You'll sign a three- or four-year contract with a lawyer because the first year or two may generate very little money, but hopefully it will grow. Some lawyers negotiate the ways they'll be paid—less during the younger periods in an artist's career and more through the hopefully richer times."

PUBLICISTS

You want the world to know about your talent, and publicists let the world know. They get your name and music to the public through the media. They'll help you craft your story and create your image. A publicist is rarely going to be the first person on your team. You, your manager, or one of your band members usually will have to wear that hat at the start.

In the beginning, publicists will do advance press for your regional gigs, getting listings, photos, and articles in local papers so that people will know about your concerts and show up. They'll also focus on cities where record labels are located, to get a buzz going on your act so you'll draw interest from the labels.

Many record labels have staff publicists who will work most closely with you when you have a new album coming out. A record company publicist's first allegiance is to the label, and they'll be working every other act on the roster at the same time they're working you. So at some point, you may also want to hire an independent publicist who'll devote more time to you.

Publicists each have their specialties. Some work with artists from specific genres—like

Photo courtesy of Trey Fanjoy

George Strait and Trey Fanjoy reviewing a video of "The Seashores of Old Mexico"

country, indie rock, or hip-hop. Others arrange press around a tour. Some have especially good relationships with national publications or television bookers—perhaps you'll hire one of those if you're convinced you're ready to play *The Tonight Show* or be featured in *USA Today*. Others specialize in crisis management and will handle media requests in the event of a scandal, an arrest, or a tragedy.

Some publicists are real bulldogs, pressing reporters for coverage; others act more as a layer of protection around an artist who doesn't like to talk much. George Strait, for instance, does interviews only rarely; he would never want someone hustling to place magazine articles and schedule photo shoots.

Usually, you'll negotiate a flat monthly fee to hire a publicist to work a set length of time—around a tour, for instance, or in the months just before and just after an album's release.

BUSINESS MANAGERS

My business manager, Gary Haber (who also serves as Carrie Underwood's business manager), has a great description of business managers. "We're a Rent-a-CFO," he says. "It's like outsourcing all your accounting and financial functions to a third party who's a member of the team.

"The last thing an artist is going to want to do is hire accountants and bookkeepers and oversee that operation. Most artists don't have the ability to oversee financial operations. So when you hire a business manager, you get a bookkeeper, you get an account manager who is the day-to-day representative, you can get an accountant who does tax returns and financial statements, and you get the chief financial officer who's the head of the organization and analyzes the numbers to make sure that everything works.

"In our organization—not necessarily in every organization—we have an in-house royalty department, so we're able to analyze agreements and statements."

Gary recommends an artist get a business manager "the minute they sign a record deal or a publishing deal, even though the income may not justify it." Business managers typically receive a 5 percent commission on an artist's income.

TOUR MANAGERS

If you tour much at all, you'll need a tour manager pretty early in your career. Your tour manager is the person who ensures that you get to where you are going and have everything that you need on the road.

The tour manager will advance all your dates, which means he gets a list of the gigs that are confirmed. He will provide your booking agency with a rider of your needs—which, at the beginning, will be very few. He will ensure that the venue has received the rider and complies with it. He will book all the travel arrangements for a tour. He will make sure there's enough time to get to the gig, that the band has time to eat, that the singer has time to rest her voice before the show. He'll also act as the buffer between the artist and fans, radio people, or any other business contacts in each market.

YOUR TOUR MANAGER IS THE PERSON WHO ENSURES THAT YOU HAVE EVERYTHING YOU NEED ON THE ROAD.

A lot of managers come from tour-manager backgrounds. I encourage new artists, when they're interviewing road managers, to look for observant, open-minded people. Tour managers have to be detail-oriented, but if they can see the big picture, they can make a big difference for you. You want somebody who notices if there's a buzz happening in a certain region or if merchandise sales are at an all-time high because of a certain T-shirt design. If they're just in it to travel and be near the artist, they're not going to look at your career as a business. You want somebody who's perceptive and hungry enough to help you grow your business.

STYLISTS/HAIR AND MAKEUP

Stylists and hair-and-makeup artists help acts develop their image, from the cut of their hair to the clothes they wear for photo shoots and awards shows. "Usually, the record label person will find us and say, 'We want her to look like this, but we don't want her to look like that,'" says hair-and-makeup artist Debbie Dover. "You listen to the artists and what they say they like, and then be honest with them. We all think we look different than we do, and our friends tell us we look fabulous. That's what's good about having a wardrobe stylist—they can really bring out the best in someone's figure."

You probably won't have a stylist until you have a record deal or land on TV, but it's not a bad idea to hire one to help you shop for a few key outfits for your shows or for an early photo shoot. As verbal descriptions can cause misunderstandings, feel comfortable sharing with your stylist images of style, hair, and makeup that you like. If you are a jock, a true cowboy, or a budding fashionista, that's helpful information to share. Always stress what shape you think works best for your body, and start from there. Stylists do tend to be on the cutting edge of fashion trends, but if you look awful in an A-line dress, the "it" dress with that silhouette won't be what's best for you no matter how great Kate Moss looks in it. These people will become some of your best friends, so the more honesty you give them, the better the outcome will be.

FAN CLUB MANAGERS

It may seem silly to think of having a fan club manager early in your career, but if you're on MySpace or your music is getting a buzz somewhere, you want someone who can stay in contact with your early believers.

A manager is probably not going to help run your fan club. She has too much other work that needs her attention. Many artists find an enthusiastic fan with organizational skills to run their fan club. Whoever you get, make sure it's someone you know well and trust. That person should like you as a human being, not just as a performer. He shouldn't be prone to gossip, and he should have a knack for positive interaction with people and be able to make new friends easily. This person will represent you to your fans, so you want him to run the fan club in a way that will make you proud.

A good fan club manager will grow and nurture your fan base. She can tell fans when you'll be touring in their area—having that person can be the difference between a half-empty club and a sold-out show. She can also make some merchandise decisions, whether it's picking T-shirt designs or handling order fulfillment.

Fan club managers for young acts often don't get paid—many are willing to work out of sheer enthusiasm, for access to the artist, and for the thrill and the pride of having insider status. It's nice, though, if you can find a way to monetize what they do, perhaps paying them a commission on merchandise orders placed through your Web site if they make sure the orders go out in a timely fashion. Having an energetic, well-organized fan club manager can truly make a difference in your career, whether it's leading to a record deal or selling your own CDs. It's more important than you might think.

PERSONAL ASSISTANTS

When the time comes to get a personal assistant, it'll be a matter of necessity, not status. If you have one too early, then I think you have a diva lurking inside of you.

The more successful an artist is, the greater the demands placed on her. At a certain point—perhaps when an artist has multi-platinum status—a PA isn't a fancy extravagance, it's the part of a team that makes the artist's personal life manageable.

Personal assistants handle everything outside the business. They manage the personal life between the business commitments—personal travel arrangements, dinners, birthday gifts, perhaps even child help. If your church asks you to help with a fund-raiser, your personal assistant can handle that in conjunction with management. If you want to support a friend of yours who's touring or appearing in a film, they help remind you of your personal commitments. They stay informed about the business because you can make some big mistakes if everybody's not in sync.

If you're a Carrie Underwood, you may need an assistant before the show ends. But if you're not winning a major TV contest, you're not going to need a personal assistant for years. When you're in a building phase, you have to save your pennies. You never know how long that phase of your career will last. Hiring a PA just because the big stars do is not a wise decision.

CHAPTER 14

NEW CAREER STRATEGIES: THE FUTURE'S WIDE OPEN

If you follow the music industry in the press, you've seen doom-and-gloom stories about how music sales have fallen, record companies have had to lay off workers, and peer-to-peer file-sharing has wrecked the industry. It's true that the industry faces chaotic times, but where some people see confusion, others see opportunities.

For decades, an artist who wanted to be successful had to get the attention of a record label, get that label to sign her, then get on the radio in order to sell records. There were some variations in that story line—it was truer for country music than it was for, say, heavy metal—but that's pretty much the way it played out for everybody.

That story line, however, is less true now than it has been at any time since the 1950s. For this brief time at least, the music industry has become a wide-open frontier. New rules need to be written, new business models await, and new paths lie ready for discovery. Every week brings developments in technology, new alliances for music distribution, and great concepts to help people discover music to love. CD sales may be down, but music is more popular and more pervasive than ever.

"These rigid boundaries we had to work within for so many years are dissolving," says producer David Malloy. "What's happening is like two big dinosaurs fighting each other. They both look like they're going to fall, but it's all in slow motion. In the meantime, we're trying to slip in and out between them and make a living while we wait to see what's going to happen when they hit the ground."

FOR THIS BRIEF TIME AT LEAST, THE MUSIC INDUSTRY HAS BECOME A WIDE-OPEN FRONTIER.

Manager Carol Peters says today's climate reminds her of when she first got into the business, back in 1964. "Most folks who ran small labels sold albums and singles out of the backs of their cars," she says. "You had Capitol, Columbia, and RCA—those were the big three. All the other things that were really happening were happening locally. Motown broke artists in Detroit. Fantasy Records was based in San Francisco—that's where Creedence Clearwater Revival launched. Mushroom Records signed Heart out of Seattle, and they did that whole local thing."

Some new acts use their recordings as loss leaders—if they sell CDs, that's great, but they don't count on making money from them. They'll often give tunes away for free, enticing people to take a chance on their music with a goal of getting them to buy tickets to a concert and, while they're at the show, buy some merchandise.

"More and more, I'm no longer in the music business; I'm in the live touring business," Carol says. "You had better know how to play your instrument so that every time you walk into a place, people will say, 'That was so much fun I'm going to come back and bring my friends.' Because if you can't do it live, you can't do it."

When Carol thinks about how bands will break in the future, she looks at the examples of independent singer/songwriters like Bright Eyes and Ani DiFranco, who've sold hundreds of thousands of albums and built large, devoted followings without ever making much of an impact on radio or mainstream media. "These are people who just plowed the fields where they lived, away from the limelight, away from SoundScan," she says.

Some people think the days of the superstar artist—the time when a Mariah Carey, a Michael Jackson, a Garth Brooks, or a U2 could sell 10 million copies of an album—are gone completely. They predict that stars will come from different circles—whether genre-oriented like hip-hop or country, or medium-driven like radio or MySpace—but they'll rarely become as ubiquitous, as universally famous, as superstars of the past.

I would bet my career that something huge *will* break in the next ten years, but for right now, everything's changing. It's as though the dam of the old formula has broken, creating several different streams. Everybody's watching to see which one will eventually turn into a river, but any of the streams will take people where they want to go.

"It is a more confusing time than ever for aspiring artists," says Heart's Nancy Wilson. "The industry is shifting and mutating and redefining itself quickly.

"Record companies are no long investing in the development of artists. It's become so disposable that there's already a backlash. You can feel the groundswell in the new music that's coming from the underground, from the grassroots level. It's exciting nowadays, and that's why I would suggest to anyone who loves music and really wants to work and live music to stick to their music and start small.

"And there's a whole new world coming together that's visual as well as musical. When you have such groundbreaking viewership for things like YouTube, and bands are breaking out from that homegrown kind of place, it's such a refreshing change from the corporate flaked-and-formed, spoon-fed art. It's refreshing and probably the next big thing—real people at home can be good musicians or good songwriters and maybe even put together something visual as a calling card. They don't necessarily have to show their big, beautiful mugs onscreen; they just need the vibe of the music or something that's a stamp."

It's a scary time, to be sure, but also very exciting. More artists have greater opportunities to find audiences than they've ever had before. We'll look at a few of those opportunities, but don't limit yourself to these. Whether you enter a TV contest, license a song for a commercial, or sing the national anthem at a baseball game, do whatever you can. You never know what's going to work.

THE INTERNET: WORLDWIDE FROM YOUR LIVING ROOM

New artists once had to build their audiences show by show, city by city, until they developed enough of a following in one or two regions of the country that they started to draw national attention. That's still a component of career development—the country acts in Texas, for instance, have mastered it—but, today, the Internet allows you to expose your music worldwide with just a few strokes of your computer keyboard. Through sites like MySpace, Facebook, GarageBand (http://www.garageband.com), and PureVolume, bands can bypass traditional distribution channels and find fans hundreds of miles away without ever leaving their hometowns. That's a dramatic development that once was unimaginable.

THE INTERNET ALLOWS YOU TO EXPOSE YOUR MUSIC WORLDWIDE WITH JUST A FEW STROKES OF YOUR COMPUTER KEYBOARD.

"Everyone knew that a change was coming," says Don Was, who produces new music for a site called MyDamnChannel, "but I don't think anyone could have foreseen something this dramatic."

"You could see the seeds of something happening ten years ago, that people were missing the boat. I remember going to a meeting with the chairman of EMI Worldwide around 1996, saying, 'I don't know what the Internet is going to do, but let's start up a little company within EMI that explores marketing through it.' And he said, 'I'm not in the business of selling records on the Internet; I'm in the business of selling records at Tower Records.' I think that was the prevailing attitude."

The Internet has empowered thousands of aspiring artists to record their own songs and post them online, in the hope of finding an audience for them. Some, like OK Go and Colbie Caillat, have used the Internet as a launching pad for successful careers. But there's a lot of music out there, and most of it sounds the same. The more creative and unique you are, the better your chances of succeeding.

A&R people, music supervisors, and casting directors really look for talent on MySpace and those kinds of Web sites. If I'm hired as a music supervisor for a music-driven film, the producer may need a real singer to be in the film. If they need an upcoming, undiscovered singer, I turn not only to my friends that I respect in the business, but also to MySpace.

My interns use it even more than I do. For example, I've been creating a TV show with John Wayne's granddaughter, Jennifer Wayne, called *It's All in the Genes.* It's about descendants of famous people who also sing and write songs. I had Jennifer Wayne and a woman who was kin to Daniel Boone, and I needed a third girl. Obviously, I wanted her to have talent before I put her in the show, so I told my intern, Parker Welling, "I need a female under thirty-five with some kind of famous family heritage, and I need her to be a singer/songwriter." I turned the interns loose on MySpace. They sent me all kinds of links, and I looked at every one. That's how I found Tayla Lynn, Loretta Lynn's granddaughter. Her MySpace page looked great, and I loved her music. She's a bit of Loretta-meets-Gretchen Wilson, with a dash of Kelly Willis.

Colbie Caillat used MySpace to launch her career. At one point, she was the most-played unsigned musician on the site, thanks to her song "Bubbly." She didn't do well during her *American Idol* audition, but she found MySpace the perfect outlet for her music.

"It's being able to have people fall in love with your songs and relate to what you're singing about and writing about," Colbie says. "If they relate to it, they know that you've gone through the same thing they're going through. It just connects people."

Colbie had a friend help her set up her MySpace music page in February 2005.

"My friend added a few of his friends, and when I had my songs up there, people would add my songs to their pages. Then, when people would go to their pages, they'd hear my song. It just kept spreading by people adding my songs to their pages.

"We'd post bulletins that said I had a show in Hollywood or in Iowa, wherever I was. People would come to the shows, and I'd meet them, take pictures with them, and try to show them that I was just this normal girl. I would upload songs when they weren't even finished, and I'd send out bulletins asking people what they thought of them. People would write messages back, explaining what they liked about the songs and what the songs meant to them."

Working with her friend Stacy Blue, Colbie put up new music or new content every week or two, "just to keep giving them something new and interesting to come back to," she says. They'd send bulletins asking friends' opinions of new songs and respond to fans' posts on Colbie's page. MySpace became almost an obsession for her.

"When I woke up, I'd check it, and when I came home from work, I'd check it," Colbie says. "Then, after I went out with my friends, I'd come home at midnight and spend two or three hours on it. It's addicting, reading messages. When people send you messages, it makes you want to keep upgrading your page and giving them new stuff."

Colbie consciously steered clear of trying to monetize the traffic on her page. She didn't sell T-shirts or demo CDs. "That's like being a salesman," she says, "and you want people to find it on their own.

"Some people post comments or send mass e-mails, saying, 'Come listen to my music,' but people don't want to be bugged like that. Don't try promoting it, but keep your fans involved and ask them questions about everything. Keep it personal and let them see the real side of you because they enjoy knowing that you're just like them."

Just as Colbie built her audience by posting her music online, other acts have gained online followings for their videos. Tens of millions of people, for instance, have visited YouTube to watch OK Go's single-take video for "Here It Goes Again," which featured the band performing a complicated dance routine on rented treadmills. That video took a lot of work, but it cost almost nothing to make.

The explosion of online video sites like YouTube and Google Video recalls the early days of MTV, another time when a new medium opened the doors for bands who never would've had a chance at radio. Some record companies have used these sites to generate interest in their bands. Other people have gotten hundreds of thousands of views simply by singing other people's songs in front of walls in their houses.

Don't expect that climate to last too long, says video director Trey Fanjoy. While anybody with a digital camera, some editing software, and some imagination may be able to find an audience online, Trey says imagination is the key ingredient.

"If they're going to try to create their own videos, they should lean toward creating clips that are innovative," says Trey, who has directed videos for Keith Urban, Alan Jackson, Five for Fighting, Miranda Lambert, and others. "Those are the ones that get attention. In this day and age, anybody with a laptop and a camera is posting themselves with a guitar singing on YouTube, so it's almost a waste.

"If you're going to take that step to try to create something that people are going to talk about, it needs to be interesting and innovative and not just a performance-type clip. And if it is a performance, then it possibly should be some kind of live performance where the magic really happens. But it shouldn't be just you alone in a room with a guitar because the Internet is saturated with that."

Of course, pervasiveness is no substitute for quality. Colbie Caillat got more plays on MySpace than any other unsigned artist not because she was all over the site but because people identified with her music and decided they couldn't live without hearing it again. It doesn't matter how many places you put your music if nobody decides they love it. The hardest thing you'll do is get loads of fans. Once you have them, though, your life changes.

GETTING IN SYNC

More than ever, television, film, and commercials have become ways to break music. I probably get five calls a week from songwriters wanting to know how they can get their music into a film or onto a network TV show. From *Grey's Anatomy* and Apple's iPod commercials to smaller cable shows, sync licenses have become big business. And because of the wide variety of dramatic needs for the stories that film and TV tell, music of all types is benefiting.

There are middlemen who don't even work on movies who'll tell a songwriter, "I can get your song in this movie, but you have to give me a piece of your publishing." It's one thing to give a network your publishing on a song they use, but a middleman certainly doesn't deserve it, not unless they're part of a true publishing company with a track record of placing songs in movies and television. But independent middlemen deserve a percentage of the fees—and that's all.

As we discussed in an earlier chapter, you can approach some music supervisors directly with your music. You'll want to be cautious when doing this, so here are some tips for personally approaching executives like me with your music:

1. Do your homework before you make an approach. What is the subject matter of the film, commercial, or TV series? In what era/time period is it set? What part of the world is it set in? Does the supervisor need original songs or standards?
2. Be specific with your pitch. Don't state that you have a "song perfect for films"—there is no such thing. I always have a tempo, an emotional slant, or a genre in mind during my search.

3. Send two or three great songs appropriate for a specific project. They should have a feel similar to other songs that are being used, or are intended for use, in the project. (We often state our needs on our Web sites or in trade publications.)
4. Write the contact information for clearing the sync and the master recording on the CD and the CD cover, or in the e-mail containing the mp3. Keep in mind that we receive thousands of CDs and mp3s. We might lose the CD cover or even the CD once we upload it into our computers. I highly recommend including the accurate song title, the songwriter, and artist name, plus a contact number either in the "album" or "genre" columns when encoding the information on your computer. Make clearing your music as easy as possible.
5. Don't call to check whether we plan to use it. We will find you when we want to clear a song. Your call won't influence our decision; it will merely slow us down.
6. Use peers to make a follow-up call or introduction. Whether through a performing-rights organization, a publisher, an agent, an attorney, or a manager, find a common bond.
7. Make great music, play live, invite the press, and create a buzz. Remember: we are heat-seeking missiles.
8. Keep your Web site and MySpace page up to date. Post new music, press clippings, and photos every few weeks.

Just because you've sent your music to a supervisor doesn't mean it will find its way into a movie. It doesn't even mean the supervisor will listen to it. "If I'm a music supervisor, I'm getting bombarded with so much music I barely have time to listen to all the stuff the producer's telling me he needs me to get," says publisher Michael Pizzuto. "I'm trying to clear stuff someone else is telling me they need. But hopefully, I'll have some time to listen to the things people I know and trust send me."

But if you *don't* send your music to supervisors, you can be sure it won't get heard. And every once in a while, some combination of quality and sheer luck means somebody catches a break.

"I get spammed all the time by artists who get my e-mail address and send me their tracks or links to their MySpace pages," Michael says. "Recently, somebody out of nowhere e-mailed me saying he was an artist and wanted me to hear his music. I liked what he wrote—he wasn't bragging, he wasn't hyping his music, he was very humble—so I contacted the guy. That's rare, but it can happen. It's very random—I just happened to be at my desk, and his message came in while I was checking my e-mails.

"Artists should know who they're targeting. If it's, say, Alex Patsavas—whose Chop Shop Music Supervision has done shows like *Grey's Anatomy*, *The OC*, and *Gossip Girl*—they should know a little about what she likes. With a little research on the Web, they can find out the shows she does, get an idea of what her tastes are, and send her an e-mail asking whether she'd be interested in hearing their music.

"It's all about the letter you write, I think. You want it to be sincere and not hyping yourself, saying you're the greatest thing that ever happened. I get elaborate flyers all the time from bands that say too much and don't back it up. It's much more effective to say less and send one great song."

If you have a publisher, make sure they're taking advantage of these opportunities for you. If not, don't be afraid to take matters into your hands (politely, of course). Sometimes, it pays off.

CUTTING OUT THE MIDDLEMAN

In recent years, superstar acts have started signing deals to sell new music exclusively through one retailer—Garth Brooks and the Eagles cut deals directly with Wal-Mart. Paul McCartney and James Taylor signed with Starbucks' record label. Some retailers have now begun to work with lesser known, even previously unsigned, artists, hoping to break an act and share in the success.

These exclusive deals have benefits to both the artist and the retailers. A primary one, obviously, is exclusivity. If you wanted to buy the Eagles' *Long Road Out of Eden*, you had to go to a Wal-Mart or a Sam's Club to do it, and the people who run those companies hope you needed some socks or sodas while you were there.

There are also economic advantages. Artists get to put more of the price of the album into their pockets than they would if they had a record company acting as a middleman. Since the artists make more money, they can give the retailer a better deal on the cost of the music. Retailers then make a profit when they sell the music or make it more appealing to the customer by selling it at a lower price. Additionally, with large companies like Wal-Mart or Starbucks, the retailer often does what's called a one-way buy, meaning that they buy a pre-determined number of CDs at a certain price—say, two million CDs at $3.50 apiece for a top act. The artist pockets seven million dollars up front without having to worry about any of the CDs being returned, and the retailer gets a steep discount on the CDs' per-piece cost.

For years, bands have started their own labels to sell their music. Working with a retailer like Wal-Mart or Starbucks gives them additional commercial clout while avoiding the maze of record companies and distribution.

When Alana Grace's Columbia Records album *Break the Silence* didn't sell as she had hoped, the singer/songwriter and actress took matters into her own hands. Now she concentrates on developing an online audience for her music, and she has signed a deal to sell her music exclusively through Wal-Mart.

"It's really about getting out in front of people and making sure you have an online presence," says Alana, whose song "Black Roses Red" was included in the 2005 movie *Sisterhood of the Traveling Pants.* "Not only do I have my own Web site, I've started putting more time into doing MySpace, Facebook, and GarageBand. I'm on Fuzz.com and Last.fm, and people can listen to full versions of several of my songs on Facebook and Apple's iLike.

"I enter myself in contests online, which gets you heard by more people. I've done mostly Internet submission contests, and I got an honorable mention for New York Songwriting Circle and Track of the Day from GarageBand. I'm constantly trying to get my music in TV and movies—that's kind of the new radio.

"I've started to work with Wal-Mart—actually Anderson Merchandising. They want to put out two six-track EPs every year. They're buying them one way. Wal-Mart buys the product, and I can give them whatever product I want.

"When my EP comes out, I'm going to hire an Internet publicist and a normal publicist to make sure I'm out there with other people, trying to be seen, getting on tours, and getting freelance radio promoters to get me on radio in smaller markets. In time, I hope, it'll grow and I'll be in bigger markets. It really is baby steps, and there is no overnight solution. But if you have the right team, I think you can do it."

Like most independent artists, Alana has to wear a lot of hats. "People are surprised by how much time it takes," she says. "I write every day to keep in practice, and I sing as much as possible. It also takes time to blog, to shoot video blog footage and edit that, and to answer all the messages and comments from people. It's really about figuring out new ways of doing things and making sure you're on every site."

WHAT'S NEXT?

Where things are headed in the music business over the next few years is anybody's guess. The only thing certain is that the industry is changing rapidly—so rapidly it may not settle for years, if ever.

"Music and intellectual-property transmission with games, television, and film is going to change the world of our business economically and fundamentally, making it easier for consumers to listen to, communicate with, and be involved in the lifestyle of the stars they love," says attorney Joel Katz.

Joel looks for handset manufacturers to become more prominent players in the near future. "When you start thinking about how many consumers these handset manufacturers are in business with and have data about, it's extraordinary," he says. "And they're global companies, which could eliminate any need for geography. Right now, music is distributed geographically. An American act will come out in America, and music will be licensed to different territories. But what will happen is communities will be set up, like a James Taylor community, through the use of telephones. Those communities will not be geographically bound; they'll be set up all over the world."

While some people think large record companies may disappear altogether, Joel doesn't believe that will happen. He does think, however, that their future role will be much different from their present one. "I don't think record labels are going to be extinct; I just think they're going to have different functions," he says. "I don't think they'll be extinct because labels have huge catalogs of music they've acquired or created during the years, and they also have the wherewithal to promote you.

"The question becomes how should I be promoted—on YouTube, through Facebook, through radio, through extraterrestrial radio? Should I do something completely nuts that gets me promoted? How do I promote myself and create my image as an artist, and how do I get my work to as large a body of consumers as possible so I can fundamentally create a monetary transaction that works for me? That's it.

IF YOU CONSIDER YOURSELF A TRAILBLAZER, THE INDUSTRY'S CURRENT STATE SHOULD EXCITE YOU.

"I think there are going to be so many ways to do this that it will be different for different artists. What do I mean by that? If you're a country artist, you may want to use two or three different vehicles. If you're a rock artist, you might use a different vehicle. If you are a reggae artist, you may have a thoroughly different type of vehicle.

"Also I think large companies are starting to use music to sell their products, companies like Corona, a beer company that's very interested in lifestyle. Coca-Cola has been doing this for years. Companies who engage in certain lifestyle behaviors are now using the demographic of a particular artist such as a Kenny Chesney or a Madonna and figuring out how to take that lifestyle that people want to emulate to the same group of people who go to those concerts or buy those recordings."

There's never been one path to stardom for aspiring musicians. These days, it seems like nobody's even sure where the paths are anymore. If you consider yourself a trailblazer, the industry's current state should excite you. But if you hope someone will carry you down the path, then you're in for a very bumpy ride.

TOM GATES:
THE ALL-IMPORTANT STREET TEAM

Tom Gates of Nettwerk Music Group is an artist manager who works with acts including Brand New, The Format, MC Lars, and Jay Brannan. Tom specializes in street teams and shares some of his insights below.

"Street team" is a term that's abused quite a bit. A good definition of a street team is a mobilized group of core fans of your artist—that's a major-label description. What it really means is an artist directly reaching out and touching his or her fans, and in return, the fans do things to help the career of that artist grow.

The easiest way to start is on MySpace or Facebook, just messaging all the people who like your music. The most important thing is not acting generically—you should actually write e-mails directly to your supporters and try not to employ a cut-and-paste mentality. When that becomes unmanageable (which it always does if you're any good), you will have to branch out from the MySpace/Facebook world and create your own dedicated street team plan.

I created my own tool to manage the teams, but if you're a young artist who doesn't have a big management company behind you, there are services available for you to cultivate your e-mail list and manage your team. They're a Google search away. Once you are set up and getting members to join your team, simply come up with initiatives for your team to take on, as well as ways in which you can reward them. Early on, you shouldn't play a show without meeting every kid who has done something for you in that market. For example, if you book a show in Ann Arbor and you know there are ten strong supporters there, do something with them when you get to town. It can be as simple as grabbing pizza with them or inviting them backstage. It's important that you always try to take care of those initial ten fans, even if you're playing the Ann Arbor Enormodome three years later. If you super-serve the first ten thousand people on your street team, you can still maintain some credibility, even if you're a pop star.

(cont.)

We manage Sarah McLachlan, and early on she didn't have a street team per se, but she had a fan club item called *Murmurs*—complete with a special CD just for the people who really helped get the word out about her. This was before the Internet, so it was a physical disc that was mailed out to people. It was a series of rarities and b-sides—she did several of them. Not only would this core group of fans have done anything to get on that mailing list, they were also the people who were incredibly vocal and supportive of her early career. This concept is quite easy to take into the digital age, and many people have.

Brand New and The Format have huge street teams. We have a little world on The Format's site called The Living Room, where fans can hang out. That's another effective idea, to create the street team's own space on your Web site where you can have rarities, b-sides, live versions, and message boards. We even have a section called "Dear Nate," a Q&A with the singer just for street team members. Monitoring the street team section is quite a bit of work, but it's also a true community, if you build it correctly.

You should start cultivating your street teams from day one. You can do it easily on your MySpace just by adding friends, but you should always make sure you have your own e-mail list going on, too. Simple contests are excellent ways to build your list. There are a million different contests that you can imagine, and you should try the ones that you feel fit your style. Even a prize as (relatively) inexpensive as an iPod Nano can garner up to ten thousand new e-mail addresses. Take it a step further and preload your songs into the Nano and send it, autographed, to a contest winner. Those are ways to build your list, and your mailing list will always be your best friend when it comes to sharing information.

Right before The Format went on a tour, we started a street team contest where teamers could pick ten out of fifteen helpful tasks, which they could do over the course of a few weeks. Tasks included handing out flyers, promoting the tour on their MySpace page through bulletins, and even covering one of the band's songs on YouTube. The buzz that resulted helped it become one of their first sellout headline tours. The band met with the winners of this contest at every tour stop, often taking them on the bus for some serious Guitar Hero hang time. You just can't beat the good will that is created if you support your fans just as much as they support you. Given the opportunity, they'll be there for you every time.

There are so many examples of incredible things that kids have done for the bands I've worked with. We had one kid in Colorado who was a fan of Brand New who asked the pastor of his church if he could change the sign out front for a day. He wrote his pastor a letter about how the band had been a positive force in his life and how he wanted to help spread the word for them. So for a day in front of this church we had this little letterbox that said Brand New was appearing at the local venue. That's a promotion you couldn't even dream up.

Always be clear, though, that other people shouldn't be doing anything illegal on your behalf. Our worst nightmare is a kid putting flyers in devious places or going above and beyond by spray-painting the band's name on a police station. Always remember to set boundaries for just how far your fans can go!

A few other guidelines to keep in mind:

Do's:

★ Know your audience. What would motivate your specific audience, as opposed to Kenny G's?

★ Make sure that your members feel special and get the inside scoop first. Got a camera in the studio? Give your teamers a special YouTube link of their own.

★ Offer incentives for hard work (special ticket prices, special hang time—heck, play their living room!).

★ As an artist, always make sure you are involved and that everything has your seal of approval. Keep a direct connection with the people who help you.

★ Have contests. People love contests—no kidding.

★ Join every street team you can find. You'll snag tons of ideas.

(cont.)

Don'ts:

- ★ Don't e-blast fans too much! You're just asking for people to bail.
- ★ Don't forget that your teamers in Fiji are not going to care about promoting your show in Nebraska. Focus on each region individually.
- ★ Don't charge money for street team members. These people are helping you for free. Ripping them off is evil.
- ★ Don't forget to try new things. It's the strangest idea that always connects.
- ★ Don't forget that your first thousand fans are always your most important.

CHAPTER 15

YOUR NEXT STEP . . . AND BEYOND

BE CAREFUL WHAT YOU WISH FOR

When people watch the entertainment tabloid shows or read magazines in the grocery-store checkout lines, they don't see the reality. They see beautiful people looking happy.

If you want to know the life of a musician, think of a truck driver or an airline pilot—that's the amount of traveling you'll be doing. And are those professions glamorous? Not particularly.

After ten years, you might travel first class. After fifteen, you might travel in your own G4. But very few people ever get to do that. And before you ever get to first class, you're likely to spend years jammed into a car, an RV, or a van of questionable quality, schlepping from one little town to the next, hoping you'll make enough money from the seven dollars cover to pay for the gas to the next town. Some nights you pay the band. Some nights nobody gets paid. On a good night, you'll pocket fifty bucks and some free beer.

After the show, you don't relax with celebrities in the VIP area of an exclusive club. If you're smart, you're signing autographs and talking with every fan who wants a little face time. After that, you're back in the van, heading for the next town, hoping for a full house and more than fifty bucks this time.

After you get your record deal, you might fly to radio stations where you perform in a conference room with pizza on the table for five people who barely listen to you, on the off chance they might decide to play your single. You do that again and again, until the faces and names all start to run together. But you have to keep them straight because if you don't remember their names the next time you see them, they might take the slight personally, and then you'll make the challenge of getting your song on their station even more difficult.

IF YOU NEED TO PLANT YOUR ROOTS IN ONE PLACE, THIS PROFESSION IS NOT FOR YOU.

You're a gypsy. You travel 80 percent of your life. If you need roots, this profession is not for you.

There's also a lot of expense. Before you get your team in place, you're in charge of figuring out how to buy your equipment, fund your performances, and pay for your travel. At the beginning, you're going to be your own business manager, booking agent, and tour manager. Be glad if you took business courses in school—they'll come in handy. So will your psychology class, as you try to figure out how to keep a broke band happy and prevent them from going to another artist who can pay more. You're scraping together every penny, working to keep your musicians happy, and trying to sound your best and develop your material.

One thing I like about talent contests is they help singers learn covers. Most people shouldn't play unfamiliar original songs for an entire show, or they'll be playing to empty rooms. Familiar material helps keep an audience's attention. If you perform covers with a new approach, giving them your own sound, you'll practically create a new song that's a crowd pleaser, too. That's one similarity between the contests and real life—you have to win over a crowd, and you have to do it quickly. That's where charisma comes into play—some people ooze it from their pores, and some people don't. Some artists naturally connect with an audience; some don't.

When you start playing clubs, you'll find that some don't have dressing rooms and you wind up in a disgusting, dirty bathroom, fixing your hair in a stall with poor lighting. Your back will ache from carrying your gear, and if your string breaks, there's no guitar tech to fix it.

When you reach the middle of your career, there's maybe 10 percent music and glamour and 90 percent hard work. But at the beginning, there's zero glamour—all you get are great stories and amazing memories. "It's way better than when I used to move office furniture," Matt Nathanson says. "But it's also all I've got."

When people ask Matt for his advice on becoming a performing musician, he often tells them, "You've got to be smart enough to navigate and too stupid to stop."

WHEN YOU BECOME A STAR, LIFE IS NO LONGER SIMPLE.

Eventually, if you succeed, you deal with a different set of issues. Carrie Underwood values the times when she can stay at home long enough to buy a jug of milk and drink it all before it spoils in her refrigerator. At a certain point in his career, Kenny Chesney could trade his cowboy hat for a baseball cap and go most places he wanted, with the exception of malls, Wal-Marts, and Cracker Barrels. Just a couple years later, though, he couldn't go anywhere without causing a scene.

When you become a star, life is no longer simple. It takes humility, patience, planning, and the willingness to give up much of your privacy. You have to learn to be slow to anger, to endure insults and criticism from complete strangers without retaliating or letting it get to you, to deal with people taking the details of your personal life out of context, and to learn to accept criticism without letting it eat away at your soul.

"Fame sucks," says Scott Borchetta. "It sucks because everybody wants your time and attention, and you don't stay yourself if you're not grounded. I see people who wanted to be famous, and they're just shells—they're not real people.

"Being criticized constantly in tabloids and *People* magazine is absolutely demeaning. Unless you're powerful enough in your belief in yourself and your talent, if you can't ignore it and pretend it doesn't exist, then you're going to be miserable. You have to say, 'I've got my songs, I've got my fans, and I love doing this, so I don't care what you say. Actually, tell me again, because I'm going to do it better now. I believe in myself that much.'"

DON'T EQUATE "THE DEAL" WITH SUCCESS

A lot of bad deals get signed because artists just want to sign something. They get lonely and insecure, and they need some activity to give them a confidence boost. Even though you'll measure your progress by certain benchmarks—like a publishing deal or a record deal—don't jump at one just so you can say you've met that goal.

In art, as in tortoise/hare races, slow and steady wins. You don't have to come in to a music town planning to take over in a day. The people who are already there are looking for signs of persistence and endurance—after all, this is our *life*. We've spent a long time doing it, and we hope to spend a long time more. We've seen people come in and give up after a year even though almost nobody finds what they want that quickly. Frankly, we've got better things to do than spend time, energy, and money on someone who's going to give up when life gets tough. We didn't give up through our tough times; why should we want to invest in someone who might?

The worst thing you can do is put a timeline on your goals. You don't need to sign a publishing contract within four months. If you have only enough money to last six months, then give it six months. Then get a job and pursue your dream part-time. If you tell people you're giving yourself a year to "make it," you've just told them you're not in it for the long haul. This tells them that you might be more interested in fame than music.

REBA McENTIRE: STRIVE FOR BALANCE

Plan your career, but plan the fun times, also. If you don't have fun, that's when you'll resort to getting in trouble. If it's all work and no play, you're going to get rebellious, and you're going to start screwing up. You're going to hate it, you're going to resent it, and you're going to do things that will tick everybody off and ruin your career. Then you won't have those good people around anymore. So plan your work and plan your play.

WHEN "PLAN A" FAILS

We've made a big deal in this book about not having a Plan B, that back-up option in case your life doesn't work out the way you dreamed it. The brutal reality is this: most people who go into this business, even without a Plan B, will not succeed with their original Plan A.

Sometimes your Plan A evolves naturally as you do. At that point, you have a choice: should you keep pursuing your original dream, or should you follow a new course that feels more comfortable deep inside your soul?

When I think of our journeys toward success, I'm reminded of Bruce Lee paraphrasing an Eastern proverb in *Enter the Dragon*: "It's like a finger pointing a way to the moon. Don't concentrate on the finger, or you will miss all the heavenly glory." We can become so obsessed with our society-fueled preconceptions of success that we miss the beauty in our dreams.

At the beginning of this book, I said this book wasn't intended to give you a career checklist. Here's the kind I meant:

1. Get a publishing deal.
2. Get a record deal.
3. Get a manager.
4. Get an agent.
5. Buy a tour bus.
6. Have a hit single.
7. Sell a bunch of CDs.
8. Get hordes of screaming fans.
9. Get a platinum record.
10. Buy Mom a house.

If you must have a checklist, though, try this one instead:

1. Learn to play an instrument.
2. Sing.

3. Write or analyze why you like songs.
4. Sing.
5. Live.
6. Sing, and maybe write some songs.
7. Enjoy life.
8. Question your motives and direction.
9. Sing.
10. Buy Mom a house.

If we buy into society's standards, our definition of success can confuse our perception of our joy. After plenty of years of confusion, I finally started using what I call "a passion meter" as my internal radar. When I feel excited or happy or have a natural focus on a new project, that's when I know I'm on the right path. Money or status usually doesn't figure into it. Of course, realities come into play—sometimes I have to work on a "pay the bills" project, but I never lose focus on the passion project. So when life gets you confused, down, or distracted, use your passion as your compass.

If you have followed the traditional routes in the industry and you've failed, time and again, to get support from others in the industry—whether managers, publishers, or record labels—that could be a sign that you haven't found your voice, your song, or your sound. It could also be a sign that you're pursuing the wrong dream. If you get no response for years from anyone besides members of your family and the people who want to take your money, you're either not doing something right or you're totally on the wrong path.

There might come a day when you wonder if you should "give up your dream" of being a "star." If you eventually feel that strong pull away from your original dream, don't feel like a quitter. Richard Nixon said, "Defeat doesn't finish a man—quit does. A man is not finished when he's defeated. He's finished when he quits." I'd add one thing to Nixon's quote: Sometimes defeat is God's way of guiding you to your proper path.

Everything in your career might seem confusing when you're in the middle of it, but when you look back years later with 20/20 hindsight, it will start to make sense. Staying in the dance is half the race; the other half is good decision-making. God gave you your talents and your dreams—the experiences you gain from how you use them will prepare you for your ultimate career, whatever that is. It may be that original dream, it may be an alternative career in the entertainment industry, or it may be something completely different. Every so often, reality hits you in the face and makes you change your focus. If you start feeling a lot of doubts and everyone is telling you no, then your internal doubts are probably a good sign you should redirect or refocus your goals.

Most people naturally fall into other career paths by finding the specific focus within a general industry they really love—and just hadn't clearly defined for themselves. Many successful songwriters thought they wanted to be stars, but when that didn't work out, they focused on writing. I know literally dozens of people who started out as performers and wound up spending most of their careers doing something else. Some of them are songwriters; some are musicians. Others are producers, managers, publicists, A&R executives, journalists—the list goes on and on.

Pursue your dreams, but don't be so stubborn that you miss out on doing what you love because you're determined to do what you thought you wanted. It takes experience to determine what really motivates you. By stepping up to bat—even if you miss the ball time and again—you put yourself in the game. That's the only way to learn that hitting isn't your strength. Spotting talent might be your strength, so the revelation of becoming an agent hits you hard, and this curvy path leads you to success.

SO YOU THINK YOU WANT TO BE A STAR? **CYNDI THOMSON** ON THE DREAM VERSUS THE REALITY

Cyndi Thomson arrived on the country music scene in early 2001 with a delightful Southern accent and an album's worth of equally lovely songs. Her first single, "What I Really Meant to Say," reached Number One on the country charts, and two other singles made the Top 40. From the outside, it looked like a great start to a promising career. But even as her album, My World, *went gold, Thomson knew all was not right in her world. In fact, her dream was turning into her nightmare. In the fall of 2002, Thomson did what many singers consider the unthinkable: she decided to give up her recording career.*

In an open letter to her fans and the music industry, she wrote: "Being in the music business necessitates change in the life of a person in ways that can only be realized through experience. I made those changes to become successful.

"Now I have come to a crossroad," she continued. "The next step in my career would be to make a new album, thus making a commitment to see the project through with the many obligations that go along with it. I have now realized I cannot commit to those obligations. I love music; I love the way it makes me feel, but the timing is right for me to walk away from being a recording artist."

Thomson continued to write songs. She co-wrote Gary Allan's 2006 single "Life Ain't Always Beautiful," using her married name, Cyndi Goodman. And eventually, she began recording again. But Thomson's perspective on what being a star means would never be the same. Now she says:

"I never really imagined the life of a star when I was young. I had no real concept of "celebrity." All I knew was that I wanted to sing in front of people and I wanted to change lives. I had no concept of tour buses, radio, corporate decision-making, regional promotions, and sleep deprivation. I just had a true, pure desire to sing and perform at a different level.

"The problem with pursuing a career in the music industry is that from the outside you only see what the media portrays—the stars and the glamour. It saddens me because the misperception is that you need to be a star to do something grandiose and valid with your life. There's such a beauty in it to young girls, and it's marketed toward them, but it's a skewed image of reality. And when you're fifteen, you lack the wisdom and hindsight of a thirty-year-old to separate the fantasy from the reality.

"I don't think anybody could accurately depict the life of an artist to you over lunch or a cup of coffee, but it's just like anything else—the grass is always greener, and you simply have to walk in those shoes to understand the good and the bad. Don't get me wrong—I know that most people would kill for some of the opportunities I've been afforded. I get it, I really do. But the reality is, in this line of work, nobody really knows what they're getting themselves into.

"When it came time to make my first album, I was fortunate that Capitol Records involved me in the creative process. I had always had a vision for my album, and I was intensely focused on what the entire package would look like. Every ounce of my being wanted to get the album out to the public and then to work really hard on the road.

"I remember those first two years well, when life on the road was almost nonstop. It was exciting and new, and to some extent the lack of sleep I was getting simply made me more excitable. I was working hard and incredibly long hours, sometimes flying on three planes a day, shaking hundreds of hands. The problem, however, was that while I was pouring myself into my work and into other people, I was neglecting myself and my own need for balance.

"One minute I'd be wearing the most beautiful shoes on stage and having a wonderful performance, but in the next moment I might find myself backstage engaged in an argument with my manager. All the while I was missing the birthday parties, my nephews' little league games, dinner parties with friends. Sometimes it felt like the world was spinning forward without me. All anybody saw was the smile and all the glitter, and that I was getting the opportunity to sing the songs that I had written. It looked really great because there were lots of people around me to make it all appear pristine.

"I found it really hard to be what everybody else wanted me to be. I just felt spent. When you're going that hard for so long, it's like, 'Can I get some sleep so that I can be nice to people, so that I can do what you need me to do?' It was a reality check the first time I realized that it didn't matter to some people if I didn't sleep or that I was moving so fast that I'd forget to eat. The prevailing attitude always seemed to be, 'We have to keep the momentum going,' but it came off like, 'How dare you ask for time off?' Not everyone was that hard-core, but oftentimes there was a serious lack of balance and understanding.

(cont.)

"To me, it's self-defeating because I believe it's impossible to do your best work without maintaining some semblance of balance in every area of your life.

"It was extremely difficult for me to come to grips with the fact that I no longer enjoyed this career that I'd always aspired to. I'd never not wanted to be a singer.

"At the height of it all, I had the opportunity to appear on shows like *The Tonight Show* and *Live with Regis and Kelly*. My songs were performing well on the charts. Everything looked great. Inside, though, I felt like my dream was being crushed, in spite of the success. It was truly perplexing to me. For the first time in my life, I was bitterly unhappy, even though I was living out the dream I'd had since I was twelve. I had achieved many of my goals, and yet it didn't matter. Maybe it was just because I was so tired—I cannot begin to express to you just how tired I was. Every bone in my body ached. I cried myself to sleep every night. And I was so lonely.

"I don't know exactly what went wrong, or which straw broke the proverbial camel's back. It certainly didn't have anything to do with the fans, and it didn't have anything to do with the music. I was actually mourning all that. There was simply no balance in my life; I was not refilling my tank in any way. I knew that, in order to continue, I had to make some time for myself. I even began to despise music. I kept the radio off for a long time after that.

"I was immediately bombarded with phone calls—artists, executives, producers, and other people in my life—who all said to me, 'You do realize what you're doing?

"'You are giving up everything! You could be a millionaire within a couple of years!' But it was never about money from my perspective, and I felt like I had lost sight of the truly important things in life.

"I've always said that the music business is not for those who don't know who they are. By that I mean you really have to possess a strong sense of identity. When I first achieved some level of fame, I was so thankful that I knew who I was because these can be dangerous waters to tread. I was around twenty years old, but I believe I had such a great upbringing that the values my family instilled in me far outweighed the influences and temptations on the periphery. You have to be really secure with having it all or having nothing. You have to be able to be content with either situation.

"It has been difficult, since I stepped away, to attend certain industry functions and see the new women perform, and even some of my former peers who got their start around the same time as me. It makes me imagine what my career would have been like if I had stayed put. I have to admit, there is a slight sense of regret. But when I really lay it all out for consideration, I think, I probably wouldn't be married, I wouldn't have my beautiful daughter, and I wouldn't be as mentally sound as I am right now. I needed to be able to get back to the simpler things in life. I needed to clean my bathroom. I needed to bake cookies. I just needed to be normal.

"It may perplex people, but now I'm taking another shot at it, making my second record. Choosing to come back was both difficult and interesting. I spent several years weighing the possibility, prayerfully and cautiously considering the implications the decision would have on my family. When I was first signed to Capitol, I was a young girl who possessed this fantastic and crazy dream. At some level, I'm not sure that I really thought it would ever happen! There is no way to really prepare for this type of life; there's no internship, no class you can take. And sometimes it just happens really fast. When the success comes quickly, you had better be prepared to get thrown into the machine, operating at full tilt. But this time, I have no misgivings about what to expect. These days I have a healthy appreciation for the good qualities of the job and reasonable expectations about the not-so-great aspects of the life.

"Without trying to sound cheesy, I know we all have a destiny. We were all designed for something. I know some of you reading this book may even believe you were designed to be the next big thing. Maybe you are, and maybe you're not. In reality, the odds of that happening are very, very small. It reminds me of Simon Cowell—to all those people who really can't carry a tune, he would say: 'You are not supposed to be doing this. There's something else you're obviously supposed to be doing.'

"I talked to a lot of girls when I was on the road. They'd look at me with stars in their eyes and see my earrings and my shoes, and they'd say, 'I want to be you.' And I'd say, 'No, you need to be you.' I believe each of us has been created for a unique

(cont.)

task, that we all have a path in life. I hope that I can always be an encouragement to people to seek out their destiny, whatever that may be. So if you think you want to get into this business, first and foremost, make sure this is what you are meant to be doing with your life. Make sure you're following your destiny."

DO YOU STILL WANT TO BE A STAR?

I called this book *Make Me a Star* because I know so many young people see celebrity as a validation of their creativity and as a dramatic departure from their everyday lives. They desire attention; they crave recognition. It's the reason guys pick up guitars. It's why girls enter beauty pageants.

The truth is, though, no one can *make* you a star. You can become one—it's extremely difficult work, as I hope this book has shown you, but it does happen. If you want it badly enough, if you're willing to put forth the effort and make the necessary sacrifices, if you're willing to give as much of yourself back to the audience as they want to give to you, then you may find some of the success you want.

If all you want is the fame, though, you'll find it very disappointing. That double-edged sword, celebrity, seems wonderful and glamorous from a distance, but it can quickly turn nasty on someone who doesn't know how to handle it. The artists who handle celebrity best are the ones who love what they do whether or not anybody else knows them. They love the hours spent practicing, they love the process of creation, and they love the time spent on stage. Usually, they even love the traveling. Above all, though, they love the music.

In a movie I recently worked on called *August Rush*, a character played by Robin Williams tells a young musician:

"You've got to love music more than food.
More than life.
More than yourself."

That's the level of devotion you've got to have if you want to make this dream come true. The people whom I interviewed for this book have all made that commitment—that's the reason I asked them to share their experiences and their opinions. When you put together a team with that much dedication, great things can happen. But in the end, it's up to you and only you. After all, they're *your* dreams.

Music is a big dream—a worthy and respectable one—and you never know how you ultimately will fit into it. If you remain focused and open-minded, you'll be able to make dreams come true, even if some of your dreams and goals change along the way. Embrace the true art, with all the confusion and the insanity, and learn to roll with it—for the sake of *your* sanity. Love the music, do the work, and you'll find what you love—whether it's stardom or something you decide you like even better.

By the way, when I gave you the lines from *August Rush* earlier, I intentionally omitted part of it. To me, it's the part that changes everything, the line that separates the dreamers from the doers.

Here it is. Commit it to memory.

"You've got to love music more than food.
More than life.
More than yourself.
Can you feel it?
Then show me."

Credit: Elizabeth Fladung

BETTYE LAVETTE: IT'S NOT YOUR CAREER, IT'S YOUR LIFE

R&B singer Bettye LaVette made her first record as a sixteen-year-old in Detroit in 1962. Over the next forty-plus years, she recorded for labels like Atlantic, Motown, and Epic with only occasional success. While Bettye has never become a household name, she's never worked outside of music. Her career has seen small hit records, a six-year Broadway stint, years of destitution, and a rediscovery in her fifties. After more than forty years as a singer, Bettye finally began to find an audience for herself with her 2005 album, I've Got My Own Hell to Raise, *which featured her versions of songs by artists like Fiona Apple, Lucinda Williams, Sinead O'Connor, and Dolly Parton. Bettye's 2007 album* The Scene of the Crime *continued to bring her acclaim, prompting Mojo magazine to state, "Few make their best record four-and-a-half decades into their careers, but this 61-year-old Detroit soul singer may have done just that."*

I hesitate to even call myself an artist—my views about doing this and how I do it and why I do it are just so different from most people I know. I never had any plan of any kind.

You're committed to this on a daily basis, or a gig-to-gig basis, or a record-to-record basis, or a success-to-failure basis. Nobody sat down and said, "I'm going to try this for five years, and if this doesn't go, I'm going to go back and get my law degree." I've never had those thoughts—I'm committed to this, I'm not going to do anything else. I don't even think like that. It's just when the next thing comes up, I try to be prepared to do it.

When I made my very first record, I'd never sung before—I was trying to be a groupie, I was just trying to hang where the entertainers were. One entertainer was like, 'Come here, little girl, I'm going to make you a star.' It was strictly his evil notion that even made him want to tell me that I could sing. And it just turned out well. But I never sat home with one of those, "One day I'm going to grow up and I'm going to . . . " In 1962, and certainly before that, if you were a black child in the ghetto or a black child on one of those farms of sharecroppers down in the South, you just wanted to grow up first of all, and then you wanted to just have some money.

I started hanging with these guys, we started rehearsing this song, we recorded it on a Sunday, they changed my name on Thursday, it was on the air that Friday—just the test pressing because they hadn't even had it pressed. Before it could even come out on the local label, Atlantic bought it, and I was on the road with Clyde McPhatter and Ben E. King. Circumstances were extremely right in Detroit for that kind of thing to happen.

For the first ten years, the thing that kept me in it was just the notion of being Bettye LaVette. I'd never been anybody, and nobody in my family had ever been anybody. So that's what kept me in it: I was somebody. And then when things didn't work out after that first ten years, I was still more important than the average person—people in Detroit knew who I was and little things kept happening, so I knew that was who I wanted to be. I wanted to be Bettye LaVette for ten dollars or ten thousand. I knew that was what I liked. And I believed that people believed I was good at it. People kept saying it, and they kept helping me and kept recording me. But it was a long time before I believed I was good at it, and that little fact caused a lot of trouble. That's what killed Elvis Presley; that's what caused all the big stars to get strung out on drugs. You've got to believe it. Throngs of millions cannot make you believe it. You've got to believe it yourself.

Only about 2 percent of us ever do anything, and only about 2 percent of those people ever do anything big. It's really hard to be a singer, just to be a singer. You can be taught to do anything else except sing. You can be taught to play a violin, all these other things. You can be taught to sing correctly, but you can't be taught to sing. Either you can sing or you can't. I felt to be able to do it was unique and I should do it. The only thing that made me not want to do it was that I was not making any money; other than that, everything was going great.

How could you have told me it was going to be extremely hard? That's like telling children, "Don't smoke," or whatever. No one could tell me how hard it would be. There wouldn't be any children if women really knew what labor pain felt like. It's that percentage that doesn't know that keeps everything going.

By staying in the business, I lost my daughter—well, I didn't lose her, my mother took

(cont.)

care of her. As my daughter became more educated and got a college degree, and my career still wasn't working, then she began to be like, "I'm bigger than you are." That was a great, great sacrifice. I'll never forget one time we were arguing, and I said, "As I think about it, even knowing the way you feel, if I had this to do all over again, I'd do it exactly like this." It made her so angry, but I was really telling the truth.

My mother and my sister wanted me to be Bettye LaVette—they were so proud of that, and it was the only thing they'd ever had in their lives. They took care of my daughter and probably gave her lots of problems trying to make her happy and trying to make sure she didn't want for anything. It wasn't a thing where my mother and sister wished I'd come home and take care of my child; they just wanted me to make some money so I could take care of everybody.

My worst times were the years from about 1984 to 2004. The bar in Detroit where I hung out, The Locker Room—I didn't even want to be there, I had to be there. I could go there and laugh and drink, but I wanted to be off being Bettye LaVette. Being there and being ignored as Bettye LaVette was extremely painful. Those twenty years of being totally ignored were just the worst of my life.

There wasn't a time in show business when I didn't see myself as a star—I started off as a star. It wasn't like I used to work at a factory and then started singing. I went to school, and then I had a record on the charts. I didn't have anything to relate to but being Bettye LaVette. It was hard for me to be broke, to not have pretty clothes, or to not think I was supposed to have them. I remember running into the O'Jays at one point, and I went to the dressing room and they said, "What are you doing?" I said, "I'm starving to death," and they said, "Wow, it looks good on you." When I was in humiliating situations, I thought of myself as a star being humiliated. So I don't know what I would've done if I had another plan—I just never did. I don't know how I could've devoted any time to becoming proficient at something else—this has taken every day of my life for forty-something years.

How many American Idols have there been? If I live, my career is going to outlive most of them. You can't do it that fast. If I had done it, maybe I would have been the star that my contemporaries became, but in retrospect I feel good because I became such a versatile person. Otherwise, I would've been this one-dimensional star who followed these hit records and whose show was exactly the same all the time. But mine was never the same. Sometimes it was tap dancing, sometimes it was jazz, sometimes it was rhythm and blues, sometimes it was big band, and sometimes it was one musician. One time it was a trumpet and a piano.

I had given up on finding any big success. I knew I'd be able to work—I was feverishly just trying to find an agent. I knew if I found anybody who knew where a gig was, if he sent me to it I could get that one and another one. So I was just trying to find an agent. I had a friend who introduced me to the agent I have now, and that was all I was looking for. The records were a total surprise. I never thought I'd record again, not for a major label. But I knew I could work. I knew how the show looked; I knew it would sell. I knew that if I could get a booking agency, I could work. And I haven't always known that. You've got to know that. If you can know that, even without a record, even without anybody telling you, then you've arrived at a great place. I had to eventually know that—with no record, with no one calling for a gig, no one giving me a contract, I had to know that for myself.

A music career is a pimp. It's another guy. Approach it that way. You will have to give up an awful lot for it, whether it succeeds or fails. It takes one thing if it fails and another if it succeeds, but neither leaves much time for babies or husbands, unless they're all in it with you.

Try to be good; find out what exactly it is you do and try to be good at it. I tried so very long to sound like a girl, then I found I sound like I do, and I've spent the last twenty years just working on the way I sound. This is a whole new voice to me because I thought eventually I'd sound beautiful. But that being gone, I have to settle for this here. Work with what you got. Be true to it, and if you know how to do anything else better than you know how to do this, you should do that instead.

ACKNOWLEDGMENTS

You should know that you wouldn't have read this book were it not for Deb Barnes because we almost certainly wouldn't have finished it yet. Deb kept us on track and on deadline and probably saved our marriages and our reputations. We quite literally could not have written this book without her.

Anastasia wishes to thank:

- ★ Most important, the foundation of my life and the anchor of my heart, Tony Brown; Wilson Pruitt (who unknowingly saved a key interview by leaving his cassette recorder where it could be found); my amazing parents, Katrina and Dave Wilson; Tatianna and Natasha Troutman; Kristina Wilson; and Brandi, Josie, and Brennan Brown; Chippy; and Blu.
- ★ Brian Mansfield, who works great under pressure and stands his ground while allowing me to stand mine. There could not have been a better person to write this book with, and I could not have done it without him.
- ★ My 821 Entertainment Group team, who helped with research, interviews, and holding down the fort during deadline crunch time—Eric Geadelmann (I'm proud to be your partner), Carrie Simons, Denise Johnson, Parker Welling, Tanya Taylor, Graham Chalfant, Tessa Atkins, Ben Horton, Dub Cornett, and Andrea Robinette.
- ★ Meg Davis, who put up with me as I was writing away at home; Andy Norwood; my CAA family, who believed in Eric and me from the start—Rod Essig, Jon Levin, and Steve Tellez; the *Nashville Star* team—Ben Silverman, Howard Owens, Libby Hansen, Jeff Wachtel, Jon Small, Jeff Boggs, Trevor O'Neil, Kristi Smith, Randy Owen, Blake Shelton, and Jewel.
- ★ My girlfriends, who are near and dear to my heart: Trey Fanjoy, Jo Ainlay, Kathy Anderson, Beverly Keel, Renee White, Janet Miller, Lisa Wilson, Laura Ellis, Leah

Sohr, Genia Winwood, Janine Dunn, Claudia Church, Reba, Laura Stroud, Hope Stringer, Nancy Jarecki, Maria Caldwell, Tanza Farr, Cassidy Bentley, Julia Michels, Denise Draper, Jill Pullen, Mindy Smith, Holly Williams, Lee Ann Womack, Norma Strait, Donna Summer, Amy Matson, Gina Maltese, Heather and Bonnie, Matreca Berg, Jessi Alexander, Collie Daily, Carla McCombs, Kathi Whitley, Elisa Sanders, Kim Carnes, and Deana Carter.

★ Artists, peers, and friends who impacted my life and career: Waylon Jennings, Jessi Colter, Peter Frampton, Sting, Tanya Rae and Junior Brown, Paul Jefferson, Leon Russell, Robin and John Berry, Keith Urban, Jerry Flowers, Peter Clarke, Rodney Crowell, Lucas Reynolds, Emmylou Harris, Buddy Miller, Allison Moorer, Steve Earle, Blue Mother Tupelo, Kaki King, Gerry House, Ansel Davis, Jim Ed Norman, Jeff Pringle, Wyatt Easterling, Roger Osborne, Melanie Shelley, Jewel and Barry Coburn, Carey Nelson Burch, Marc Oswald, Ken Levitan, Greg Oswald, Marc Abraham, Richard Lewis, Clarence Spalding, Manuel, Gary Haber, Dawn Nepp, Les Bohem, Kirsten Sheridan, Mark Mancina, Marty Bowen, Danielle Diego, Doug Frank, Darren Higman, G Marq Roswell, Katrina Bronson, Mike Judge, T Bone Burnett, Sheryl Crow, Pam Worthiemer, Larry Mortoff, Sally Singer, Valerie Boster, Julia Reed, John Huie, Amy and Judge Reinhold, Amy and Richard Stevens, Hunt Lowry, Perry Gibson, Phil Martin, Ree Guyer, Brian Loucks, Teenah Hunt, Erv Woolsey, Joe Galante, Stacie Standifer, Debra White, John Hamlin, David Jaworski, Steven Gaydos, Josh Renkens, Teri Argo, Teresa Rowlett, Blake McDaniel, Karen Conrad, Kristin Barlowe, Darin Murphy, David Ross, Chuck Ainlay, Jim Sohr, Howard Stringer, Steve Winwood, Jim Horn, George Strait, Jon Randall, Billy Ray Caldwell, Jeff Hanna, Andrew Jarecki, Mike Jones, Mark Knopfler, John Rich, Bret James, Pam DeWoody, Whitney Sutton, Jason Quillan, Barbara Orbison, Dan Gordon, Hank Williams Jr., Jett Williams, Bruce Sudano, Phil Martin, and Dick Brown.

★ Eddie Perez, one of Nashville's greatest guitarists, for the arrangements and production of the valuable CD included in this book.

Brian wishes to thank:

★ My exceptionally forbearing wife, Nancy Mansfield; the kids—Nick, Zach, Gracelyn, and Annalise Mansfield; and my parents, John and Betty Mansfield.

★ Anastasia Brown for meaning it when she said she wanted to do a project together and for talking me back into the project when I was ready to back out.

★ Ken Barnes, Kim Willis, Ann Oldenburg, and Bill Keveney from *USA Today*, who provided understanding and expertise, especially when it came to *American Idol.* If you haven't yet read Ken's Idol Chatter blog (http://blogs.usatoday.com/idol-chatter), check it out.

Anastasia and Brian truly appreciate those people who gave their time and knowledge by agreeing to let us interview them: Anastasia's mentor Miles Copeland, Keith Urban, Don Was, Nancy Wilson, Dierks Bentley, Trey Fanjoy, Rodney Crowell, Reba McEntire, David Malloy, Ronnie Dunn, Phil Ramone, Bo Bice, Scott Borchetta, Gary Borman, Gary Burr, Colbie Caillat, David Conrad, Bucky Covington, Diana D'Angelo, Debbie Dover, Sara Evans, Tom Gates, Alana Grace, Tom Higgenson of Plain White T's, Jennifer Hanson, Buddy Jewell, Joel Katz, Shelby Kennedy, Bev Lambert, Bettye LaVette, Renee Layher, John Mason, Reen Nalli, Matt Nathanson, Jake Owen, Carol Peters, Michael Pizzuto, Cyndi Thomson, and Chris Young.

The following people made introductions and facilitated interviews: Narvel Blackstock, Renee Bell, Diana Baron, Betsy Cook, Jenny Bohler, Sarah Brosmer, Billy Craven, Cindy Heath, Chad Jensen, Abby Johns, Mark Jourdian, Kevin Kiley, Tara Leasure, Martha Luttrell, Sue Marcus, Nancy Munoz, Lisa Perez, Tresa Redburn, Jessie Schmidt, Sharrin Summers, Whitney Sutton, Brenner Van Meter, and Sue Wood.

We'd also like to thank the people at Thomas Nelson who helped make this project happen—Pamela Clements, David Dunham, Geoffrey Stone, and Emily Prather—as well as copyeditor Michelle Adkerson and proofreaders Sally Graham and Denver Sherry.

The folks on the in3words mailing list are appreciated for their willingness to make suggestions and weigh in on all sorts of topics. They include Tom Goldsmith, Roy Kasten, Barry Mazor, Nina Melechen, Ron Warnick, Jon Weisberger, Chris Willman, Carl Wilson, and Carl Zimring.

Others who provided much needed help, whether they knew it or not, include Nancy Apple, Kristi Barnes, Rob Bleetstein, Beth Blenz-Clucas, Craig Campbell, Kelly Clarkson, Kay Clary, Brad Crisler, Benson Curb, Anthony DeCurtis, Kim Dettwiller, Marty Dodson, Jon Grimson, Vince Hans, Steve Holtje, Andy Leitner, Lynne Margolis, Cassie McConnell, Laura Morgan, Al Moss, Ed Pettersen, Johnny Rose, Mark Rubin, Ronna Rubin, Jay Samit, Mark Satlof, Tamara Saviano, Perry Serpa, Lisa Shively, Dave Steunebrink, Chris Thomas,

Jon Tiven, and Rob and Becky Waggoner. Thank you all, especially those of you who helped without ever meeting us.

To our readers: Those of you who follow your dreams into the music industry should consider yourselves fortunate when you encounter any of the people listed above. We certainly do.

APPENDIX A:
SAMPLE CONTRACTS

The forms and commentaries are provided for informational purposes only and do not constitute legal advice. It is recommended that you always seek the advice of a qualified attorney before entering into a binding legal contract.

SAMPLE RECORD CONTRACT
Courtesy of Dr. David Herrera, Belmont University

AGREEMENT BETWEEN A NEW ARTIST AND A MAJOR RECORD COMPANY

Term; Recording Obligation; Procedures; Delivery Procedure; Rights; Advances; Royalties; Accountings; Mechanical Copyright Licenses; Artist's Additional Warranties and Representations; Failure of Performance; Additional Remedies; Definitions; Miscellaneous; Group Artist

Agreement made as of the ___________ day of___________, 20__, by and between________________ RECORDS, INC., (RI) at___________________________________ Avenue, New York, New York and___________________ and____________________ p/k/a___________________ c/o_________________ at_____________, P.O. Box ______, (individually and collectively referred to as the "Artist").

1. *Term:*

1.01. The term of this agreement (the "Term") will begin on the date hereof and continue, unless extended as provided herein, for a first Contract Period (sometimes referred to as the "Initial Period") ending nine (9) months after delivery of the Master Recordings comprising the Recording Obligation for such Period.

1.02. Artist grants RI six (6) separate options to extend the Term for additional Contract Periods (sometimes referred to as "Option Periods"). RI may exercise each of those options by sending Artist a notice at any time before the expiration of the Contract Period then in effect. If RI exercises such an option, the Option Period concerned will commence upon the end of the current Contract Period (or, if RI so advises, such period will begin on the date of such exercise notice) and end nine (9) months after delivery of the last Master Recordings comprising the Recording Obligation for such Option Period, provided however, that if, in any Contract Period, such delivery is made in September or October, the months of November and December shall not be included when computing the ending date of that particular Contract Period and said Contract Period shall be automatically extended accordingly.

(b) Notwithstanding anything to the contrary expressed or implied herein.

(i) If, by the date (the "Determination Date") which is thirty (30) days prior to the last date on which RI may exercise the option for the First Option Period (the "Exercise Date"), the first Album of the Minimum Recording Obligation has not achieved Net Sales through Normal Retail Channels in the United States in excess of One Hundred Thousand (100,000) units, as estimated in good faith by RI in its sole discretion, by taking into account, among other things, sales figures reflected in the latest monthly trial balance prepared prior to the Determination Date, then RI shall have the obligation to either:

(A) By the Exercise Date, exercise such option; or

(B) Within thirty (30) days following the Exercise Date, pay Artist, as an additional Advance hereunder, the sum of Twenty-Five Thousand Dollars ($25,000), in which event the Term shall be terminated and all parties shall be deemed to have fulfilled all of their obligations hereunder, except for those obligations which survive the end of the Term such as warranties, re-recording restrictions, the obligation to accrue and pay royalties, if payable, and to render royalty statements; or

(ii) If, by the Determination Date, the first Album of the Minimum Recording Obligation has achieved Net Sales through Normal Retail Channels in the United States in excess of One Hundred Thousand (100,000) units, as estimated in good faith by RI in its sole discretion, by taking into account, among other things, sales figures reflected in the latest monthly trial balance prepared prior to the Determination Date, then RI shall have the obligation to exercise the option for the first Option Period hereunder.

2. *Recording Obligation:*

2.01. RI hereby engages the exclusive services of Artist and the services of individual producers to produce and deliver to RI Master Recordings as provided for herein. Artist warrants that during the Term Artist shall perform for the purpose of making Phonograph Records exclusively for RI.

2.02. During each Contract Period, Artist will perform for, record and deliver a minimum number of Master Recordings ("Minimum Recording Obligation") specified in the following schedule:

Contract Period	Minimum Recording Obligation
Initial	One (1) Album
First Option	One (1) Album
Second Option	One (1) Album
Third Option	One (1) Album
Fourth Option	One (1) Album
Fifth Option	One (1) Album
Sixth Option	One (1) Album

3. *Procedures:*

3.01. Artist shall be responsible for coordination of recording sessions and Artist and the individual producers shall render their services subject to the terms and conditions hereof to the best of their ability and in accordance with first-class standards of performance for production in the Phonograph Record industry.

3.02. Prior to making each Recording, Artist shall obtain RI's approval, of each of the following in order, before proceeding further: (i) selection of the individual producer(s) of the Master Recordings hereunder, (ii) selection of Compositions to be recorded, (iii) specification of accompaniment, arrangement and copying services, and (iv) selection of dates of recording and studios where recording is to take place. At least fourteen (14) days prior to the date of the first recording session for the recording of any Master Recordings, Artist will submit to RI for its written approval, a written proposed budget setting forth, in itemized detail, all anticipated Recording Costs. The scheduling and booking of all studio time will be done by RI. Artist shall notify the appropriate local of the American Federation of Musicians in advance of each recording session. Artist shall reasonably allow RI representatives to attend any or all recording sessions hereunder.

3.03. With respect to Master Recordings hereunder, Artist shall simultaneously deliver to RI stereo mixed down tape masters of the original multi-track recordings which are of a quality reflecting then-current "state of the art" analog and/or digital recording techniques. Such stereo mixed down tape masters shall be satisfactory for the production of lacquers and reference discs for phonograph record manufacturing, equalized tape transfers for cassette manufacturing, digital transfers for compact disc and digital cassette manufacturing, and such elements of future technology as may hereinafter be utilized in the phonograph recording industry. Upon RI's request, Artist shall re-record any Composition until a satisfactory Master Recording shall have been obtained. Artist shall edit, sequence, and leader multi-track master tapes for Master Recordings hereunder, in parallel sequence to any two-track master tapes delivered hereunder, and shall further deliver same to RI. All tapes and work parts of whatever nature (including, without limitation, out-takes or other tracks recorded during the Term) shall be delivered to RI concurrently with delivery of the foregoing items under this paragraph 3.03 or maintained at a recording studio or other location designated by RI in RI's name and subject to RI's control.

3.04. Artist shall furnish RI in writing with all information, consents and clearances required for the manufacture and distribution of Phonograph Records hereunder including, without limitation, the label copy (including song titles and any subtitles), names of composers and lyricists, complete publisher line, music performing rights organizations (BMI, ASCAP, etc.), timings, any credits to arrangers or accompanists, names of engineers, list of musicians with instruments played, exact recording date(s), studio location(s), album liner credits, and any information required to be submitted to unions, guilds or other third parties.

3.05. Artist shall secure on behalf of RI from the copyright proprietors of Compositions not subject to compulsory license, and embodied on Recordings to be delivered to RI hereunder, executed mechanical licenses, on the terms provided in Article 9 of this agreement, granting RI the right to make and distribute Phonograph Records embodying such Recordings.

3.06. Artist's performances hereunder shall be reasonably consistent in concept and style and Master Recordings delivered hereunder will be similar in general artistic concept and style to Master Recordings previously delivered hereunder. Artist further agrees that neither "live" performances nor multiple LP Albums, or joint recordings with other royalty-receiving artists, or instrumental recordings or recordings which were not made in compliance with the provisions of this agreement shall be recorded as part of the Minimum Recording Obligation without RI's prior written consent. Without limitation of the generality of the foregoing, any multiple LP Album delivered hereunder shall be deemed a single LP for the purposes of product delivery and payment of Advances unless RI specifically agrees otherwise in writing. RI agrees that it shall not require Artist to record any multiple LP Album hereunder.

3.07. In the event of a dispute between Artist and RI in connection with the procedures described in this Article 3, the decision of RI shall be controlling.

4. *Delivery Procedure:*

4.01. The Minimum Recording Obligation with respect to each Contract Period shall be delivered no later than one hundred and twenty (120) days following commencement of such Period.

4.02. Satisfactory completion by Artist of the procedures in Article 3 and this Article 4 shall be among the necessary conditions to determine whether any Recording has been delivered within the meaning of this agreement. RI's election to make a payment which was to have been made upon delivery of Recordings or release such Recording shall not be deemed to be its acknowledgment that such delivery was properly made, and RI shall not be deemed to have waived either its right to require such complete and proper performance thereafter or its remedies for Artist's failure to perform in accordance herewith.

4.03. All Master Recordings delivered hereunder shall be recorded no earlier than six (6) months prior to delivery to RI and shall not embody Compositions which have been previously recorded by Artist (whether as a group or an individual) without RI's prior written consent. Artist shall not commence recording any Album (other than the first Album) prior to ninety (90) days after delivery to RI of Master Recordings constituting the immediately preceding Album without RI's prior written consent.

4.04. (a) RI shall send Artist written notice of the date which RI deems to be the applicable delivery date of Master Recordings hereunder. If Artist disputes the date of such notice, Artist shall give notice in writing to RI within thirty (30) days of RI's notice to Artist. Artist's failure to so notify RI shall be deemed Artist's acceptance of the date contained in RI's notice.

(b) If Artist has not received any notice from RI pursuant to paragraph 4.04(a) above within thirty (30) days after the date Artist deems to be such applicable delivery date, then Artist shall notify RI within ten (10) days after such thirty (30) day period of the date Artist deems the applicable delivery date. RI shall have the right to object to such date within thirty (30) days after receipt of Artist's notice.

(c) If either party objects to the date contained in the notice given by the other party, RI and Artist shall mutually and in good faith agree in writing on the date to be deemed the delivery date. If the parties do not reach such agreement or if neither party gives notice of the delivery date of Master Recordings as provided above earlier than thirty (30) days prior to the date of initial release in the United States of such Master Recordings, then the delivery date of such Album shall be deemed to be thirty (30) days prior to such date of initial release.

4.05 Artist shall prepare and deliver to RI the artwork for all Records (i.e., all configurations, including without limitation, Albums, tape cassettes, compact discs and their accompanying long cards, and Singles) used in connection with the initial release in the United States of each Album of the Minimum Recording Obligation (hereafter, the "Artwork"), upon the following conditions:

(a) Artist will consult with RI regarding the Artwork, and Artist and RI shall agree with respect to the budget therefor not to exceed five thousand dollars ($5,000). Such Artwork will be delivered by no later than thirty (30) days prior to the required delivery date of the Master Recordings for such Album; it being understood that delivery of such Album shall not be deemed complete without such Artwork in the form of mechanicals and art conforming to specifications of RI, together with all licenses and consents required in connection therewith. Provided Artist delivers to RI, together with such Artwork, an itemized statement of Artist's actual costs in connection with the preparation of such Artwork, RI shall promptly thereafter reimburse Artist the amount of such costs up to the aforesaid amount. Without limiting the generality of the foregoing, it is understood and agreed that if RI elects to pay any costs in connection with the preparation of Artwork hereunder for which Artist is responsible, then RI shall have the right to demand reimbursement therefor from Artist (and Artist shall immediately make such reimbursement) and/or the right to deduct such costs from any payments to Artist.

(b) RI may reject such Artwork if (i) RI would be required to incur Album cover manufacturing costs in excess of manufacturing costs for a single-fold disc Album jacket with a standard white sleeve and no inserts; or (ii) in the sole opinion of RI's counsel, such Artwork is objectionable on the basis of obscenity, or might constitute a defamation, libel, potential violation of any law or governmental regulation, or potential violation of any personal, property or other rights of any Person; or
(iii) such Artwork has not been delivered within the time prescribed.

(c) If RI rejects any Artwork for the reasons specified in paragraph 4.05(b) above, RI will have the right to prepare and use its own artwork without consultation with Artist, and RI shall have no obligation to make any payment to Artist or any other Person in connection with Artwork prepared by Artist with respect to the applicable Album.

(d) If RI elects to use a modified version of any Artwork rejected pursuant to paragraph 4.05(b) above, or if RI elects to prepare its own artwork in accordance with paragraph 4.05(c) above, then RI shall have the right to demand reimbursement from Artist and/or to deduct from all payments to Artist hereunder all costs incurred in connection with any changes or corrections to said Artwork, or in connection with the preparation of new artwork.

(e) Matters relating to trademarks, copyrights or other notice elements of the Artwork or background thereof, including, without limitation, UPC symbols (i.e., bar-coding), or any disclosures deemed advisable by RI's attorneys, and any matter other than the Album cover layout and the picture or art to be used on the cover, shall be determined by RI in its sole discretion. The Artwork and all related material delivered pursuant to this paragraph 4.05, including the copyrights and renewals and extensions of copyright therein and thereto, shall be the property of RI throughout the world in perpetuity.

5. *Rights:*

5.01. (a) Each Master Recording recorded hereunder shall be considered a "work made for hire." All Master Recordings delivered hereunder or recorded by Artist during the Term and the performances contained thereon and Recordings derived therefrom shall from inception of their creation be entirely the property of RI in perpetuity throughout the world, under copyright and otherwise, free of any claim whatsoever by Artist or any other Person, and RI shall have the right to register the copyrights in such Master Recordings and Recordings derived therefrom in RI's name or in the name(s) of RI's designee(s) and to secure any and all renewals and extensions thereof. Without limiting the generality of the foregoing, Artist hereby assigns to RI all of Artist's right and title to the copyrights in perpetuity throughout the world in and to such Master Recordings, Recordings derived therefrom and any and all renewals and extensions of such copyrights, and RI and its subsidiaries, affiliates, and licensees shall have the sole, exclusive and unlimited right throughout the world to manufacture Records, by any method(s) now or hereafter known embodying any portion(s) or all of the performances embodied on Master Recordings hereunder; to publicly perform such Records; to import, export, sell, transfer, lease, license, rent, deal in or otherwise dispose of such Master Recordings and Records derived therefrom throughout the world under any trademarks, trade names or labels designated by RI; to edit or adapt the Master Recordings hereunder to conform to the technological or commercial requirements of Phonograph Records in various formats now or hereafter known or developed, or to eliminate material which might subject RI to any civil or criminal action; to use the Master Recordings hereunder for background music, synchronization in motion pictures and television soundtracks and other similar purposes, including, without limitation, use on transportation facilities, without any additional payments to Artist other than as expressly set forth in paragraph 7.06 hereof; or, notwithstanding the provisions of this agreement, RI and its subsidiaries, affiliates and licensees may, at their election, delay or refrain from doing any one or more of the foregoing.

(b) Notwithstanding anything to the contrary contained in paragraph 5.01(a) above, with respect to sales of Records in the United States during the Term:

(i) Except with respect to promotional Records, Records in the form of compact discs, Audio-Visual Recordings or Records used in connection with public transportation carriers or facilities, RI will not, in the United States, during any one (1) calendar year of the Term, couple more than three (3) Master Recordings delivered hereunder with Master Recordings not embodying Artist's performances without Artist's written consent, which shall not be unreasonably withheld;

(ii) If RI elects to edit any Master Recordings hereunder in connection with the initial United States release of Records embodying such Master Recordings, then RI shall offer to Artist the first opportunity to edit such

Master Recordings (unless same would interfere with a scheduled release date), which editing must be completed by Artist within five (5) days following RI's notice to Artist, and which offer shall be deemed rejected if Artist does not respond and/or complete such editing within said five (5) day period. If Artist does not so edit such Master Recordings within said five (5) day period, RI shall have the right to so edit such Master Recordings without further consultation with Artist.

(iii) Without limiting the generality of the terms of paragraph 5.01(a) above, during the Term (or after the Term, if, and only if, Artist account is in a fully recouped position) RI will not release "outtakes" on Phonograph Records without Artist's consent. ("Outtakes" are preliminary, unfinished or alternate versions of Master Recordings made under this agreement.) This subparagraph 5.01(b) shall not apply if Artist has not timely fulfilled the Minimum Recording Obligation or is otherwise in material breach of this agreement.

(iv) In connection with the initial release in the United States of each Album of the Minimum Recording Obligation, Artist shall have the right to consult with RI regarding the preparation of artwork for the Album cover ("Artwork") and the right to approve such Artwork, provided that such approval shall not be unreasonably withheld, and provided further that the giving of such approval shall not conflict with the scheduled release date of the applicable Album. Artist shall be responsible for arranging appointments with RI, at a mutually convenient time, sufficiently far in advance of the scheduled release date of the applicable Album to allow Artist to timely exercise the above right of consultation and approval. Artist's approval shall be deemed given within five (5) days following Artist's receipt of RI's request therefor unless Artist notifies RI of Artist's specific objections within such five (5) day period. After Artist's exercise of such right of consultation and approval (or failure to exercise such right), RI shall have the right to prepare and use such Artwork without any further right of consultation or approval by Artist. All rights in and to any Artwork or related material furnished by Artist or at Artist's request, including the copyright and renewals and extensions thereof, shall be RI's property throughout the world in perpetuity. All matters relating to trademarks, notices, including, without limitation, UPC symbols (i.e., bar-coding), or disclosures deemed advisable by RI's attorneys, and any matter other than the Album cover layout and the picture or art to be used on the cover, will be determined in RI's sole discretion.

v) RI will not, without Artist's prior written consent which shall not be unreasonably withheld, release as a Mid-Price Record in the United States during the Term any Album delivered hereunder as part of the Minimum Recording Obligation until twelve (12) months after the initial release of such Album provided, however, that if any such Mid-Price Record is so released by RI during such twelve (12) month period and RI accrues to Artist's account hereunder the so-called "top-line" basic royalty rate set forth in paragraph 7.02, then RI shall not be deemed to have breached the terms of this subparagraph.

(vi) RI will not, without Artist's prior written consent which shall not be unreasonably withheld, release as a Budget Record in the United States during the Term any Album delivered hereunder as part of the Minimum Recording Obligation until eighteen (18) months after the initial release of such Album provided, however, that if any such Budget Record is so released by RI during such eighteen (18) month period and RI accrues to Artist's account hereunder the so-called "top-line" basic royalty rate set forth in paragraph 7.02, then RI shall not be deemed to have breached the terms of this subparagraph.

(c) The provisions of paragraph 5.01(b) above shall not apply if Artist has not timely fulfilled Artist's material delivery obligations described in Articles 3 and 4 above with respect to any Master Recordings hereunder within the time periods set forth in such Articles, or any of Artist's other obligations hereunder.

(d) Provided that Artist has timely fulfilled all of Artist's material obligations hereunder, and the Master Recordings for each Album of the Minimum Recording Obligation hereunder are delivered within the time periods set forth in Article 4 above, if RI does not release any Album of the Minimum Recording Obligation in the United States on or before ninety (90) days following the date of delivery to RI of such Album, then Artist may, within thirty (30) days following the expiration of such ninety (90) day period, give RI notice of such failure so to release such Album. RI shall either cure such failure within sixty (60) days after RI's receipt of such notice, or Artist shall have the right by written notice to RI within thirty (30) days following the expiration of such sixty (60) day period to terminate the Term of this agreement. In the event of such termination, the parties shall be deemed to have fulfilled all of their obligations hereunder except for those obligations which survive the end of the Term, such as warranties, re-recording restrictions, and the obligation to account and pay royalties, if payable, and such termination shall be Artist's sole remedy for RI's failure to release Records derived from the said Master Recordings. If Artist fails to give RI either of the notices specified in this paragraph, Artist's right to terminate as to the Album concerned hereunder shall lapse. The running of each of the aforementioned sixty (60) and ninety (90) day periods will be suspended for the period of any suspension of the Term of this agreement. For purposes of computing said periods, the months of October, November and December shall not be counted.

5.02. (a) Without limiting the generality of paragraph 5.01, RI shall have the exclusive right to publicly perform and otherwise to utilize Artist's performances in connection with Audio-Visual Recordings for promotional and commercial purposes, including without limitation, release on Audio-Visual Devices and/or CD/Video. Artist shall perform for said Recordings upon RI's request provided that Artist shall not be required to perform in any Contract Period for the recording of Audio-Visual Recordings greater in playing time than the playing time of the sound Recordings constituting the Recording Obligation in such Contract Period.

(b) Artist's compensation in connection with Artist's performances for Audio-Visual Recordings, including, without limitation, those performances referred to in paragraph 10.07 hereof, shall be limited to any minimum amounts required to be paid for such performances pursuant to any collective bargaining agreements pertaining thereto, provided, however, that Artist hereby waives any right to receive such compensation to the extent that such right may be waived in connection with any applicable collective bargaining agreement.

(c) Artist shall procure for RI an irrevocable written consent, by the copyright proprietor of each Composition embodied in any Audio-Visual Recording, to such recording and uses thereof without payment.

(d) Notwithstanding anything to the contrary contained herein, provided that Artist has timely fulfilled the Minimum Delivery Requirements of the applicable Contract Period, RI shall be obligated with respect to each Album of the Minimum Recording Obligation to produce one (1) video production at a cost of not less than Forty Thousand dollars ($40,000) per video.

5.03. Artist shall execute and deliver promptly to RI any instruments of transfer and other documents RI may reasonably request to carry out the purposes and effects contemplated by this agreement. Artist hereby irrevocably appoints RI as Artist's agent and attorney-in-fact to sign any such documents in Artist's name and to make appropriate disposition of them consistent with this agreement and irrevocably authorizes RI to proceed, whether in RI's name or Artist's name, with any appropriate action necessary to enforce RI's rights hereunder (including, without limitation, all rights of exclusivity). Artist acknowledges that RI's agency and power are coupled with an interest.

5.04. (a) RI shall have the perpetual right, without any liability to any Person, to use and to authorize other Persons to use Artist's name and biographical material and the names (including any professional names or sobriquets), and any likenesses, whether or not current, (including pictures, portraits, caricatures and stills from any Audio-Visual Recordings made hereunder), autographs (including facsimile signatures) and biographical material relating to the Artist and any producer for purposes of advertising, promotion and trade and (subject to paragraph 5.04(b) below) in connection with other merchandising of any kind, including the making and exploitation of Records hereunder and in general goodwill advertising. Artist warrants and represents that Artist owns the exclusive rights to so use such names, likenesses, autographs (including facsimile signatures) and biographical materials and that the use of same will not infringe upon the rights of any Person. If any Person challenges the Artist's right to use a professional name or sobriquet, RI may, at its election and without limiting its rights, require Artist to adopt another professional name or sobriquet approved by RI without awaiting the determination of the validity of such challenge. Furthermore, during the Term, the Artist will not change the name by which Artist is professionally known without the prior written approval of RI.

(b) The merchandising rights granted to RI pursuant to paragraph 5.04(a) above are limited to the exclusive right to use the names, biographical material and likenesses described in paragraph 5.04(a), alone or together with other elements, solely in items derived from or embodying the artwork of Records hereunder, and/or in connection with merchandising utilized directly in connection with the sale of Records hereunder.

(c) RI agrees that Artist shall have the non-exclusive right to use and to authorize the use by others of artwork of Albums embodying solely the Master Recordings in connection with the exploitation of merchandising rights, and further agrees to supply to Artist, at Artist's sole cost, duplicate negatives of such artwork for such purpose at Artist's request. Artist's exploitation of such merchandising rights shall be subject to any and all restrictions of which RI may advise Artist, and Artist shall exercise the merchandising rights only in accordance with such restrictions. In no event shall Artist have the right to reproduce any trademark, trade name (except as necessary in RI's copyright notice) or logo of RI without RI's express written consent, which may be withheld for any reason whatsoever. For the rights granted to Artist pursuant to this paragraph 5.04(c), Artist agrees that it shall do nothing to derogate from RI's copyright in said artwork, and Artist agrees further to reproduce RI's copyright notice at all times in conjunction with reproduction of such artwork. Artist shall pay to RI fifty percent (50%) of the gross amounts earned by Artist from the exploitation of merchandising rights in conjunction with artwork prepared by RI subject to this paragraph 5.04(c), and shall pay such monies to RI on or before ten (10) days following Artist's receipt of the applicable amounts.

RI will have the right to examine Artist's books and records for the purpose of verifying the accuracy of the payments made to RI by Artist pursuant to this paragraph 5.04(c).

6. *Advances:*

6.01. RI shall pay, as Advances to be charged against and be recoupable from royalties (excluding mechanical copyright royalties) accruing to Artist's account hereunder, the following:

(a) All Recording Costs in the approved budget. Artist shall be responsible for the payment of all Recording Costs or other costs in connection with making Master Recordings which costs have not been specifically approved in writing by RI. If RI elects to pay any such costs for which Artist is responsible, then RI shall have the right to demand reimbursement therefor from Artist (and Artist shall immediately make such reimbursement) and/or the right to deduct such costs from any payments to Artist.

(b) (i) With respect to the first Album of the Minimum Recording Obligation, RI will pay to Artist an Advance equal to the excess of the applicable amount set forth below ("Recording Fund") over Recording Costs for such Album. Such Advance shall be payable as follows: Forty Thousand dollars ($40,000) within fourteen (14) days of the complete execution of this agreement and the balance, if any, shall be paid within thirty days following delivery of all Master Recordings and other materials required to be delivered pursuant to Articles 3 and 4 in connection with the First Album.

Album of the Minimum Recording Obligation	Recording Fund
First Album	$100,000

(ii) With respect to each of the second through seventh Albums of the Minimum Recording Obligation, RI will pay to Artist an Advance equal to the excess of the applicable amount ("Recording Fund") set forth below over Recording Costs for such Album. The Recording Fund shall be that amount, calculated as of the end of the accounting period immediately preceding the period in which the Master Recordings constituting the applicable Album are delivered, equal to with respect to the second Album of the Minimum Recording Obligation, sixty-six and two thirds percent (66-2/3%) of the royalties earned on Net Sales through Normal Retail Channels in the United States of the First Album of the Minimum Recording Obligation, and with respect to each of the third through the seventh Albums of the Minimum Recording Obligation, sixty-six and two-thirds percent (66-2/3%) of the average of the royalties earned on Net Sales through Normal Retail Channels in the United States of the immediately preceding two (2) Albums of the Minimum Recording Obligation, provided that such Recording Fund shall not be less than the minimum amounts set forth below nor more than the maximum amounts set forth below with respect to each such Album with respect to each such Album or sixty-six and two thirds percent (66-2/3%) of the royalties earned on Net Sales through Normal Retail Channels in the United States of the previous Album.

Album of Minimum Recording Obligation	Minimum Recording Fund	Maximum Recording Fund
Second Album	$125,000	$187,500
Third Album	$135,000	$202,500
Forth Album	$145,000	$217,500
Fifth Album	$150,000	$225,000
Sixth Album	$175,000	$262,500
Seventh Album	$200,000	$300,000

Costs in excess of the applicable Recording Fund shall be Artist's responsibility and, to the extent RI elects to pay any of such costs, RI shall have the right to demand reimbursement therefor from Artist (and Artist shall immediately make such reimbursement) and/or RI may deduct such amounts from any and all monies otherwise payable to Artist hereunder (excluding mechanical copyright royalties). If any of the second through seventh Albums of the Minimum Recording Obligation is not delivered within ninety (90) days following the time periods set forth in Article 4 above, the Recording Fund for the applicable Album will be the minimum Recording Fund above set forth for such Album.

6.02. (a) Any monies paid to Artist during the Term and any monies paid by RI on Artist's behalf or at Artist's direction, other than royalties paid pursuant to this agreement shall be deemed Advances.

(b) Provided RI consults with Artist prior thereto, any monies other than royalties paid by RI on Artist's behalf shall be deemed Advances. Notwithstanding the foregoing, RI shall not be obligated to consult with Artist prior to making any payments required to be paid by RI pursuant to the terms of union agreements or legal or other obligations in connection herewith, and such payments shall be deemed Advances.

6.03. All costs of video productions incurred by RI with respect to each Album of the Minimum Recording Obligation hereunder shall be deemed Advances, provided however, only fifty percent (50%) of such costs shall be recoupable from audio-only Record royalties (excluding mechanical copyright royalties) payable pursuant to the provisions of Article 7 hereof.

7. *Royalties:*

RI shall accrue to the account of Artist in accordance with the provisions of Article 8 below the following royalties for the sale of Phonograph Records derived from Master Recordings hereunder provided, however, no royalties shall accrue (except for accounting purposes) or be due and payable to Artist until such time as all Advances, as defined in Article 6 above, have been recouped by or repaid to RI:

7.01. (a) A royalty of eight percent (8%) of the Royalty Base for Net Sales of all Singles sold by RI for distribution through Normal Retail Channels in the United States.

(b) For Net Sales through Normal Retail Channels in the United States of any such single in excess of one hundred thousand (100,000) units, the royalty shall be ten percent (10%) in lieu of the royalty rate provided in paragraph 7.01(a).

7.02. (a) With respect to each of the first through the third Albums of the Minimum Recording Obligation, if any:

(i) A royalty of thirteen percent (13%) of the Royalty Base for Net Sales of all such Albums sold by RI for distribution through Normal Retail Channels in the United States.

(ii) For Net Sales through Normal Retail Channels in the United States of any such Album in excess of five hundred thousand (500,000) units, the royalty rate for such excess units shall be thirteen and one-half percent (13 1/2%) in lieu of the royalty provided in paragraph 7.02(a)(i) above.

(iii) For Net Sales through Normal Retail Channels in the United States of any such Album in excess of one million (1,000,000) units, the royalty rate for such excess units shall be fourteen percent (14%) in lieu of the royalty rate provided in paragraphs 7.02(a)(i) and 7.02(a)(ii) above.

(b) With respect to each of the fourth through the sixth Albums of the Minimum Recording Obligation, if any:

(i) A royalty of thirteen and one-half percent (13 1/2%) of the Royalty Base for Net Sales of all such Albums sold by RI for distribution through Normal Retail Channels in the United States.

(ii) For Net Sales through Normal Retail Channels in the United States of any such Album in excess of five hundred thousand (500,000) units, the royalty rate for such excess units shall be fourteen percent (14%) in lieu of the royalty rate provided in paragraph 7.02(b)(i) above.

(iii) For Net Sales through Normal Retail Channels in the United States of any such Album in excess of one million (1,000,000) units, the royalty rate for such excess units shall be fourteen and one-half percent (14 1/2%) in lieu of the royalty rate provided in paragraphs 7.02(b)(i) and 7.02(b)(ii) above.

(c) With respect to the seventh Album of the Minimum Recording Obligation, if any:

(i) A royalty of fourteen percent (14%) of the Royalty Base for Net Sales of all such Albums sold by RI for distribution through Normal Retail Channels in the United States.

(ii) For Net Sales through Normal Retail Channels in the United States of any such Album in excess of five hundred thousand (500,000) units, the royalty rate for such excess units shall be fourteen and one-half percent (14 1/2%) in lieu of the royalty rate provided in paragraph 7.02(c)(i) above.

(iii) For Net Sales through Normal Retail Channels in the United States of any such Album in excess of one million (1,000,000) units, the royalty rate for such excess units shall be fifteen percent (15%) in lieu of the royalty rate provided in paragraphs 7.02(c)(i) and 7.02(c)(ii) above.

7.03. (a) The royalty rate with respect to Net Sales of all Records sold in Canada, the United Kingdom, West Germany and Holland shall be seventy-five percent (75%) of the otherwise basic royalty rate set forth in paragraph 7.01 or 7.02.

(b) The royalty rate with respect to Net Sales of all Records sold in Australia, New Zealand, Japan and the rest of Western Europe (i.e., those countries in Western Europe other than the countries referred to in paragraph 7.03(a) above) shall be sixty-six and two-thirds percent (66-2/3%) of the otherwise applicable basic royalty rate set forth in paragraph 7.01 or 7.02.

(c) The royalty rate with respect to Net Sales of all Records sold in the rest of the world (i.e., outside the United States and countries referred to in paragraphs 7.03(a) and 7.03(b) above) shall be fifty percent (50%) of the otherwise applicable royalty rate set forth in paragraph 7.01 or 7.02.

7.04. (a) With respect to Net Sales of Records sold in the form of compact discs or other new Record configurations (but expressly excluding CD/Video), RI shall have the option to accrue, at its sole discretion, with respect to each such Record, either a royalty equal to the same dollars-and-cents (or other currency) royalty amount as is accrued hereunder with respect to an equivalent Record not in the form of a compact disc or other new Record configuration, or a royalty computed at the same percentage of the Royalty Base of such compact disc or other new Record configuration as the percentage of the Royalty Base utilized to compute the royalty for an equivalent Record not in the form of a compact disc or other new Record configuration.

(b) Notwithstanding the foregoing, it is agreed that after two (2) years following the end of the accounting period which contains the date of commencement of recording of the first Album of the Minimum Recording Obligation hereunder, upon notice by Artist to RI, RI and Artist shall negotiate in good faith regarding an adjustment of the royalty to be paid thereafter for Net Sales of Records sold in the form of compact discs, taking into account industry-wide standards, it being further understood and agreed, however, that until the conclusion of such negotiations, the terms of paragraph 7.04(a) above shall continue to be operative.

7.05. (a) The royalty for Net Sales of EP Records shall be accrued at two-thirds (2/3) of the otherwise applicable Album royalty rate and shall be computed based on the particular Royalty Base of each EP Record.

(b) The royalty for Net Sales of Long-Play Singles shall be accrued at one-half (1/2) of the otherwise applicable Singles royalty rate and shall be computed based on the particular Royalty Base of each such Long-Play Single.

(c) The royalty for Net Sales of premium Records, Budget Records, special configuration Singles (i.e., Singles and/or Long-Play Singles sold at two for the price of one, manufactured in colored vinyl and/or sold with a four-color poster included) or Records other than Albums not otherwise specifically referred to herein shall be accrued at one-half (1/2) of the otherwise applicable royalty rate and shall be computed based on the particular Royalty Base of each such Record.

(d) The royalty for Net Sales of Mid-Price Records shall be accrued at two-thirds (2/3) of the otherwise applicable Album royalty rate and shall be computed based on the particular Royalty Base of each such Record.

(e) The royalty for Net Sales of Records sold in Armed Forces Post Exchanges shall be accrued at one-hundred percent (100%) of the otherwise applicable royalty rate and shall be computed based on the particular Royalty Base of each such Record.

(f) The royalty rate with respect to Net Sales through Normal Retail Channels of Multiple-Record Albums sold by RI for distribution shall be calculated by multiplying the otherwise applicable royalty rate by a fraction, the numerator of which shall be the Royalty Base for such Multiple-Record Album, and the denominator of which shall be the Royalty Base applicable to RI's or its licensees' top-line single-disc LPs multiplied by the number of disc LPs in the Multiple-Record Album.

(g) For purposes of this paragraph 7.05, the sales escalations provided in paragraph 7.01 and 7.02 above shall not apply.

7.06. (a) With respect to the following Records and/or exploitation of Master Recordings, the royalty to be accrued hereunder shall be a sum equal to fifty percent (50%) of RI's net receipts with respect to such exploitation: (i) Records derived from Master Recordings hereunder sold through Non-Affiliated Third Party record clubs or similar sales plans operated by Non-Affiliated Third Parties; (ii) licenses of Master Recordings to Non-Affiliated Third Parties for sales of Records by such licensees through direct mail, mail order or in conjunction with TV or radio advertising, including through methods of distribution such as "key outlet marketing" (distribution through retail fulfillment centers in conjunction with special advertisements on radio or television), or by any combination of the methods set forth above or other methods; (iii) licenses of Master Recordings on a flat-fee or other royalty basis; (iv) licenses to Non-Affiliated Third Parties for promotional or commercial use of Audio-Visual Recordings described in paragraph 5.02, excluding blanket licenses to exploit RI's Audio-Visual Recording catalog; and (v) use of the Master Recordings for background music, synchronization in motion pictures and television soundtracks and Records derived therefrom and/or use on transportation facilities.

(b) The terms "net receipts" and "net amount received" and similar terms in this paragraph 7 shall mean amounts received by RI in connection with the subject matter thereof which are solely attributable to the Master Recordings hereunder (excluding catalog and/or administrative fees payable to RI for the licensing of Audio-Visual Recordings hereunder), after deduction of any costs or expenses or amounts which RI is obligated to pay to third parties (such as, without limitation, production costs, mechanical copyright payments, AFofM and other union or guild payments).

7.07. As to Net Sales of Records derived from Master Recordings hereunder sold through RI's affiliated record clubs or similar sales plans operated by parties affiliated with RI, Artist shall receive a royalty equal to three percent (3%) of eighty-five percent (85%) of the Royalty Base of such Records. No royalty shall be payable with respect to Records distributed to members of record clubs as "Bonus" or "Free" Records as a result of joining the club, and/or recommending that another join the club and/or purchasing a required number of Records; provided, however, no more than fifty percent (50%) of such Records shall be non-royalty bearing.

7.08. As to Net Sales by RI or its affiliated licensees of Records derived from Master Recordings by direct mail, mail order or in conjunction with radio or TV advertising, including through methods of distribution such as "key outlet marketing," or by any combination of such methods, the royalty to be accrued hereunder shall be a royalty of five percent (5%) of the Royalty Base for Net Sales of such Records.

7.09. If any Recordings made hereunder embody Artist's performances together with the performances of any other Persons to whom RI is obligated to pay royalties, then the royalty due hereunder for such joint performances shall be the royalty provided for herein divided by the number of royalty-earning artists participating therein including Artist.

7.10. As to Records not consisting entirely of Master Recordings delivered hereunder, the royalty to be accrued hereunder shall be pro-rated on the basis of the number of Master Recordings hereunder which are on such Records compared to the total number of Master Recordings on such Records.

7.11. (a) With respect to Net Sales of Audio-Visual Devices sold by RI for distribution in the United States, a royalty of twelve percent (12%) of the lowest wholesale price, exclusive of excise, sales and similar taxes, payable by RI's customers in respect of such Audio-Visual Device.

(b) With respect to Net Sales of Audio-Visual Devices sold by RI and/or its affiliates for distribution outside of the United States, a royalty of seven percent (7%) of the lowest wholesale price, exclusive of excise, sales and similar taxes, payable by RI's customers in respect of such Audio-Visual Device.

7.12. (a) With respect to Net Sales of Records sold by RI for distribution in the United States in the form of CD/Videos, a royalty of ten percent (10%) of the CD/Video Royalty Base.

(b) With respect to Net Sales of Records sold by RI and/or its affiliates for distribution outside the United States in the form of CD/Videos, a royalty of ten percent (10%) of the CD/Video Royalty Base multiplied by a fraction, the numerator of which is the royalty rate set forth in this agreement for Net Sales of disc Albums sold by RI for distribution in the applicable country, and the denominator of which is the royalty rate set forth in this agreement for Net Sales of disc Albums sold by RI for distribution in the United States. For purposes of this paragraph 7.12(b), the sales escalations provided in paragraph 7.02 above shall not apply.

(c) The "CD/Video Royalty Base" shall mean the lowest wholesale price, exclusive of excise, sales and similar taxes, payable by RI's customers in respect of such CD/Video, less thirty-five percent (35%) of such lowest wholesale price. No Container Charge or automatic free goods (as set forth in paragraph 13.15(a)(ii) below) shall apply in respect of CD/Videos.

8. *Accountings:*

8.01. Accountings as to royalties accruing or which otherwise would have accrued hereunder shall be made by RI to Artist on or before September 30th for the period ending the preceding June 30th, and on or before March 31st for the period ending the preceding December 31st, or such other accounting periods as RI may in general adopt, but in no case less frequently than semi-annually, together with payment of accrued royalties, if any, earned by Artist during such preceding half-year, less Advances or other recoupable and/or deductible amounts hereunder. RI shall have the right to hold reasonable reserves in respect of sales hereunder. In no event, will reserves of one hundred percent (100%) for seven-inch Singles be considered unreasonable. Each royalty reserve will be liquidated not later than the end of the fourth semi-annual accounting period following the period during which such reserve is initially established. A royalty reserve will not be established for any Album or CD/Video, during any semi-annual accounting period in excess of fifty percent (50%) of the aggregate number of units of that Album distributed. A royalty reserve will not be established for any Audio-Visual Device during any semi-annual accounting period in excess of twenty five percent (25%) of the aggregate number of units of that Audio-Visual Device distributed. Without limitation of RI's right to recoup all Advances hereunder against royalties earned hereunder, RI shall not charge against royalties earned with respect to a semi-annual accounting period a Recording Fund Advance which is paid after the end of such accounting period but before such royalties are actually paid, provided that such Advance is being paid solely in connection with an Album of the Minimum Recording Obligation being timely delivered.

8.02. Royalties for Records sold for distribution outside the United States shall be computed in the same national currency as RI is accounted to by its licensees and shall be paid at the same rate of exchange as RI is paid, and shall be subject to any taxes applicable to royalties remitted by or received from foreign sources, provided, however, that royalties on Records sold outside the United States shall not be due and payable by RI until payment therefor has been received by or credited to RI in the United States in United States Dollars. If RI shall not receive payment or credit in the United States, or in United States Dollars, and shall be required to accept payment in a foreign country or in foreign currency, RI shall deposit to the credit of Artist (at Artist's request and expense), in such currency in a depository in the country in which RI is required to accept payment, Artist's share of royalties due and payable to Artist with respect to such sales. Deposit as aforesaid shall fulfill the obligations of RI as to Record sales to which such royalty payments are applicable. If any law, government ruling or any other restriction affects the amount of the payments which RI's licensee can remit to RI, RI may deduct from Artist's royalties an amount proportionate to the reduction in such licensee's remittances to RI.

8.03. (a) All royalty statements rendered by RI to Artist shall be binding upon Artist and not subject to any objection by Artist for any reason unless specific objection in writing, stating the basis thereof, is given to RI within two (2) years from the date rendered. Failure to make specific objection within said time period shall be deemed approval of such statement.

(b) All statements hereunder will be deemed conclusively to have been rendered on the due date set forth in paragraph 8.01 unless Artist notifies RI otherwise within forty five (45) days after such due date.

8.04. (a) Artist shall have the right at Artist's own expense to audit RI's books and records only as the same pertain to distribution under this agreement for the two (2) accounting periods prior to such audit. Artist may make such an examination for a particular statement only once, and only within two (2) years after the date when RI renders said statement under paragraph 8.01. Such audit shall be conducted during RI's usual business hours, and at RI's regular place of business in the United States where RI keeps the books and records to be examined. Such audit shall be conducted by an independent certified public accountant. If such accountant or his or her firm has begun an examination of RI's books and records for another party or pursuant to an agreement other than this agreement, the examination on Artist's behalf shall not be undertaken until such other examination is concluded and any applicable audit issues relating to such other examination have been resolved.

(b) Notwithstanding the last sentence of paragraph 8.04(a), if RI notifies Artist that the representative designated by Artist to conduct an examination of RI's books and records under paragraph 8.04(a) is engaged in an examination on behalf of another Person ("Other Examination"), Artist may nevertheless have Artist's examination conducted by its designee, and the running of the time within which such examination may be made shall be suspended until Artist's designee has completed the Other Examination, subject to the following conditions:

(c) Artist acknowledges that RI's books and records contain confidential trade information. Neither Artist nor its representatives shall at any time communicate to others or use on behalf of any other Person any facts or information obtained as a result of such examination of RI's books and records (except pursuant to an order of a court of competent jurisdiction).

8.05. (a) Artist will not have the right to bring an action against RI in connection with any royalty accounting or payments hereunder unless Artist commences the suit within three (3) years from the date such statement of accounting for royalties or such payment was rendered.

(b) If Artist commences suit on any controversy or claim concerning royalty accountings rendered by RI under this agreement, the scope of the proceeding will be limited to determination of the amount of the royalties due for the accounting periods concerned, and the court will have no authority to consider any other issues or award any relief except recovery of any royalties found owing. Artist's recovery of any such royalties will be the sole remedy available to Artist by reason of any claim related to RI's royalty accountings. Without limiting the generality of the preceding sentence, Artist will not have any right to seek termination of this agreement or avoid the performance of her obligations under it by reason of any such claim. Notwithstanding the foregoing, in the event any court determines fraud or gross negligence on the part of RI in connection with any such claim, and such determination is not overturned or reversed, the limitations set forth in this paragraph 8.05(b) shall not apply.

8.06. Artist hereby authorizes and directs RI to withhold from any monies due Artist from RI any part thereof required by the United States Internal Revenue Service and/or any other governmental authority to be withheld, and to pay same to the United States Internal Revenue Service and/or such other authority. No Advances or other payments shall be made pursuant to this agreement until Artist has completed the Internal Revenue Service Form attached as Exhibit "A."

9. *Mechanical Copyright Licenses:*

9.01. The following provisions shall pertain to Controlled Compositions:

(a) Each Controlled Composition shall be and hereby is licensed to RI at a copyright royalty rate equal to seventy-five percent (75%) of the Statutory Rate prevailing at the time of the initial release of the Master Recording embodying such Controlled Composition, provided that such Master Recording is delivered within the applicable time period set forth in Article 4 above and subject to the provisions of this Article 9. With respect to any Master Recording which is not delivered within the applicable time period set forth in Article 4 above, each Controlled Composition embodied on such Master Recording shall be and hereby is licensed to RI at a copyright royalty rate equal to seventy-five percent (75%) of the Statutory Rate prevailing on the last date on which such Master Recording would otherwise have been timely delivered pursuant to Article 4 above, subject to the provisions of this Article 9. With respect to Records sold and/or distributed in the manner described in paragraphs 7.05(a), 7.05(c), 7.05(d), 7.05(e), 7.05(f) 7.06, 7.07 or 7.08, the copyright royalty rate with respect to Controlled Compositions shall be three-fourths (3/4) of the rate set forth in this paragraph 9.01(a).

(b) Copyright royalties with respect to Controlled Compositions shall be payable only on Net Sales hereunder. Copyright royalties shall not be payable with respect to Records otherwise not royalty-bearing hereunder or with respect to Compositions which are in the public domain or are arranged versions of Compositions in the public domain or for non-musical material.

(c) Notwithstanding anything to the contrary contained herein, if any Record hereunder embodies more than one (1) Master Recording of a particular Controlled Composition, then RI shall only be obligated to pay the copyright royalty rate(s) referred to in paragraph 9.01(a) with respect to only one (1) such Master Recording.

(d) The provisions of this Article 9 shall constitute and are accepted by Artist, on Artist's own behalf and on behalf of any other owner of any Controlled Composition(s) or of any rights therein, as full compliance by RI with all of its obligations under the compulsory license provisions of the applicable copyright law, arising from any use by RI of Controlled Compositions as provided for herein, and shall constitute a mechanical license. RI shall have the right to hold reasonable mechanical royalty reserves in respect of sales hereunder. Mechanical royalty reserves maintained by RI against anticipated returns and credits shall not be held for an unreasonable period of time; retention of a reserve for two years after it is established shall not be considered unreasonable in any case. If RI makes any overpayment of mechanical royalties on Controlled Compositions (including without limitation, by means of an accounting error or by paying mechanical royalties on Records returned), RI shall have the right to demand reimbursement of such excess from Artist (and Artist shall immediately make such reimbursement) and/or the right to deduct the amount of such overpayment from any and all monies due hereunder. RI shall account for mechanical royalties on a quarterly basis. Artist's right to audit RI's books and records as the same relate to copyright royalties for Controlled Compositions shall be subject to the terms and conditions set forth in Article 8 in connection with Artist's audit rights.

(e) Any assignment made of the ownership or copyright in any Controlled Composition shall be made subject to the provisions of this Article 9.

9.02. Notwithstanding anything to the contrary contained herein, Artist warrants, represents, and agrees that RI shall have no obligation whatsoever to pay an aggregate copyright royalty rate in respect of any Record hereunder regardless of the number of Controlled Compositions and/or other Compositions contained thereon, in excess of the following sums:

(a) In respect of an Album or twelve-inch CD/Video: ten (10) times the applicable amount set forth in paragraph 9.01 above.

(b) In respect of a Single, EP Record, Long Play Single or any Record other than as expressly provided for in this paragraph 9.02: three (3) times the applicable amount set forth in paragraph 9.01 above.

(c) In respect of a five-inch CD/Video: three (3) times the applicable amount set forth in paragraph 9.01 above.

(d) In respect of an eight-inch CD/Video: five (5) times the applicable amount set forth in paragraph 9.01 above.

(e) In respect of a Multiple-Record Album: the aggregate copyright royalty rate set forth in paragraph 9.02(a) above multiplied by a fraction, the numerator of which shall be the Royalty Base for such Multiple-Record Album, and the denominator of which shall be the Royalty Base applicable to RI's or its licensees' top-line single-disc LPs.

9.03. Without limitation of the generality of clause 9.02 above, if the aggregate of copyright royalties in respect of any Record hereunder exceeds the applicable amounts set forth in this Article 9, then, without limitation of RI's rights, RI shall have the right, at its election, if it elects to release such Recording, to demand reimbursement from Artist of such excess and/or to deduct the amount of such excess from payments due hereunder, including copyright royalties.

9.04. If any Recordings made under this agreement contain copyrighted non-Controlled Compositions which are not available to RI under compulsory license as a result of the "first use" provisions of the copyright laws, Artist will obtain mechanical licenses on the standard form used by the Harry Fox Agency, Inc. or on any other form approved by RI, at the compulsory license rate prevailing at the time of recording of the Master Recording embodying such Composition.

10. *Artist's Additional Warranties and Representations:* Artist warrants and represents the following:

10.01. (a) Artist is authorized, empowered and able to enter into and fully perform its obligations under this agreement. Neither this agreement nor the fulfillment thereof by any party infringes upon the rights of any Person. Artist owns and controls, without any limitations, restrictions or encumbrances whatsoever, all rights granted or purported to be granted to RI hereunder, and Artist has obtained all necessary licenses and permissions as may be required for the full and unlimited exercise and enjoyment by RI of all of the rights granted and purported to be granted to RI herein. RI will own, possess and enjoy such rights without any hindrance on the part of any Person, firm or entity whatsoever.

(b) Artist has no knowledge of any claim or purported claim which would interfere with RI's rights hereunder or create any liability on the part of RI.

10.02. There now exist no prior unreleased recorded performances by Artist, except as listed on Exhibit B attached hereto.

10.03. The Master Recordings hereunder and performances embodied thereon shall be produced in accordance with the rules and regulations of the American Federation of Musicians and the American Federation of Television and Radio Artists and in accordance with the rules and regulations of all other unions having jurisdiction. Artist is or will become and will remain to the extent necessary to enable the performance of this agreement, a member in good standing of all labor unions or guilds, membership in which may be required for the performance of Artist's services hereunder.

10.04. Artist will perform exclusive services hereunder. Artist will not perform for (or license, or consent to, or permit the use by any Person other than RI of Artist's name or likeness for or in connection with) the recording or exploitation of any Phonograph Record (including, without limitation, any Audio-Visual Device) embodying any Composition recorded by Artist under this agreement prior to the later of the date five (5) years subsequent to the date of delivery to RI of the Master Recording embodying that Composition hereunder, or the date three (3) years subsequent to the expiration or termination of the Term.

10.05. Neither Master Recordings hereunder nor the performances embodied thereon, nor any other Materials, as hereinafter defined, nor any use thereof by RI or its grantees, licensees or assigns will violate or infringe upon the rights of any third party. "Materials," as used in this paragraph, means: Artwork, all Controlled Compositions; each name or sobriquet used by Artist, individually or as a group; and all other musical, dramatic, artistic and literary materials, ideas, and other intellectual properties furnished or selected by Artist or any producer and contained in or used in connection with any Recordings made hereunder or the packaging, sale, distribution, advertising, publicizing or other exploitation thereof.

10.06. Artist shall be solely responsible for and shall pay all sums due the individual producer of the Sides, and all other Persons entitled to receive royalties or any other payments in connection with the sale of Phonograph Records derived from Master Recordings hereunder, and the royalties set forth in Article 7 hereof include all monies due all such parties. Notwithstanding the foregoing, RI shall be responsible for all so-called "per Record payments."

10.07. (a) Subject to Artist's prior professional commitments, Artist shall be available from time to time to appear for photography, poster, and cover art, and the like, under the direction of RI or its nominees and to appear for interviews with representatives of the communications media and RI's publicity personnel. RI shall reimburse for the reasonable travel and living expenses incurred by Artist in connection with the rendition by Artist of services requested by RI pursuant to this paragraph based upon a budget approved by RI in advance.

(b) Artist shall be available from time to time at RI's request to perform for the purpose of recording for promotional purposes by means of film, videotape, or other audio-visual media performances of Compositions embodied on Master Recordings hereunder.

10.08. (a) Artist shall not authorize or knowingly permit Artist's performances to be recorded for any purpose without an express written agreement prohibiting the use of such recording on Records in violation of the restrictions herein, and Artist shall take reasonable measures to prevent the manufacture, distribution and sale at any time by any Person other than RI of such Records. Neither Artist, nor any Person deriving any rights from Artist, shall use or authorize or permit any Person other than RI to use Artist's name (including any professional name or sobriquet), likeness (including picture, portrait or caricature), autograph (including facsimile signature), or biography in connection with the manufacture and/or exploitation of Master Recordings or Records.

(b) Notwithstanding anything to the contrary contained in paragraph 10.08(a), Artist may perform services as a producer for the purposes of making Phonograph Records for third parties during the Term, provided that (i) Artist has fulfilled all of Artist's obligations under this agreement, and such engagement does not interfere with the continuing prompt performance of Artist's obligations to RI; (ii) Artist will not record any material which Artist has then recorded for RI, or which are Controlled Compositions; and (iii) the name of the member of Artist performing such services may not be used, except in a standard producer credit on the labels or liner notes of such Records; without limiting the generality of the foregoing, in no event may the likeness of the member of Artist, or the group or professional name of Artist be used in connection with such Records.

(c) Notwithstanding anything to the contrary contained in paragraph 10.08(a), Artist may perform as a background musician ("sideman") accompanying a featured artist for the purpose of making Recordings for Phonograph Record purposes for third parties during the Term provided that:

(i) Artist has fulfilled all of her material obligations under this agreement, and such engagement does not interfere with the continuing prompt performance of Artist's obligations to RI;

(ii) Artist shall not perform solo or step-out performances on Recordings for such parties in excess of ten (10) seconds or be separately identified in connection with any solo or step-out performances on such Recordings;

(iii) The name of Artist performing may not be used except in a courtesy credit to RI or its designee on the liners used for such Phonograph Records, which courtesy credit shall appear in the same position as the credits accorded to other sidemen and in type identical in size, prominence and all other respects; without limiting the generality of the foregoing, in no event may the likeness of Artist, or the group or professional name of Artist be used in connection with such Phonograph Records.

10.09. Neither Artist, nor any Person deriving any rights from Artist, shall at any time, do, or authorize any Person to do, anything inconsistent with, or which might diminish or impair, any of RI's rights hereunder. Artist shall not endorse any products whose use would be detrimental to the Phonograph Record industry, including but not limited to, blank tapes and tape recording equipment.

10.10. Artist agrees to and does hereby indemnify, save and hold RI harmless of and from any and all liability, loss, damage, cost or expense (including reasonable attorneys' fees) arising out of or connected with any breach or alleged breach of this agreement or any claim which is inconsistent with any of the warranties or representations made by Artist in this agreement, provided the said claim has been settled with Artist's consent, not to be unreasonably withheld, or has been reduced to final judgment, and agrees to reimburse RI on demand for any payment made or incurred by RI with respect to any liability or claim to which the foregoing indemnity applies. Notwithstanding anything to the contrary contained herein, RI shall have the right to settle without Artist's consent any claim involving sums of Five Thousand Dollars ($5,000) or less, and this indemnity shall apply in full to any claim so settled; if Artist does not consent to any settlement proposed by RI for an amount in excess of Five Thousand Dollars ($5,000), RI shall have the right to settle such claim without Artist's consent, and this indemnity shall apply in full to any claim so settled, unless Artist obtains a surety bond from a surety acceptable to RI in its sole discretion, with RI as a beneficiary, assuring RI of prompt payment of all expenses, losses and damages (including attorneys' fees) which RI may incur as a result of said claim. Pending final determination of any claim involving such alleged breach or failure, RI may withhold sums due Artist hereunder in an amount reasonably consistent with the amount of such claim, unless Artist obtains a surety bond from a surety acceptable to RI in its sole discretion, with RI as a beneficiary, in an amount reasonably consistent with the amount of such claim. If no action is filed within two (2) years following the date on which such claim was first received by RI, RI shall release all sums withheld in connection with such claim, unless RI, in its reasonable business judgment, believes an action will be filed. Notwithstanding the foregoing, if after such release by RI of sums withheld in connection with a particular claim, such claim is reasserted, then RI's rights under this paragraph 10.10 will apply *ab initio* in full force and effect. RI will give Artist prompt notice of any lawsuit instituted with respect to such a claim, and Artist shall have the right to participate in the defense thereof with counsel of Artist's choice and at Artist's expense provided, however, that RI shall have the right at all times to maintain control of the conduct of the defense.

10.11. Artist warrants and represents that, as of the date hereof, no member of Artist is a resident of the State of California. Artist shall notify RI immediately in the event that any member of Artist becomes a resident of the State of California.

11. *Failure of Performance:*

11.01. RI reserves the right by written notice to Artist to suspend the operation of this agreement and its obligations hereunder for the duration of any contingencies by reason of which RI is materially hampered in its recording, manufacture, distribution or sale of Records, or its normal business operations become commercially impracticable: for example, labor disagreements; fire; catastrophe; shortage of materials; or any cause beyond RI's control. A number of days equal to the total of all such days of suspension may be added to the Contract Period in which such contingency occurs and the dates for the exercise by RI of its options as set forth in Article 1, the dates of commencement of subsequent Contract Periods and the Term shall be deemed extended accordingly. No suspension imposed under this paragraph 11.01 shall exceed six (6) months unless such contingency is industry-wide, in which event RI shall have the right to suspend the applicable Period for the duration of such contingency. If such suspension is not industry-wide, Artist may request RI by notice in writing given at any time after the expiration of such six (6) month period to terminate the suspension within sixty (60) days following RI's receipt of Artist's said notice. If RI does not so terminate the suspension, the Term of this agreement will terminate at the end of such sixty (60) day period, or at such earlier date as RI may designate in writing, and the parties shall be deemed to have fulfilled all their obligations hereunder except those obligations which survive such termination, such as warranties, re-recording restrictions, and the obligation to pay royalties, if payable.

11.02. If in respect of any Contract Period RI, except for reasons set forth in paragraph 11.01 above, refuses without cause to allow Artist to fulfill the Minimum Recording Obligation for such Period, and if no later than thirty (30) days after that refusal takes place, Artist notifies RI in writing of Artist's desire to fulfill such Minimum Recording Obligation, then if RI does not allow Artist either to record sufficient Master Recordings to fulfill the Minimum Recording Obligation within sixty (60) days of receipt of such notice, or to commence recording of such Minimum Recording Obligation if it cannot be recorded within said sixty (60) days, the Term of this agreement shall terminate upon the expiration of such sixty (60) day period. Upon such termination of the Term of this agreement all parties shall be deemed to have fulfilled all of their obligations hereunder except for those obligations which survive the end of the Term such as warranties, re-recording restrictions, and the obligation to accrue and pay royalties, if payable, and RI shall pay, in full settlement of its obligations in connection with such unrecorded Album(s), the applicable amounts set forth below, which amounts shall constitute Advances against royalties payable hereunder. This shall be Artist's sole remedy in connection with RI's failure to allow Artist to fulfill the Minimum Recording Obligation. If Artist shall fail to give notice to RI within the period specified therefor, RI shall be under no obligation for its failure to allow Artist to fulfill such Minimum Recording Obligation:

(a) If such unrecorded Album is the First Album of the Minimum Recording Obligation for the Initial Period, such payment shall be equal to the applicable Recording Fund, less any amount previously paid to Artist in connection with such Album hereunder;

(b) If such unrecorded Album is other than the First Album of the Minimum Recording Obligation, such payment shall be equal to the difference between the Recording Fund for the applicable Album and the Recording Costs for the immediately preceding Album, less any amounts previously paid to Artist in connection with such Album hereunder, provided that in no event shall such payment exceed forty percent (40%) of the Recording Fund payable with respect to such Album; in the event Recording Costs for the prior Album were paid by Artist, such calculation will not be made until Artist has provided satisfactory documentation to establish the amounts of such Recording Costs.

12. *Additional Remedies:*

12.01. Without limitation of any other rights and remedies of RI, if Artist fails to record and deliver

Recordings in accordance with Articles 3 and 4, then RI may, at its election, suspend its obligations hereunder for a number of days equal to the number of days between the last date on which Artist is scheduled to deliver Master Recordings and the date on which Artist actually delivers such Master Recordings. If any such failure exceeds one hundred twenty (120) days, RI may, in addition to its other rights and remedies, terminate the Term of this agreement by written notice to Artist, and upon such termination RI shall have no obligations to Artist hereunder except the obligation to pay royalties, if due.

12.02. Without limiting any other rights of RI, it is specifically understood and agreed that in the event of the liquidation of Artist's assets, or the filing of a petition in bankruptcy or insolvency or for an arrangement or reorganization by, for or against Artist, or in the event of the appointment of a receiver or a trustee for all or a portion of Artist's property, or if Artist shall make an assignment for the benefit of creditors or commit any act for or in bankruptcy or become insolvent or if Artist shall fail to fulfill its obligations under this agreement, RI shall have the option by notice to Artist to terminate the Term of this agreement.

12.03. It is recognized that Artist's services are of special, unique, unusual, extraordinary and intellectual character involving skill of the highest order which gives them a peculiar value, the loss of which cannot be reasonably or adequately compensated for by damages in an action at law. Inasmuch as any breach of this agreement with respect to such services would cause RI irreparable damage, RI shall be entitled to injunctive and other equitable relief, in addition to whatever legal remedies are available to RI, to prevent or cure any such breach or threatened breach.

12.04. The rights and remedies of RI as specified in this agreement are not to the exclusion of each other or of any other rights or remedies of RI; RI may decline to exercise any one or more of its rights and remedies as RI may deem fit, without jeopardizing any other rights and remedies of RI; and all of RI's rights and remedies in connection with this agreement shall survive the expiration or other termination of the Term. Notwithstanding anything in this agreement, RI may at any time exercise any right which it now or at any time hereafter may be entitled to as a member of the public as though this agreement were not in existence.

13. *Definitions:*

13.01. *"Master," "Recording," "Master Recording":* Any recording of sound, whether or not coupled with a visual image, by any method and on any substance or material, whether now or hereafter known, including Audio-Visual Recordings, intended for reproduction in the form of Phonograph Records, or otherwise.

13.02. *"Records," "Phonograph Records":* Any device now or hereafter known, on or by which sound may be recorded and reproduced, which is manufactured or distributed primarily for home and/or consumer and/or juke box use and/or use on or in means of transportation including "sight and sound" devices or Audio-Visual Devices.

13.03. (a) *"Audio-Visual Devices":* All forms of reproductions of Audio-Visual Recordings, excluding CD/Video, now or hereafter known, manufactured or distributed primarily for home and/or juke box use and/or use on or in means of transportation.

(b) *"Audio-Visual Recordings"* means every form of recording embodying performances of Artist wherein are fixed visual images, whether of Artist or otherwise, together with sound.

13.04 (a) *"Side"*: A Recording of sufficient playing time to constitute one (1) side of a 7 inch, 45 rpm disc Phonograph Record, but not less than two and one-half (2-1/2) minutes of continuous sound, embodying performances of Artist.

(b) *"Single"*: A 7 inch, 45 rpm Phonograph Record or equivalent embodying thereon at least one (1) Side, and expressly including a compact disc or pre-recorded tape embodying the same two (2) Sides on each of side "A" and side "B."

(c) *"Album"*: One or more LPs, sold in a single package (an Album of more than one LP sometimes being referred to as a "Multiple-Record Album").

(d) *"LP"*: A 12 inch, long-play Phonograph Record or the equivalent thereof embodying thereon the equivalent of not fewer than nine (9) Sides, and having not less than thirty-three (33) minutes playing time.

(e) *"EP Record"*: A 12 inch, 33-1/3 rpm or 45 rpm, double-sided long-play disc Phonograph Record or equivalent embodying thereon five (5) or six (6) Sides and not less than twenty (20) minutes of playing time.

(f) *"Long Play Single"*: A 12 inch 33-1/3 rpm or 45 rpm double-sided long play disc Phonograph Record or equivalent usually embodying three (3) or four (4) Sides.

(g) *"CD/Video"*: A Phonograph Record in laser-read compact disc form embodying Audio-Visual Recordings, which may, without limitation, include additional audio-only Sides.

(h) As used herein, the phrase "or equivalent" shall mean every form of pre-recorded tape, compact disc or any other Record equivalent.

13.05. *"Base Price"*: With respect to Records other than Audio-Visual Devices and CD/Videos, the Base Price is the "Retail List Price," defined as RI's suggested retail list price (or the equivalent price category) in the United States for records sold in the United States, and, with respect to Records sold outside the United States, RI's or its licensee's suggested or applicable retail price in the country of manufacture or sale, as RI is paid, or, in the absence in a particular country of such suggested retail price the price as may be established by RI or its licensee(s) in conformity with the general practice of the Record industry in such country, or otherwise, provided that RI may but shall not be obligated to utilize the price adopted by the local mechanical copyright collection agency as the basis for the collection of mechanical copyright royalties.

13.06. *"Container Charge"*: Twelve and one-half percent (12-1/2%) of the Retail List Price for a single-fold disc Album in a standard sleeve with no inserts, for a compact disc or for any other Record other than as hereinafter provided; fifteen percent (15%) of the Retail List Price for an Album in a double fold jacket or non-standard sleeve or jacket or with inserts; and twenty percent (20%) of the Retail List Price for a pre-recorded tape or any non-disc configuration.

13.07. (a) *"Royalty Base":* The Base Price less all excise, sales and similar taxes and less the applicable Container Charges.

(b) RI may at any time and from time to time change the method by which it computes royalties in the United States from a retail basis to some other basis (the "New Basis"), such as, without limitation, a wholesale basis. The New Basis will replace the then-current Royalty Base and the royalty rates shall be adjusted to the appropriate royalty which would be applied to the New Basis so that the dollars-and-cents royalty amounts payable with respect to the top-line product through Normal Retail Channels as of the date of such change would be the same as that which was payable immediately prior to such New Basis; for sales other than top-line product, for which there is a New Basis, the adjusted royalty rate shall be reduced in the ratio of the royalty rate for such sales to the royalty rates for sales of top-line product. If there are other adjustments made by RI that would otherwise make the New Basis more favorable (a particular example of which might be the distribution of smaller quantities of free goods than theretofore distributed) then the benefits of such other adjustments will be taken into consideration in adjusting the royalty rate.

(c) Notwithstanding anything to the contrary contained herein, the Royalty Base for premium Records shall, at RI's election, be RI's actual sales price of such Records.

13.08. *"Recording Costs":* All costs including preproduction and post-production costs incurred for and with respect to the production of Master Recordings. Recording Costs include without limitation, union scale; payments for musicians, vocalists, conductors, arrangers, orchestrators, copyists, etc.; payments required by an agreement between RI and any labor organization; producer's fees; studio charges; costs of tape, editing, mixing, mastering to tape, reference discs, and engineering; expenses of travel, per diems and rehearsal halls; costs of non-studio facilities and equipment; dubbing; costs and transportation of instruments including cartage and rental fees; and other costs and expenses incurred in producing Master Recordings and other costs which are customarily recognized as recording costs in the Phonograph Record industry. With respect to the preparation of a lacquer master from a fully-edited and mixed tape master, an amount equal to the normal engineering charges which would reasonably be incurred in connection with the production of one (1) such lacquer master on a real-time basis will be excluded in the calculation of Recording Costs, but all costs in excess of said normal engineering charges will be included in that calculation.

13.09. *"Composition":* A musical composition or medley consisting of words and/or music, or any dramatic material, whether in the form of instrumental and/or vocal music, prose or otherwise, irrespective of length.

13.10. *"Controlled Composition":* Any Composition written, composed, owned or controlled directly or indirectly by Artist and/or any individual producer of Master Recordings and/or any Person affiliated with one or more of the foregoing or in which one or more of the foregoing has a direct or indirect interest.

13.11. *"Advance":* An "Advance" constitutes a prepayment of royalties and shall be charged against and shall be recoupable from all royalties accruing hereunder excluding mechanical royalties.

13.12. (a) *"Budget Records":* Albums sold in a particular country of the Territory outside the United States at a Retail List Price which is eighty percent (80%) or less of the Retail List Price in such country of the Territory for top pop single LP Albums; and Albums sold in the United States at a Retail List Price which is seventy percent (70%) or less of the Retail List Price in the United States for top "pop" single LP Albums.

(b) *"Mid-Price Records":* Albums sold in the United States at a Retail List Price which is less than eighty percent (80%) but more than seventy percent (70%) of the Retail List Price in the United States for top "pop" single LP Albums.

13.13. *"Person":* Any individual, corporation, partnership, association, or other business entity, or the legal successors or representative of any of the foregoing.

13.14. *"Non-Affiliated Third Parties":* Persons other than members of the GROUP as now or hereafter constituted, and other than Persons as to which RI now or hereafter directly or indirectly holds at least a fifty percent (50%) interest or control (including joint ventures) or Persons in which the principals of RI or any of the GROUP now or hereafter collectively hold at least a fifty percent (50%) interest or control.

13.15. *"Net Sales":* Sales of Records hereunder, paid for, less returns and credits. Net Sales shall specifically exclude the following:

(a) (i) Records given away gratis or sold for fifty percent (50%) or less of the Gross Price (as hereinafter defined); Records distributed to disc jockeys, radio or television stations, publishers, distributors, dealers, consumers, or others for publicity, advertising, or promotional purposes; and Records sold as cutouts, surplus or for scrap.

(ii) Free or bonus Records given away together with Records sold for monetary consideration (sometimes referred to as "free goods"). The number of Records automatically deemed not sold for royalty purposes under this paragraph 13.15(a)(ii) shall be, for Singles, 23.08% of the gross total distributed and, for Albums, 15% of the gross total distributed. This paragraph 13.15(a)(ii) shall not be applicable to CD/Video or to Audio-Visual Devices.

(iii) Free or bonus Records given away pursuant to special sales plans in addition to free goods.

(iv) To the extent that Records hereunder are sold subject to a sales plan entailing a selling price for such Records reduced by a percentage discount from RI's "Gross Price" (i.e., the selling price to distributors before any discounts or free goods or bonus plans), the number of such Records deemed to be Net Sales shall be determined by reducing the number of Records actually sold by the percentage of discount granted applicable to such sale.

(b) Without limitation of the generality of paragraph 13.15(a) above, RI shall have the right to deduct from the number of Records sold returns and credits of any nature, including without limitation: (i) those on account of any return or exchange privilege; (ii) defective merchandise; and (iii) errors in billing or shipment, provided that returns shall be pro-rated between royalty-bearing and non-royalty bearing Records on the assumption that such Records were shipped pursuant to RI's standard basic sales plan as described in subparagraph 13.15(a)(ii) above.

(c) Without limitation of the foregoing, royalties shall not be payable with respect to distributions which are not Net Sales and the terms "Net Sales" and/or "net royalty-bearing sales" shall not include the sales described in paragraphs 13.15(a) and 13.15(b) and shall not include any sales which are being held as royalty reserves.

13.16. *"Normal Retail Channels":* Normal retail distribution channels excluding sales of Records described in paragraphs 7.05, 7.06, 7.07, 7.08, 7.09, 7.10, 7.11 and 7.12 herein.

13.17. *"Contract Period":* The Initial Period or an Option Period as defined in Article 1 above.

13.18. *"Statutory Rate":* The minimum statutory compulsory license rate applicable to a Composition of less than five (5) minutes under the copyright laws of the applicable country.

13.19. *"Armed Forces Post Exchanges":* United States military posts, ships' stores or other United States armed forces facilities, including, without limitation, federal, state and/or local governments.

14. *Miscellaneous:*

14.01. Wherever Artist's approval or consent is required, Artist shall give RI written notice of approval or disapproval (the reasons for such disapproval being specifically stated) within five (5) business days after RI requests same. If Artist shall fail to give such notice to RI as aforesaid, Artist shall be deemed to have given such consent or approval.

14.02. Any promotional efforts or expenditures made by Artist or by any Person on behalf of Artist in connection with any Records hereunder shall be in accordance with applicable legal standards, including Sections 317 and 507 of the Communications Act of 1934, as amended. In the event Artist is in breach of the preceding sentence, RI may, without limiting its rights, terminate the Term of this agreement.

14.03. Artist recognizes that the sale of Records is speculative and agrees that the judgment of RI with regard to any matter affecting the sale, distribution and exploitation of Records hereunder shall be binding and conclusive upon Artist. Nothing contained in this agreement shall obligate RI to make, sell, license, or distribute Records manufactured from the Sides recorded hereunder other than as specifically provided herein. The method, manner and extent of release, packaging, promotion, advertising, distribution and exploitation of Master Recordings and Records shall be within the sole discretion of RI unless otherwise herein specifically provided.

14.04. (a) RI may, at its election, assign this agreement or any of its rights hereunder.

(b) Artist may assign its rights under this agreement only to another corporation owned or controlled by Artist, subject to the following conditions: (1) the assignee will be subject to RI's approval in RI's sole discretion; (2) the assignment will not be effective until Artist has delivered to RI an instrument satisfactory to RI in its sole discretion effecting the assignment and the assignee's assumption of Artist's obligations, and RI has executed that instrument to evidence RI's approval of it; (3) no such assignment will relieve Artist of its obligations under this agreement; (4) Artist and the assignee shall both be responsible for the representations and warranties on the part of Artist hereunder, whether such representations and warranties are made before or after the date of such assignment; and (5) if such an assignment takes place, any further transfer of the rights assigned will be subject to the same conditions as provided in this paragraph 14.04(b).

14.05. All notices required to be given to RI shall be sent to RI at its address first mentioned herein, and all royalties, royalty statements and payments and any and all notices to Artist shall be sent to Artist at its address first mentioned herein, or such other address as each party respectively may hereafter designate by notice in writing to the other. All notices sent under this agreement shall be in writing and, except for royalty statements shall be sent by registered or certified mail, return receipt requested, and the day of mailing of any such notice shall be deemed the date of the giving thereof (except notices of change of address, the date of which shall be the date of receipt by the receiving party). RI will undertake to send a copy of all notices sent to Artist to______________, Attn:______________, provided that RI's failure to send any such copy shall not be deemed a breach of this agreement or impair the effectiveness of the notice concerned. All notices to RI shall be served upon RI to the attention of the Senior Vice President, Business Affairs, with a copy to the Senior Vice President, Legal Affairs.

14.06. It is expressly understood and agreed that, in the event of a breach or purported breach by RI hereunder, Artist's rights shall be limited to an action at law for money damages, if any, actually suffered by Artist as a result thereof, and in no event shall Artist be entitled to rescission, injunction or other equitable relief of any kind. Moreover, Artist shall not be entitled to recover damages or to terminate the Term of this agreement by reason of any breach by RI of its material obligations hereunder, unless RI has failed to remedy such breach within a reasonable time following receipt of Artist's notice thereof.

14.07. This agreement is entered into in the State of New York and shall be construed in accordance with the laws of New York applicable to contracts entered into and to be wholly performed therein. The parties agree that any action, suit or proceeding based upon any matter, claim or controversy arising hereunder or relating hereto shall be brought solely in the State Courts of or the Federal Court in the State and County of New York; except that in the event RI is sued or joined in any other court or in any other forum in respect of any matter which may give rise to a claim by RI hereunder, the parties hereto other than RI consent to the jurisdiction of such court or forum over any claim which may be asserted by RI therein. The parties hereto irrevocably waive any objection to the venue of the above-mentioned courts, including any claim that such action, suit or proceeding has been brought in an inconvenient forum. Any process in any action, suit or proceeding arising out of or relating to this agreement may, among other methods permitted by law, be served upon Artist or RI by delivering or mailing the same in accordance with paragraph 14.05 hereof. Any such process may, among other methods, be served upon Artist or any other Person who approves, ratifies, or assents to this agreement to induce RI to enter into it, by delivering the process or mailing it to Artist or the other Person concerned in the manner prescribed in paragraph 14.05.

14.08. The invalidity or unenforceability of any provision hereof shall not affect the validity or enforceability of any other provision hereof. This writing sets forth the entire understanding between the parties with respect to the subject matter hereof, and no modification, amendment, waiver, termination or discharge of this agreement shall be binding upon RI unless confirmed by a written instrument signed by the Senior Vice President of Business Affairs of RI.

15. *Group Artist:*

15.01. (a) Artist warrants, represents and agrees that, for so long as this agreement shall be in effect, Artist will perform together as a group for RI. If any individual comprising Artist refuses, neglects or fails to perform together with the other individuals comprising Artist in fulfillment of the obligations agreed to be performed under this agreement or leaves the group, Artist shall give RI prompt written notice thereof. (The term "leaving member" shall hereinafter be used to define each individual who leaves the group or no longer performs with the group, or each member of the group if the group disbands.) RI shall have the right, to be exercised by written notice to Artist within ninety (90) days following its receipt of Artist's notice:

(i) To continue with the services of any such leaving member pursuant to paragraph 15.04 below;

(ii) To terminate the Term of this agreement with respect to the remaining members of Artist whether or not RI has exercised its right to continue with the services of a leaving member;

(iii) To treat all the members of Artist as leaving members, and have the right to exercise its rights with respect to each in accordance with this Article 15.

(b) In the event that RI fails to send notice of RI's exercise of rights pursuant to paragraph 15.01(a) above, the Term of this agreement shall be deemed terminated with respect to such leaving member.

15.02. A leaving member, whether or not his engagement is terminated hereunder, may not perform for others for the purpose of recording any selection as to which the applicable restrictive period specified in paragraph 10.04 of this agreement has not expired.

15.03. A leaving member shall not, without RI's consent, use the professional name of the group in any commercial or artistic endeavor; the said professional name shall remain the property of Artist and those members of the group who continue to perform their obligations hereunder and whose engagements are not terminated; and, the person, if any, engaged to replace the individual whose engagement is terminated shall be mutually agreed upon by RI and Artist and each such person added to Artist, as a replacement or otherwise, shall become bound by the terms and conditions of this agreement.

15.04. In addition to the rights provided in the preceding paragraphs, RI shall have, and Artist hereby grants to RI, an irrevocable option for the individual and exclusive services of each leaving member as follows: Said option, with respect to such individual, may be exercised by RI giving Artist notice in writing within ninety (90) days after RI receives Artist's notice provided for in paragraph 15.01(a) above. In the event of RI's exercise of such option, Artist and such leaving member shall be deemed to have entered into an agreement with RI with respect to such individual's exclusive recording services upon all the terms and conditions of this agreement except that: (i) the Minimum Recording Obligation in the Initial Period shall be two (2) Sides, with an overcall option, at RI's election, for sufficient additional Master Recordings to constitute up to one (1) Album, with an additional number (the "Number") of options granted to RI to extend the term of such agreement for consecutive option periods for one (1) Album each, each of which options shall be exercised within nine (9) months after delivery to RI of the Minimum Recording Obligation for the immediately preceding contract period of such leaving member's agreement. The Number shall be equal to the remaining number of Albums embodying performances of Artist which Artist would be obligated to deliver hereunder if RI exercised each of its options, but in no event shall the Number be less than four (4); (ii) the provisions contained in paragraph 6.01(b) shall not be applicable, but RI shall pay all Recording Costs for Master Recordings to be recorded by such individual up to the amount of the budget approved by RI therefor; (iii) RI's royalty obligation to Artist in respect of Recordings by such individual shall be the payment to Artist of the royalties computed as set forth in this agreement but at only three quarters (3/4) the rates set forth herein; (iv) RI shall be entitled to combine such leaving member's account with one half of the Artist account hereunder; and (v) Recordings by such individual shall not be applied in diminution of Artist's Minimum Recording Obligation as set forth in this agreement.

15.05. Changes in the individuals comprising Artist shall be made by mutual agreement between Artist and RI.

15.06 Artist shall not have the right, so long as this agreement is in effect, to assign Artist's professional name(s) or to permit its use by any other individual or group of individuals without RI's prior written consent, and any attempt to do so shall be null and void and shall convey no right or title. Without limitation of the generality of paragraph 5.04 above, Artist hereby represents and warrants that it is the owner of the professional name mentioned on the first page of this agreement, and that no other Person, firm or corporation has the right to use said professional name or to permit it to be used in connection with Phonograph Records, and that it has the authority to grant RI the right to use said professional name. RI shall have the right to use said professional name in accordance with the provisions hereof.

By__________.__________ By__________.__________

By__________.__________ By__________.__________

SAMPLE MANAGEMENT CONRACT

Courtesy of Dr. David Herrera, Belmont University

PERSONAL MANAGEMENT CONTRACT

I desire to obtain your **advice, counsel and direction** in the development and enhancement of my artistic and theatrical career. The nature and extent of the success or failure of my career cannot be predetermined and it is therefore my desire that your compensation be determined in such manner as will permit you to **accept the risk of failure and likewise benefit to the extent of my success.**

In view of the foregoing we have agreed as follows:

I do hereby engage you as my personal manager for **a period of** ____ years from date. As and when requested by me during and throughout the term hereof you agree to perform for me one or more of the services as follows: **advice and counsel in the selection of literary, artistic and musical material; advice and counsel in any and all matters pertaining to publicity, public relations and advertising; advice and counsel with relation to the adoption of proper format for presentation of my artistic talents and in the determination of proper style, mood, setting, business and characterization in keeping with my talents; advice, counsel and direction in the selection of artistic talent to assist, accompany or embellish my artistic presentation; advice and counsel with regard to general practices in the entertainment and amusement industries and with respect to such matters of which you may have knowledge concerning compensation and privileges extended for similar artistic values; advice and counsel concerning the selection of theatrical agencies and persons, firms and corporations to counsel, advise, seek and procure employment and engagements for me.**

You are authorized and empowered for me and in my behalf and your discretion to do the following: **approve and permit any and all publicity and advertising; approve and permit the use of my name, photograph, likeness, voice, sound effects, caricatures, literary artistic and musical materials for purposes of advertising and publicity and in the promotion and advertising of any and all products and services; execute for me in my name and/or in my behalf any and all agreements, documents and contracts for my services, talents and/or artistic literary and musical materials, collect and receive sums as well as endorse my name upon and cash any and all checks payable to me for my services, talents and literary and artistic materials and retain therefrom all sums owing to you; engage, as well as discharge and/or direct for me, and in my name theatrical agents and employment agencies as well as other persons, firms and corporations who may be retained to obtain contracts,**

engagements or employment for me. The authority herein granted to you is coupled with an interest and shall be irrevocable during the term hereof.

I agree to **at all times devote myself to my career** and to do all things necessary and desirable to promote my career and earnings therefrom. I shall at all times **engage proper theatrical agencies to obtain engagements and employment for me and I agree that I shall not engage any theatrical or employment agency of which you may disapprove.** It is clearly understood that you are not an employment agent or theatrical agent, that you have not offered or attempted or promised to obtain employment or engagements for me that you are not obligated, authorized or expected to do so.

This Agreement shall not be construed to create a partnership between us. It is specifically understood that you are acting hereunder as an **independent contractor and you may appoint or engage any and all other persons, firms and corporations throughout the world in your discretion to perform any or all of the services which you have agreed to perform hereunder. Your services hereunder are not exclusive** and you shall at all times be free to perform the same or similar services for others as well as engage in any and all other business activities. You shall only be required to **render reasonable services as and when reasonably requested by me.** Due to the difficulty which we may have in determining the amount of services to which I may be entitled, it is agreed that you shall not be deemed to be in default hereunder until and unless I shall first deliver to you a **written notice describing the exact service** which I require on your part and then only in the event that you shall thereafter fail for a period of fifteen consecutive days to commence the rendition of the particular service required. You shall not be required to travel or to meet with me at any particular place or places except in your discretion and following arrangements for costs and expenses of such travel.

In compensation for your services I agree to pay to you, as and when received by me, and during and throughout the term hereof, a sum equal to ____ percent of any and all compensation, **sums and other things of value which I may receive as a result of my activities in and throughout the entertainment, amusement, musical recording and publishing industries, including any and all sums resulting from the use of my artistic talents and the results and proceeds thereof and, without in any manner limiting the foregoing, the matters upon which your compensation shall be computed shall include any and all of my activities in connection with matters as follows: motion pictures, television, radio, music, literary, theatrical engagements, personal appearances, public appearances, in places of amusement and entertainment, records and recordings, publications, and the use of my name, likeness and talents for purposes of advertising and trade. I likewise agree to pay you a similar sum following the expiration of the term hereof upon and with respect to any and all engagements,**

contracts and agreements entered into during the term hereof relating to any of the foregoing, and upon any and all extensions, renewals and substitutions thereof.

In the event of any dispute under or relating to the terms of this agreement it is agreed that the same shall be submitted to arbitration to the American Arbitration Association in (Insert New York City or Los Angeles) ____________________ and in accordance with the rules promulgated by the said association. In the event of litigation or arbitration the prevailing party shall be entitled to recover any and all reasonable attorney's fees and other costs incurred in the enforcement of the terms of this agreement.

This agreement shall be deemed to be executed in the State of __________________ and shall be construed in accordance with the laws of said State. In the event any provision hereof shall for any reason be illegal or unenforceable then, and in any such event, the same shall not affect the validity of the remaining portions and provisions hereof.

This agreement is the only agreement of the parties and there is no other or collateral agreement (oral or written) between the parties in any manner relating to the subject matter hereof.

If the foregoing meets with your approval please indicate your acceptance and agreement by signing in the space hereinbelow provided.

Very truly yours,
(Artist)

I DO HEREBY AGREE TO THE FOREGOING

Manager_____________________________

Date_____________________________

APPENDIX B:
RESOURCES

WEB SITES

PERFORMING RIGHTS ORGANIZATIONS

American Society of Composers, Authors and Publishers (ASCAP): http://www.ascap.com
Broadcast Music, Inc. (BMI): http://bmi.com
SESAC: http://sesac.com

TRADE ORGANIZATIONS

American Federation of Musicians (AFM): http://afm.org
American Federation of Television and Radio Artists (AFTRA): http://aftra.com
Association of Independent Music Publishers (AIMP): http://aimp.org
Country Music Association (CMA): http://cmaworld.com
Gospel Music Association: http://gospelmusic.org
National Academy of Recording Arts and Sciences: http://grammy.org
Nashville Songwriters Association International (NSAI): http://nashvillesongwriters.com
National Music Publishers' Association (NMPA): http://nmpa.org
Recording Industry Association of America (RIAA): http://riaa.org
Songwriters Guild of America (SGA): http://songwritersguild.com

MUSIC SITES

GarageBand: http://garageband.com
Last.fm: http://www.last.fm
MyDamnChannel: http://mydamnchannel.com
PureVolume: http://www.purevolume.com

OTHER

U.S. Copyright Office: http://copyright.gov
Creative Commons: http://creativecommons.org
The Harry Fox Agency (HFA): http://harryfox.com
iLike: http://ilike.com
The International Movie Database: http://imdb.com
The Lefsetz Letter: http://lefsetz.com
The Muse's Muse: Songwriting Tips & Tools: http://musesmuse.com
SonicBids: http://www.sonicbids.com
SoundExchange: http://soundexchange.com
Volunteer Lawyers for the Arts: http://vlany.org
821 Entertainment: www.821entertainment.com
Producer of *Make Me a Star* CD: www.eddieperez.com

PUBLICATIONS

American Songwriter (http://americansongwriter.com)
Billboard (http://www.billboard.biz)
The Hollywood Reporter (http://www.hollywoodreporter.com)
Music Row (http://musicrow.com)
Performing Songwriter (http://performingsongwriter.com)
Variety (http://www.variety.com)

BOOKS

Avalon, Moses. *Confessions of a Record Producer: How to Survive the Scams and Shams of the Music Business.* San Francisco: Backbeat Books, 2002.

Davis, Sheila. *The Craft of Lyric Writing.* Cincinnati: Writer's Digest, 1985.

Krasilovsky, M. Williams, and Sidney Shemel. *This Business of Music: The Definitive Guide to the Music Industry.* 9th ed. New York: Watson-Guptill Publications, 2003.

Lovelace, Kelly. *If You've Got a Dream, I've Got a Plan: How to Get Your Songs Heard by Music Industry Professionals.* Nashville: Rutledge Hill Press, 2002.

Passman, Donald. *All You Need to Know About the Music Business.* 5th ed. New York: Simon & Schusters, 2003.

Ramone, Phil. *Making Records: The Scenes Behind the Music.* New York: Hyperion, 2007.

Slichter, Jacob. *So You Wanna Be a Rock & Roll Star: How I Machine-Gunned a Roomful of Record Executives and Other True Tales from a Drummer's Life.* New York: Broadway, 2004.

Trynin, Jen. *Everything I'm Cracked Up to Be.* New York: Harcourt, 2006.

SOURCES

"400,000 Hopefuls," *Time*, April 12, 1954, http://www.time.com/time/magazine/article/0,9171,823335,00.html (accessed December 28, 2007).

Bice, Bo, in discussion with the authors, November 2007.

Boggs, Jeff, in discussion with the authors, November 2007.

Borchetta, Scott, in discussion with the authors, November 2007.

Borman, Gary, in discussion with the authors, November 2007.

Brown, Tony, in discussion with the authors, November 2007.

Burr, Gary, in discussion with the authors, November 2007.

Cadelago, Chris. "Forget MTV – Apple's iPod Ads Are the New Music-Star Makers," *San Francisco Chronicle*, November 24, 2007, http://www.sfgate.com/cgin/article.cgi?f=/c/a/2007/11/24/MN4STFDOS.DTL (accessed December 28, 2007).

Caillat, Colbie, in discussion with Brian Mansfield, September 2007.

Caillat, Colbie, in discussion with the authors, November 2007.

Castle, Nick, and James V. Hart, screenwriters. *August Rush*. Perf. Freddie Highmore, Robin Williams. Warner Bros. Pictures, 2007.

Conrad, David, in discussion with Anastasia Brown, December 2007.

Copeland, Miles, in discussion with the authors, November 2007.

Covington, Bucky, in discussions with Brian Mansfield, February-April 2007.

Crowell, Rodney, in discussion with the authors, November 2007.

Dover, Debbie, in discussion with the authors, November 2007.

Dunn, Ronnie, in discussion with the authors, November 2007.

Essig, Rod, in discussion with the authors, November 2007.

Evans, Sara, in discussion with the authors, November 2007.

Fanjoy, Trey, in discussion with the authors, November 2007.

Gates, Tom, in discussion with Brian Mansfield, November 2007.

Goodman, Cyndi Thomson, in discussion with the authors, November 2007.

Hanson, Jennifer, in discussion with Brian Mansfield, October 2007.

Higgenson, Tom, in discussion with Brian Mansfield, June 2007.

Jewell, Buddy, in discussion with Brian Mansfield, November 2007.

Jurgensen, John. "Singers Bypass Labels for Prime-Time Exposure," *Wall Street Journal*, May 17, 2007.

Katz, Joel, in discussion with the authors, November 2007.

Kennedy, Shelby, in discussion with the authors, November 2007.

Lambert, Bev, in discussion with Brian Mansfield, November 2007.

LaVette, Bettye, in discussion with Brian Mansfield, November 2007.

Layher, Renee, in discussion with the authors, November 2007.

Malloy, David, in discussion with the authors, November 2007.

Mansfield, Brian. "Carrie Takes the Wheel," *USA Today*, November 10, 2005, http://www.usatoday.com/life/people/2005-11-09-carrie-underwood_x.htm (accessed December 28, 2005).

Mason, John, in discussion with the authors, November 2007.

McEntire, Reba, in discussion with the authors, November 2007.

McEntire, Reba, with Tom Carter. *Reba: My Story.* New York: Bantam Books, 1994.

Moss, Corey, with additional reporting by Raquel Hutchinson and Angela Lu. "The Scourge of 'American Idol': Oversingers," *MTV.com*, February 6, 2006, http://www.mtv.com/news/articles/1523040/20060202/id_o.jhtml.

Moss, Corey. "Behind the Scenes, 'Idol' Is a Singing, Dancing Boot Camp," *MTV.com*, March 21, 2006, http://www.mtv.com/news/articles/1526656/20060320/bice__bo.jhtml.

Nalli, Reen, in discussion with Anastasia Brown, December 2007.

Nathanson, Matt, in discussion with the authors, November 2007.

Owen, Jake, in discussion with the authors, November 2007.

Peters, Carol, in discussion with the authors, November 2007.

Pizzuto, Michael, in discussion with the authors, November 2007.

Ramone, Phil, in discussion with the authors, November 2007.

Roth, David Lee. *Crazy from the Heat.* New York: Hyperion Books, 1997.

Simons, Carrie, in discussion with the authors, November 2007.

St. John, Lauren. *Hardcore Troubadour: The Life and Near Death of Steve Earle.* New York: Fourth Estate/HarperCollins, 2003.

Urban, Keith, in discussion with the authors, November 2007.

Was, Don, in discussion with the authors, November 2007.

Wilson, Nancy, in discussion with the authors, November 2007.

Wynn, Ron. "Famed Producer Now Operates His Own Office," *Nashville City Paper*, September 23, 2007, http://www.nashvillecitypaper.com/news.php?viewStory=57594 (accessed December 28, 2007).

Young, Chris, in discussion with the authors, November 2007.

FINDING YOUR OWN VOICE CD

Included in the back of this book is a CD you won't find anywhere else! Broken into two parts, this CD is designed to help you 1) discover your true key, and 2) be inspired to make any song fresh and new through unique arrangements.

THE KEY REALLY IS THE KEY (FIND YOUR TRUE KEY!)

Whether or not you choose to participate in a contest, you should always sing in the key that's best for your voice. Tracks 1–9 will help you find your perfect key.

We took the song "After You've Gone" and recorded it in many keys. The lyrics are printed on the following page. Grab your most honest friend, pop in the CD, turn to the lyrics, and sing "After You've Gone" in each key until you find the one that fits. You'll know it's the right key by the way it feels—fluid and smooth—when you sing.

THE ARRANGEMENT GIVES YOU THE EDGE (OPEN YOUR MIND AND MAKE A SONG YOUR OWN!)

Making a song your own is a quick and impressive way to stand out to any judge. If you're competing in a talent contest, you will be limited in the songs you can choose to sing. Take the opportunity to transform a song into something uniquely you! We took an old song called "Down in the Valley" and rearranged it five different ways: country rock infusion, Texas infusion, New Orleans infusion, Latin infusion, and jazz infusion. Turn to the lyrics, cue the CD to tracks 10–15, and sing along to each different arrangement. You'll be inspired to make any song fresh, new, and uniquely you!

LYRICS FOR

"AFTER YOU'VE GONE" (1918)

Now won't you listen, honey, while I say,
how could you tell me that you're goin' away?
Don't say that we must part,
don't break your baby's heart.

You know I've loved you for these many years,
loved you night and day.
Oh honey, how can you leave me,
listen while I say,

After you've gone and left me cryin',
after you've gone, there's no denyin',
you'll feel blue, you'll feel sad.
You'll miss the dearest pal that you've ever had.

There'll come a time, now don't forget it.
There'll come a time when you'll regret it,
Oh baby, think what you're doin',
You know my love for you will drive me to ruin,
after you've gone, after you've gone away.

LYRICS FOR

"DOWN IN THE VALLEY" (1835)

Down in the valley, valley so low
Hang your head over, hear the wind blow
Hear the wind blow dear, hear the wind blow
Hang your head over, hear the wind blow.

Bird in a cage dear, bird in a cage
Dying for freedom, ever a slave
Ever a slave dear, ever a slave
Dying for freedom, ever a slave.

If you don't love me, love whom you please
Throw your arms 'round me, give my heart ease
Give my heart ease dear, give my heart ease
Throw your arms round me, give my heart ease.

Write me a letter, send it by mail
Send it in care of Birmingham jail
Birmingham jail dear, Birmingham jail
Send it in care of Birmingham jail.

Writing this letter, containing three lines
Answer my question, will you be mine?
Will you be mine dear, will you be mine?
Answer my question, will you be mine?

Roses love sunshine, violets love dew
Angels in heaven know I love you
Know I love you dear, know I love you
Angels in heaven know I love you.